THE SIX MILLION DOLLAR MAN

D1300709

WRITTEN BY
CHRISTOPHER HASTINGS

ART BY
DAVID HAHN

COLORS BY
ROSHAN KURICHIYANIL

LETTERS BY
ARIANA MAHER

WITH SPECIAL THANKS TO
ZACK DAVISSON

COVER ART BY
MICHAEL WALSH

COLLECTION DESIGNED BY
ALEXIS PERSSON

PACKAGED & EDITED BY
NATE COSBY

SPECIAL THANKS TO
KRISTIN CONTE OF UNIVERSAL STUDIOS

DYNAMITE®

Nick Barrucci, CEO / Publisher
Juan Collado, President / COO
Brandon Dante Primavera, V.P. of IT and Operations

Joe Rybandt, Executive Editor
Matt Idelson, Senior Editor
Kevin Ketner, Editor

Cathleen Heard, Art Director
Rachel Kilbury, Digital Multimedia Associate
Alexis Persson, Graphic Designer
Katie Hidalgo, Graphic Designer

Alan Payne, V.P. of Sales and Marketing
Pat O'Connell, Sales Manager
Vincent Faust, Marketing Coordinator

Jay Spence, Director of Product Development
Mariano Nicieza, Director of Research & Development

ISBN13: 978-1-5241-1262-2   First Printing   10 9 8 7 6 5 4 3 2 1

Online at **www.DYNAMITE.com** | On Facebook **/Dynamitecomics**
On Instagram **/Dynamitecomics** | On Twitter **@dynamitecomics**

STEVE AUSTIN. ASTRONAUT. A MAN BARELY ALIVE AFTER A HORRIBLE ACCIDENT.
REBUILT AS THE WORLD'S FIRST BIONIC MAN. BETTER THAN HE WAS BEFORE.

BETTER, STRONGER, FASTER.

THE

6,000,000

DOLLAR MAN

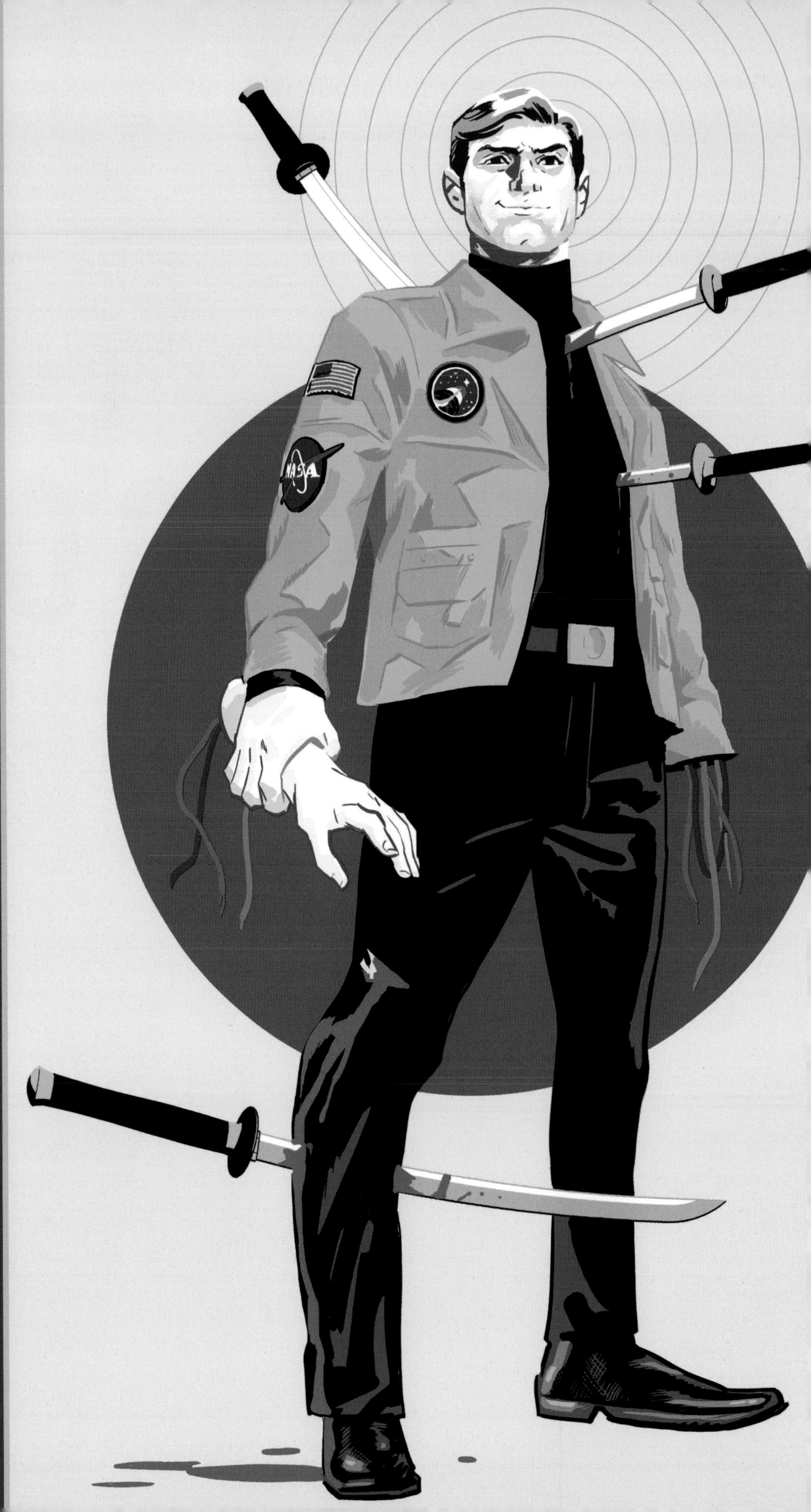
NASA
ISSUE 01 COVER ART BY MICHAEL WALSH

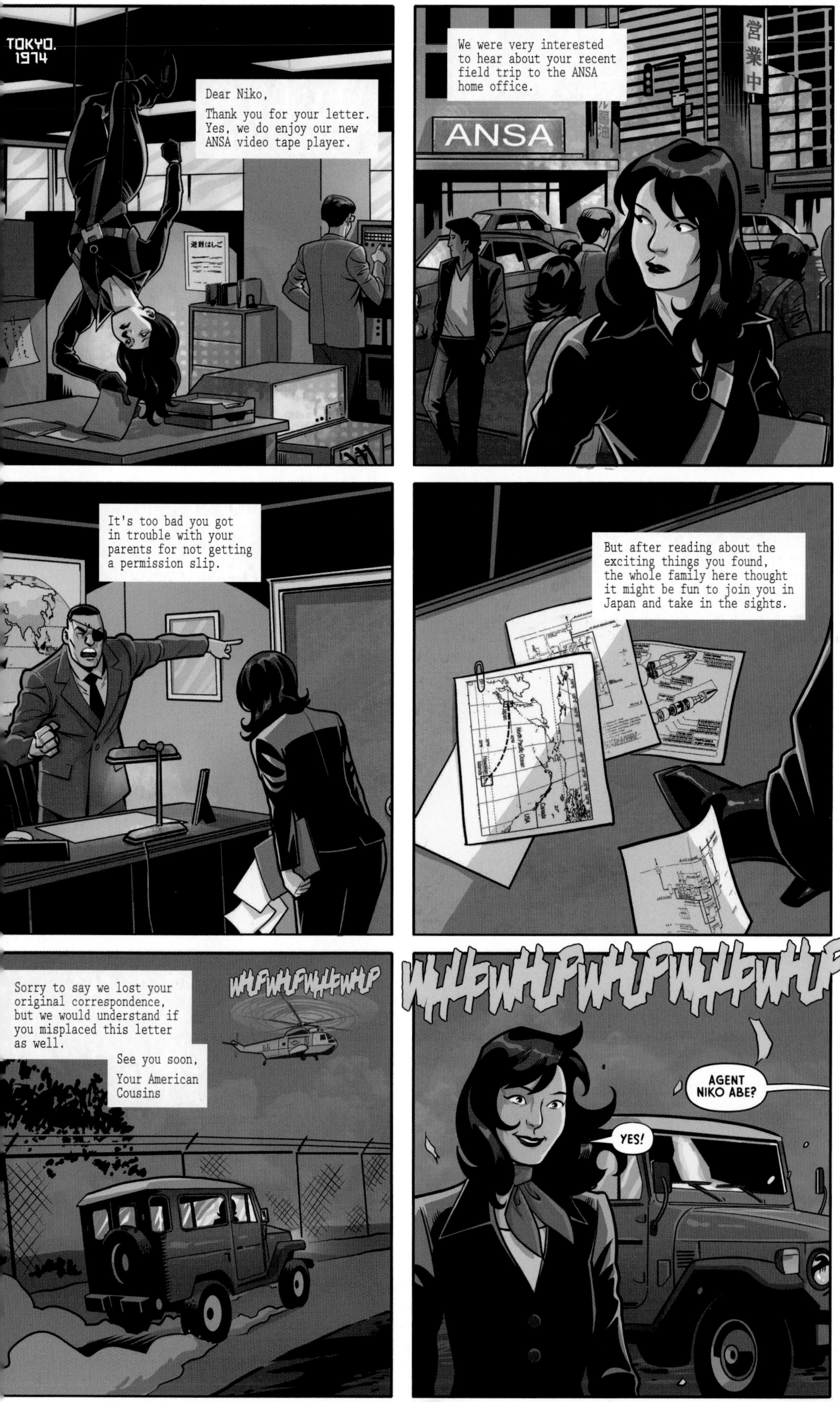
TOKYO. 1974
Dear Niko,
Thank you for your letter. Yes, we do enjoy our new ANSA video tape player.
We were very interested to hear about your recent field trip to the ANSA home office.
ANSA
営業中
It's too bad you got in trouble with your parents for not getting a permission slip.
But after reading about the exciting things you found, the whole family here thought it might be fun to join you in Japan and take in the sights.
Sorry to say we lost your original correspondence, but we would understand if you misplaced this letter as well.
See you soon,
Your American Cousins
WHUPWHUPWHUPWHUP
WHUPWHUPWHUPWHUPWHUP
AGENT NIKO ABE?
YES!

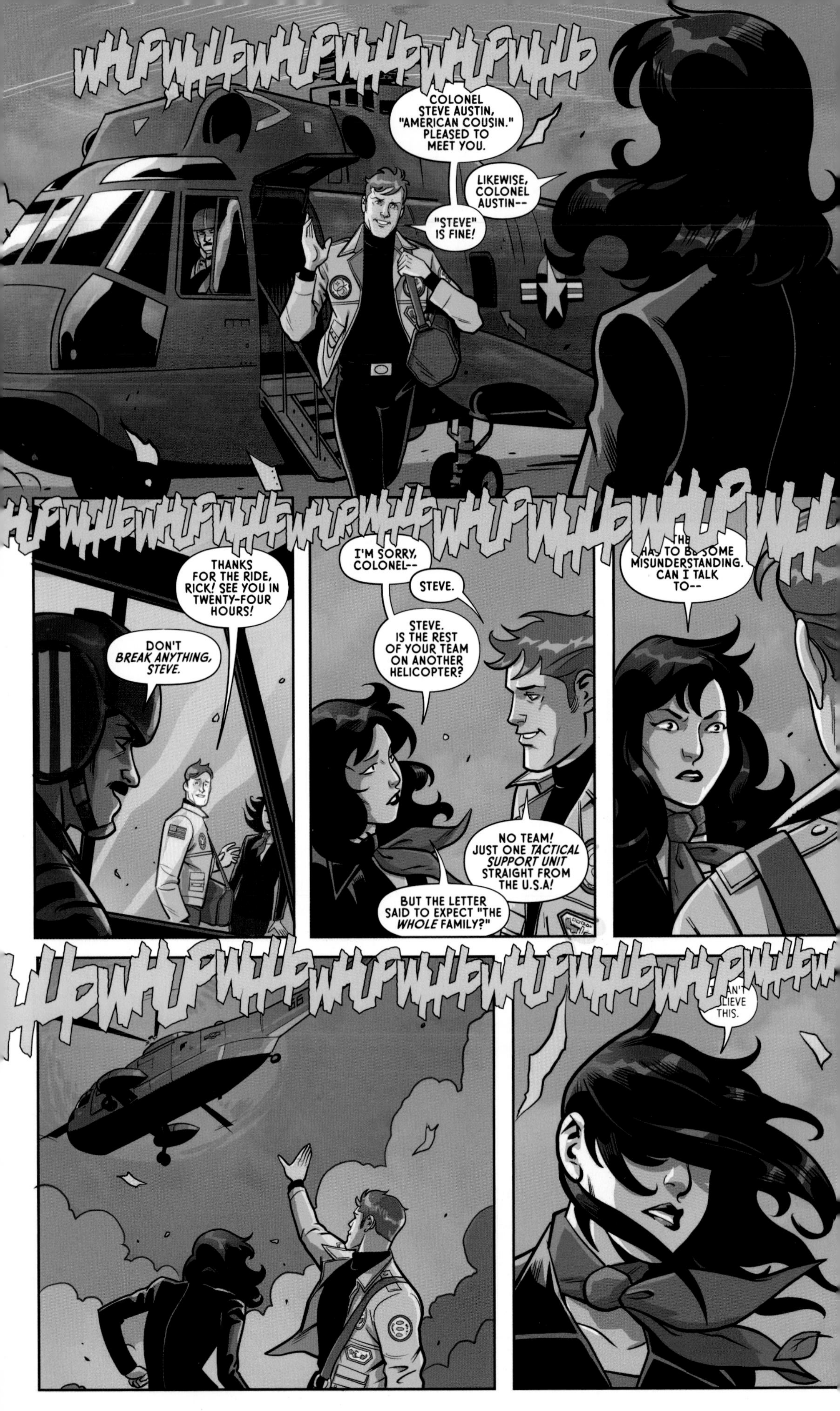
WHUPWHUPWHUPWHUPWHUPWHUP
COLONEL STEVE AUSTIN, "AMERICAN COUSIN." PLEASED TO MEET YOU.
LIKEWISE, COLONEL AUSTIN--
"STEVE" IS FINE!
WHUPWHUPWHUPWHUPWHUPWHUPWHUPWHUPWHUP
THANKS FOR THE RIDE, RICK! SEE YOU IN TWENTY-FOUR HOURS!
DON'T *BREAK ANYTHING,* STEVE.
I'M SORRY, COLONEL--
STEVE.
STEVE. IS THE REST OF YOUR TEAM ON ANOTHER HELICOPTER?
NO TEAM! JUST ONE *TACTICAL SUPPORT UNIT* STRAIGHT FROM THE U.S.A!
BUT THE LETTER SAID TO EXPECT "THE *WHOLE* FAMILY?"
HAS TO BE SOME MISUNDERSTANDING. CAN I TALK TO--
WHUPWHUPWHUPWHUPWHUPWHUPWHUPWHUPWHUP
THIS.

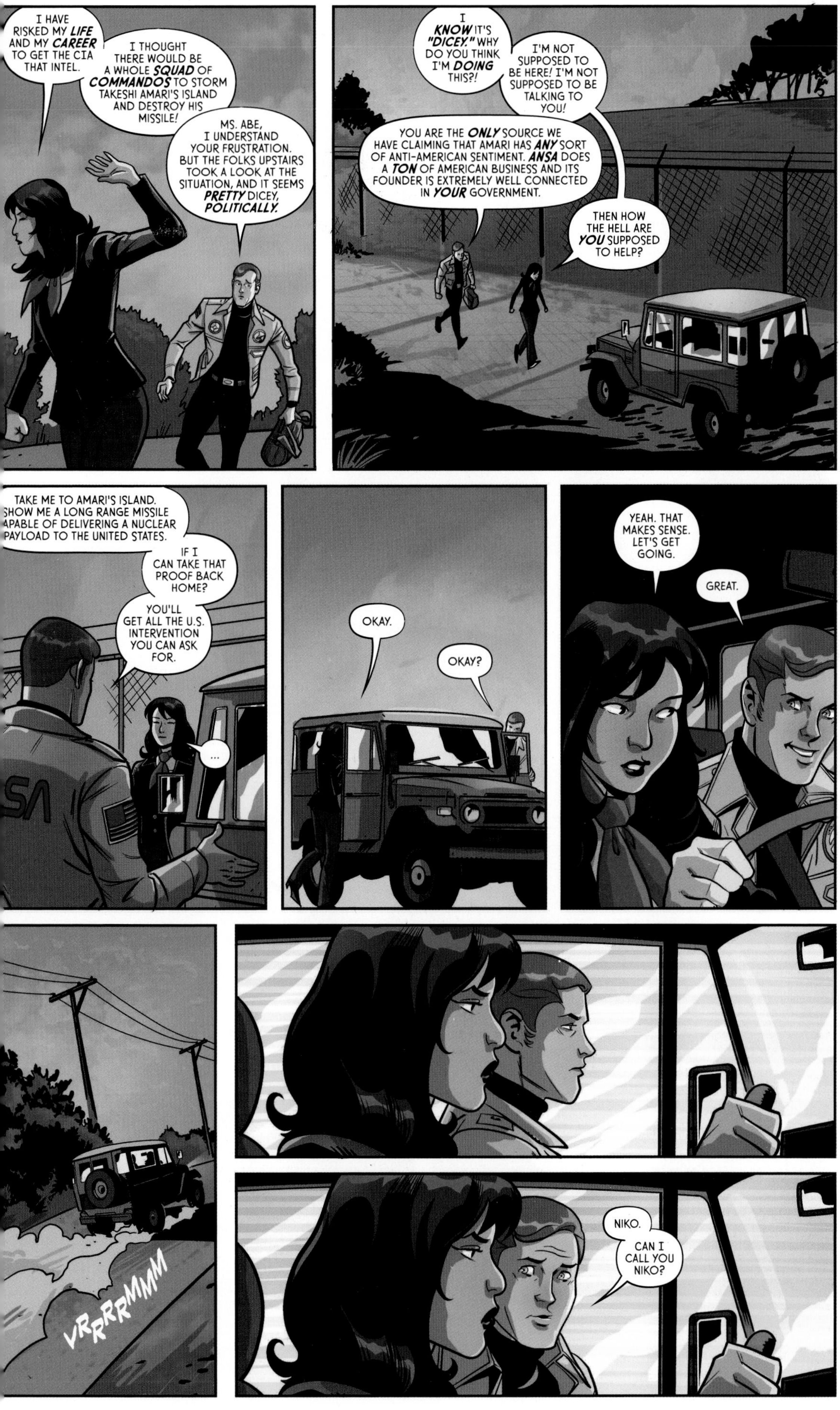
I HAVE RISKED MY LIFE AND MY CAREER TO GET THE CIA THAT INTEL.
I THOUGHT THERE WOULD BE A WHOLE SQUAD OF COMMANDOS TO STORM TAKESHI AMARI'S ISLAND AND DESTROY HIS MISSILE!
MS. ABE, I UNDERSTAND YOUR FRUSTRATION. BUT THE FOLKS UPSTAIRS TOOK A LOOK AT THE SITUATION, AND IT SEEMS PRETTY DICEY, POLITICALLY.
I KNOW IT'S "DICEY." WHY DO YOU THINK I'M DOING THIS?!
I'M NOT SUPPOSED TO BE HERE! I'M NOT SUPPOSED TO BE TALKING TO YOU!
YOU ARE THE ONLY SOURCE WE HAVE CLAIMING THAT AMARI HAS ANY SORT OF ANTI-AMERICAN SENTIMENT. ANSA DOES A TON OF AMERICAN BUSINESS AND ITS FOUNDER IS EXTREMELY WELL CONNECTED IN YOUR GOVERNMENT.
THEN HOW THE HELL ARE YOU SUPPOSED TO HELP?
TAKE ME TO AMARI'S ISLAND. SHOW ME A LONG RANGE MISSILE APABLE OF DELIVERING A NUCLEAR PAYLOAD TO THE UNITED STATES.
IF I CAN TAKE THAT PROOF BACK HOME?
YOU'LL GET ALL THE U.S. INTERVENTION YOU CAN ASK FOR.
...
OKAY.
OKAY?
YEAH. THAT MAKES SENSE. LET'S GET GOING.
GREAT.
VRRRRMMM
NIKO.
CAN I CALL YOU NIKO?

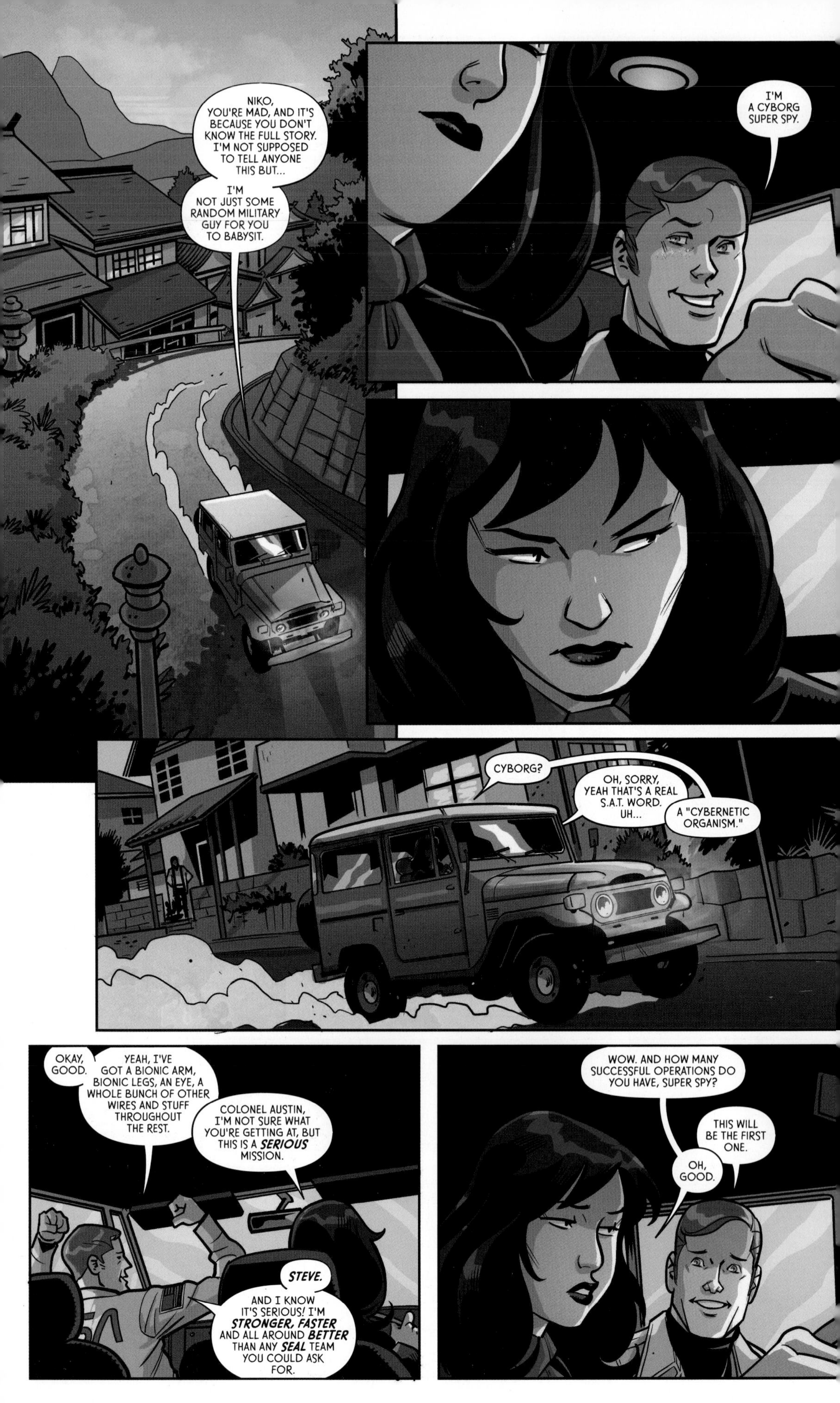
NIKO, YOU'RE MAD, AND IT'S BECAUSE YOU DON'T KNOW THE FULL STORY. I'M NOT SUPPOSED TO TELL ANYONE THIS BUT...
I'M NOT JUST SOME RANDOM MILITARY GUY FOR YOU TO BABYSIT.
I'M A CYBORG SUPER SPY.
CYBORG?
OH, SORRY, YEAH THAT'S A REAL S.A.T. WORD. UH...
A "CYBERNETIC ORGANISM."
OKAY, GOOD.
YEAH, I'VE GOT A BIONIC ARM, BIONIC LEGS, AN EYE, A WHOLE BUNCH OF OTHER WIRES AND STUFF THROUGHOUT THE REST.
COLONEL AUSTIN, I'M NOT SURE WHAT YOU'RE GETTING AT, BUT THIS IS A ***SERIOUS*** MISSION.
STEVE.
AND I KNOW IT'S SERIOUS! I'M ***STRONGER, FASTER*** AND ALL AROUND ***BETTER*** THAN ANY ***SEAL*** TEAM YOU COULD ASK FOR.
WOW. AND HOW MANY SUCCESSFUL OPERATIONS DO YOU HAVE, SUPER SPY?
THIS WILL BE THE FIRST ONE.
OH, GOOD.

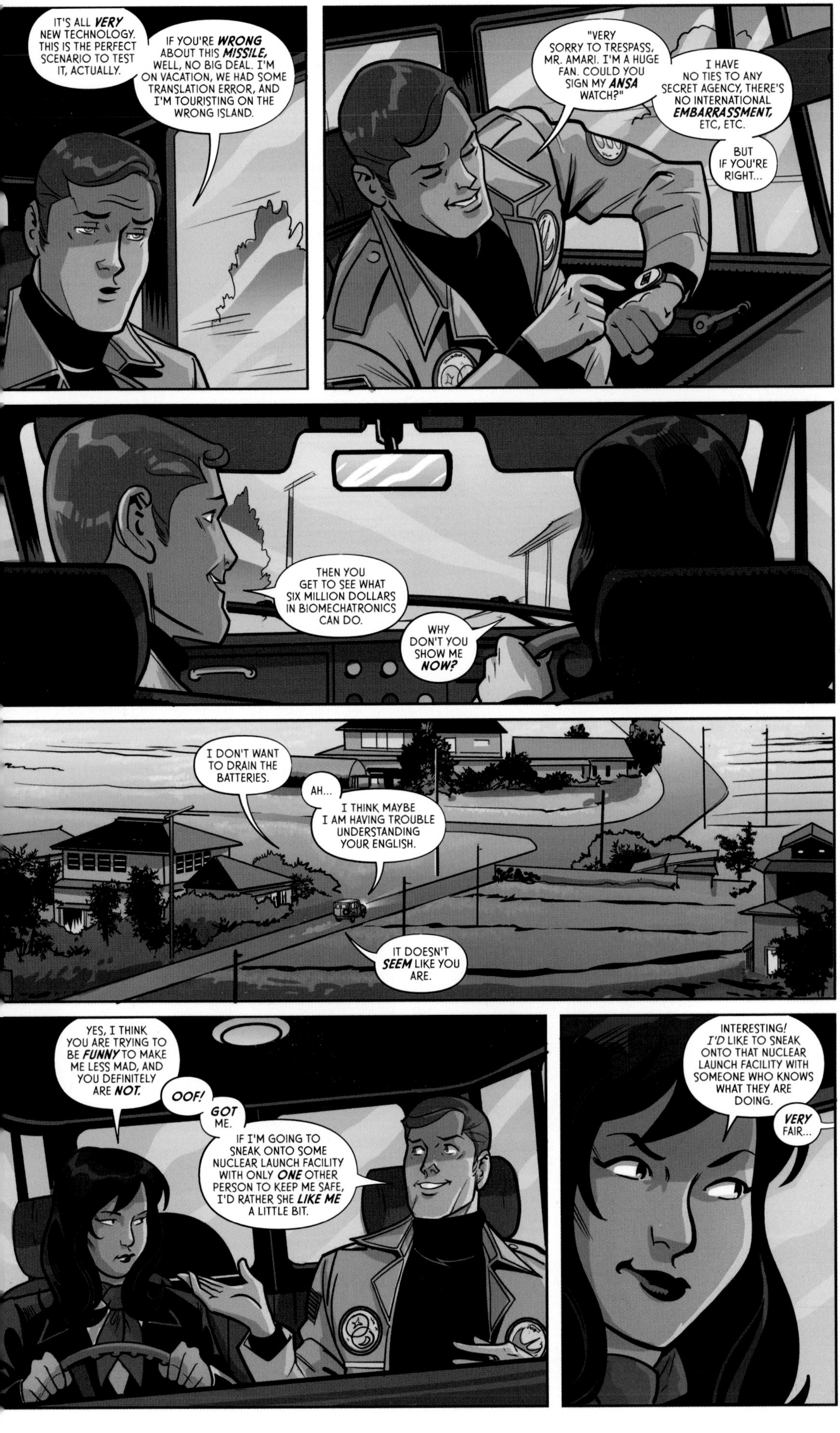

IT'S ALL VERY NEW TECHNOLOGY. THIS IS THE PERFECT SCENARIO TO TEST IT, ACTUALLY.
IF YOU'RE WRONG ABOUT THIS MISSILE, WELL, NO BIG DEAL. I'M ON VACATION, WE HAD SOME TRANSLATION ERROR, AND I'M TOURISTING ON THE WRONG ISLAND.
"VERY SORRY TO TRESPASS, MR. AMARI. I'M A HUGE FAN. COULD YOU SIGN MY ANSA WATCH?"
I HAVE NO TIES TO ANY SECRET AGENCY, THERE'S NO INTERNATIONAL EMBARRASSMENT, ETC, ETC.
BUT IF YOU'RE RIGHT...
THEN YOU GET TO SEE WHAT SIX MILLION DOLLARS IN BIOMECHATRONICS CAN DO.
WHY DON'T YOU SHOW ME NOW?
I DON'T WANT TO DRAIN THE BATTERIES.
AH...
I THINK MAYBE I AM HAVING TROUBLE UNDERSTANDING YOUR ENGLISH.
IT DOESN'T SEEM LIKE YOU ARE.
YES, I THINK YOU ARE TRYING TO BE FUNNY TO MAKE ME LESS MAD, AND YOU DEFINITELY ARE NOT.
OOF!
GOT ME.
IF I'M GOING TO SNEAK ONTO SOME NUCLEAR LAUNCH FACILITY WITH ONLY ONE OTHER PERSON TO KEEP ME SAFE, I'D RATHER SHE LIKE ME A LITTLE BIT.
INTERESTING! I'D LIKE TO SNEAK ONTO THAT NUCLEAR LAUNCH FACILITY WITH SOMEONE WHO KNOWS WHAT THEY ARE DOING.
VERY FAIR...

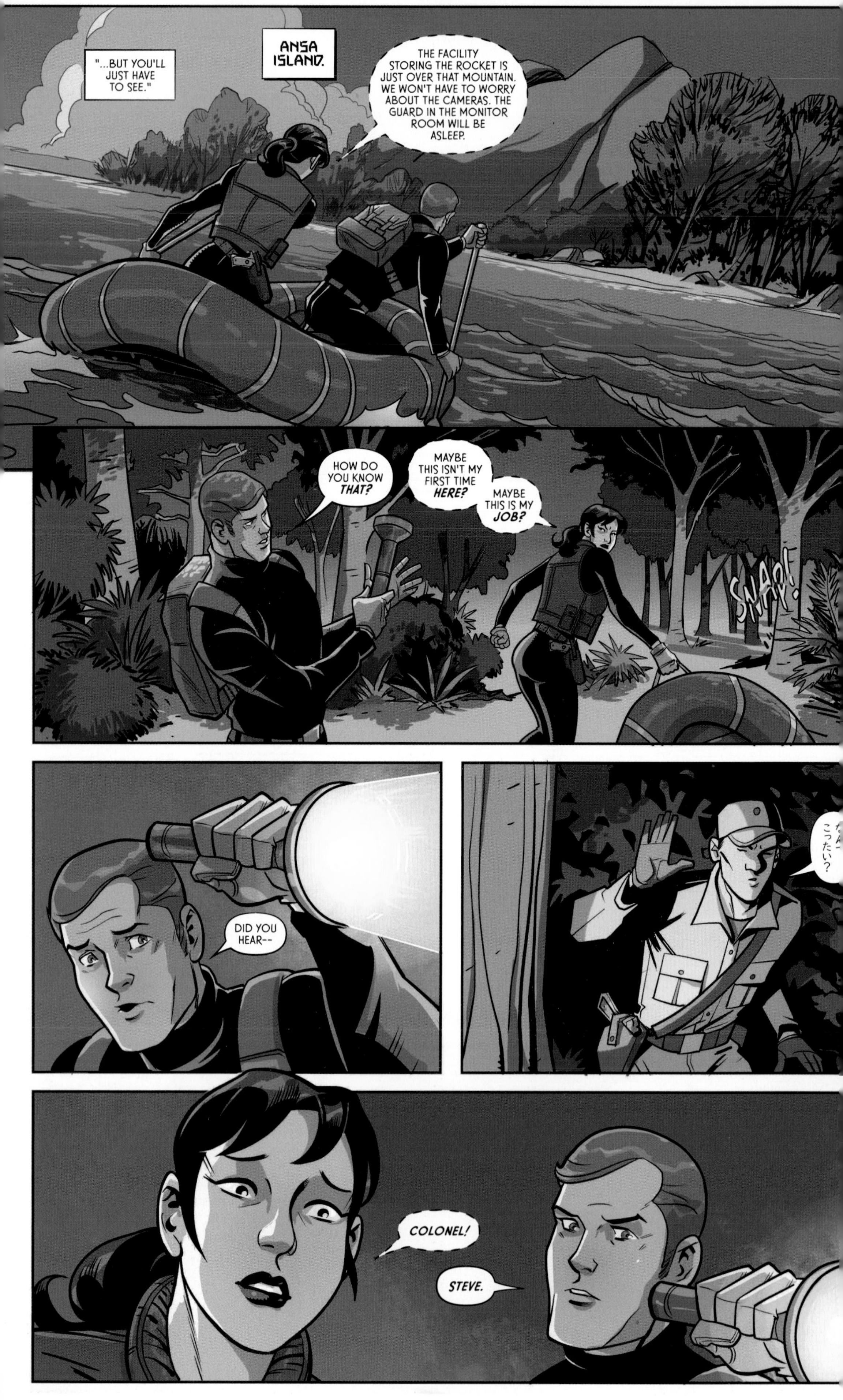
"...BUT YOU'LL JUST HAVE TO SEE."
ANSA ISLAND.
THE FACILITY STORING THE ROCKET IS JUST OVER THAT MOUNTAIN. WE WON'T HAVE TO WORRY ABOUT THE CAMERAS. THE GUARD IN THE MONITOR ROOM WILL BE ASLEEP.
HOW DO YOU KNOW *THAT?*
MAYBE THIS ISN'T MY FIRST TIME *HERE?*
MAYBE THIS IS MY *JOB?*
SNAP!
DID YOU HEAR--
こったい？
COLONEL!
STEVE.

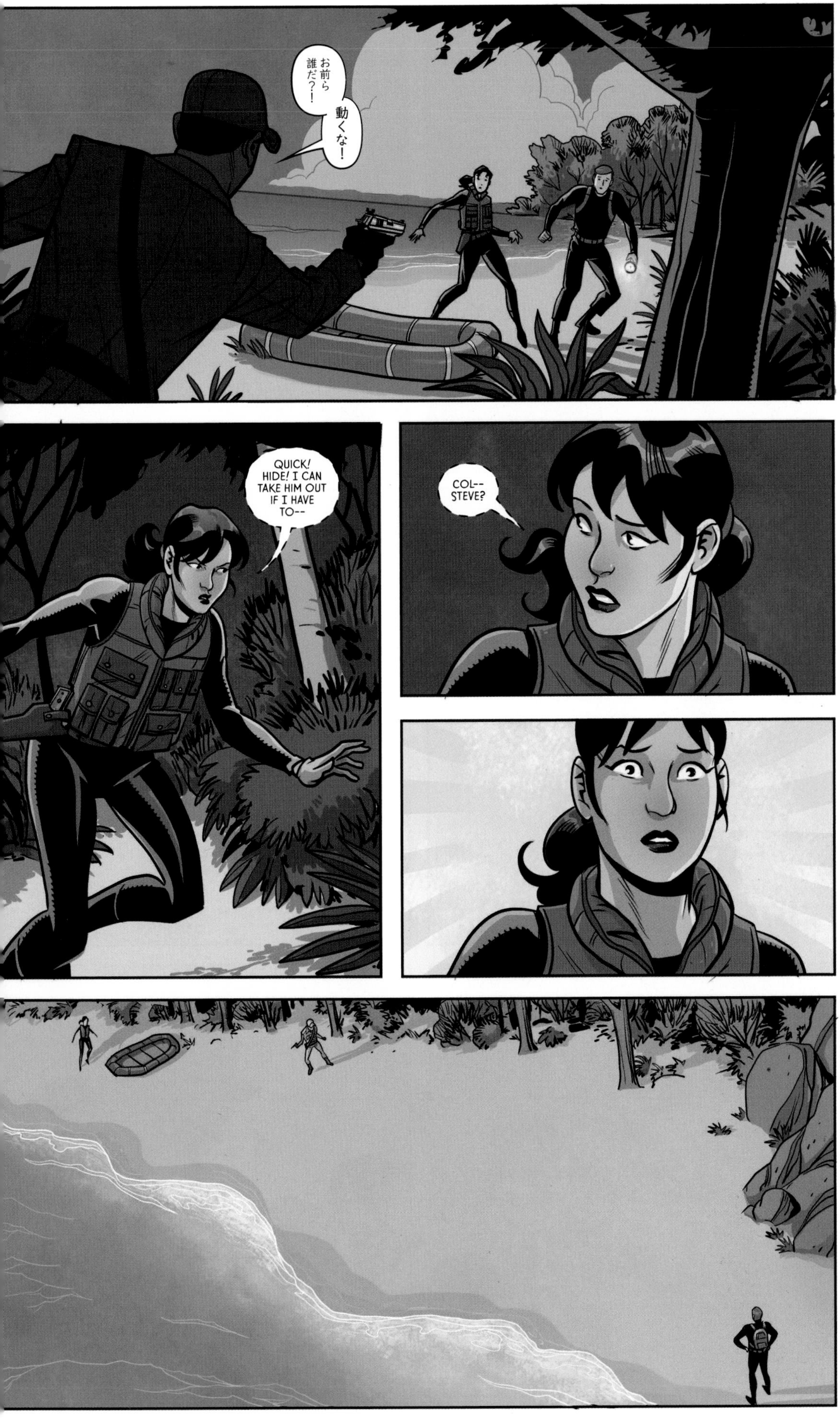
お前ら誰だ?!
動くな!
QUICK! HIDE! I CAN TAKE HIM OUT IF I HAVE TO--
COL-- STEVE?

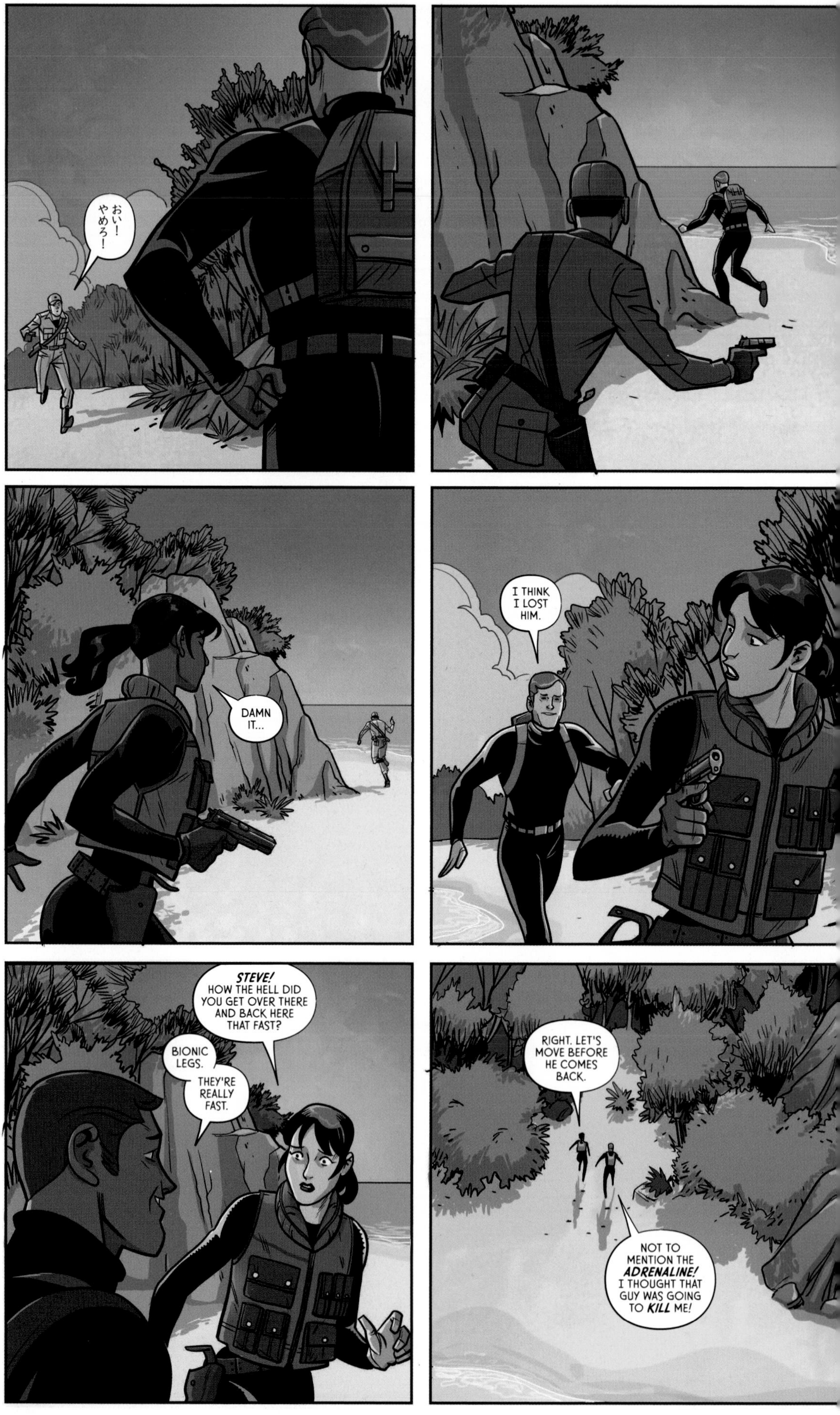
おい！
やめろ！
DAMN IT...
I THINK I LOST HIM.
STEVE! HOW THE HELL DID YOU GET OVER THERE AND BACK HERE THAT FAST?
BIONIC LEGS.
THEY'RE REALLY FAST.
RIGHT. LET'S MOVE BEFORE HE COMES BACK.
NOT TO MENTION THE ADRENALINE! I THOUGHT THAT GUY WAS GOING TO KILL ME!

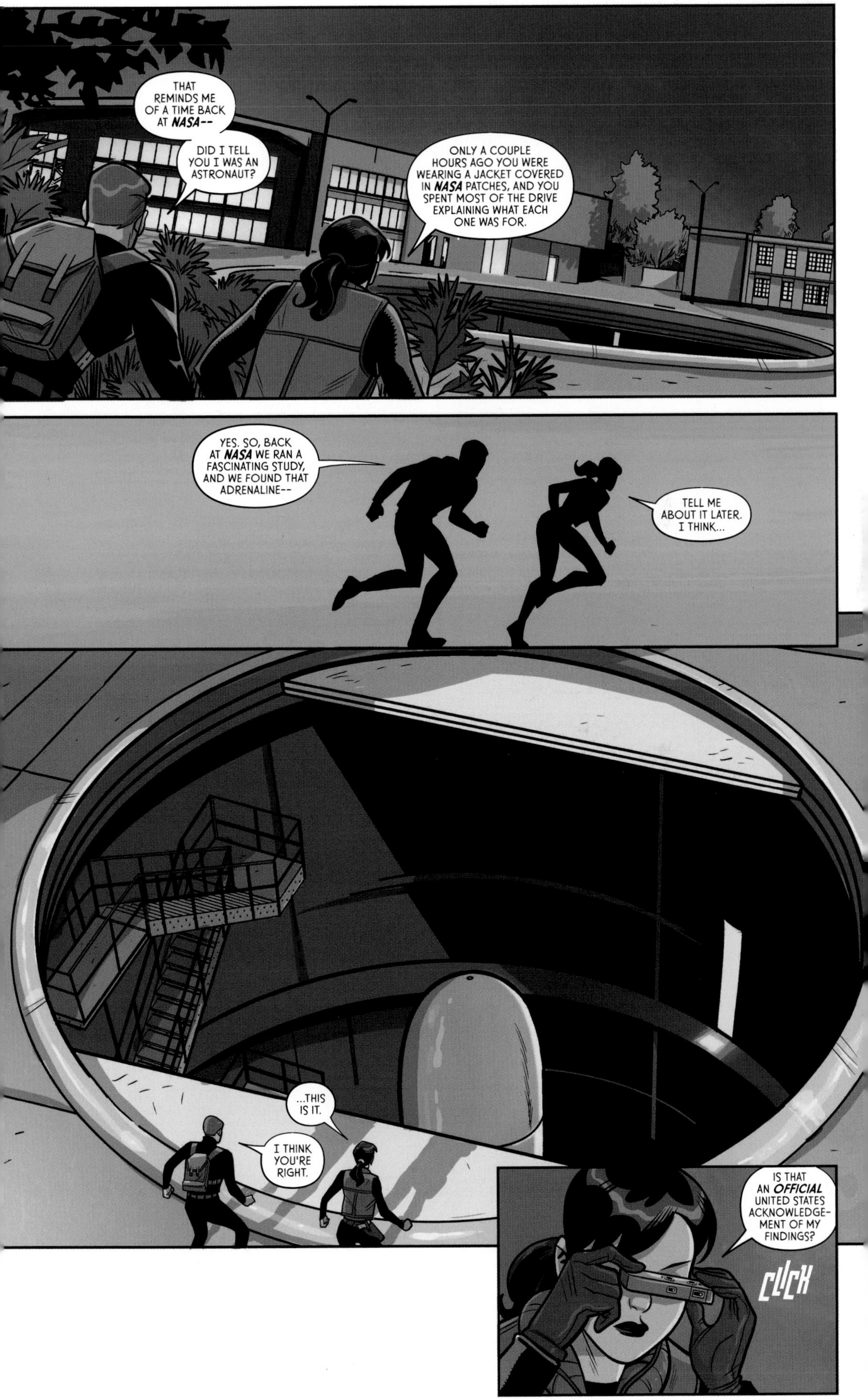
THAT REMINDS ME OF A TIME BACK AT NASA--
DID I TELL YOU I WAS AN ASTRONAUT?
ONLY A COUPLE HOURS AGO YOU WERE WEARING A JACKET COVERED IN NASA PATCHES, AND YOU SPENT MOST OF THE DRIVE EXPLAINING WHAT EACH ONE WAS FOR.
YES. SO, BACK AT NASA WE RAN A FASCINATING STUDY, AND WE FOUND THAT ADRENALINE--
TELL ME ABOUT IT LATER. I THINK...
...THIS IS IT.
I THINK YOU'RE RIGHT.
IS THAT AN OFFICIAL UNITED STATES ACKNOWLEDGE-MENT OF MY FINDINGS?
CLICK

IT WILL BE SOON...

WHRR WHRR--*CLICK*
WHRR WHRR--*CLICK*

HOW THE HELL--

IT'S NEARLY IDENTICAL TO OUR *TITAN II*'S.

INSIDE THERE'S...

AEROZINE FIFTY AND DINITROGEN TETROXIDE.

IT'S FUELED.

GET YOUR PICTURES, AND WE'LL GET OUT OF HERE. IT'S ALL WE NEED TO SHUT THIS WHOLE THING DOWN.

AT LEAST IT ISN'T ARMED.

HOW CAN YOU *TELL*?

WHFWHFWHFWH

BIONIC EYE.

WHFWHFWHFWHFWHFWH

WHAT? YOU CAN SEE *THROUGH* THINGS BECAUSE YOU HAVE A *FAKE* EYE?

IT'S NOT FAKE, IT'S *BIONIC*. AND *YES.*

"BIONIC" *WHAT?*

BIONIC COULD MEAN *ANYTHING*--

IT'S JUST REALLY GOOD, OKAY!? NOW, BE *QUIET.*

OH, NOW YOU'RE TELLING *ME* TO BE STEALTHY, THAT'S--

KGB JUST SHOWED UP.

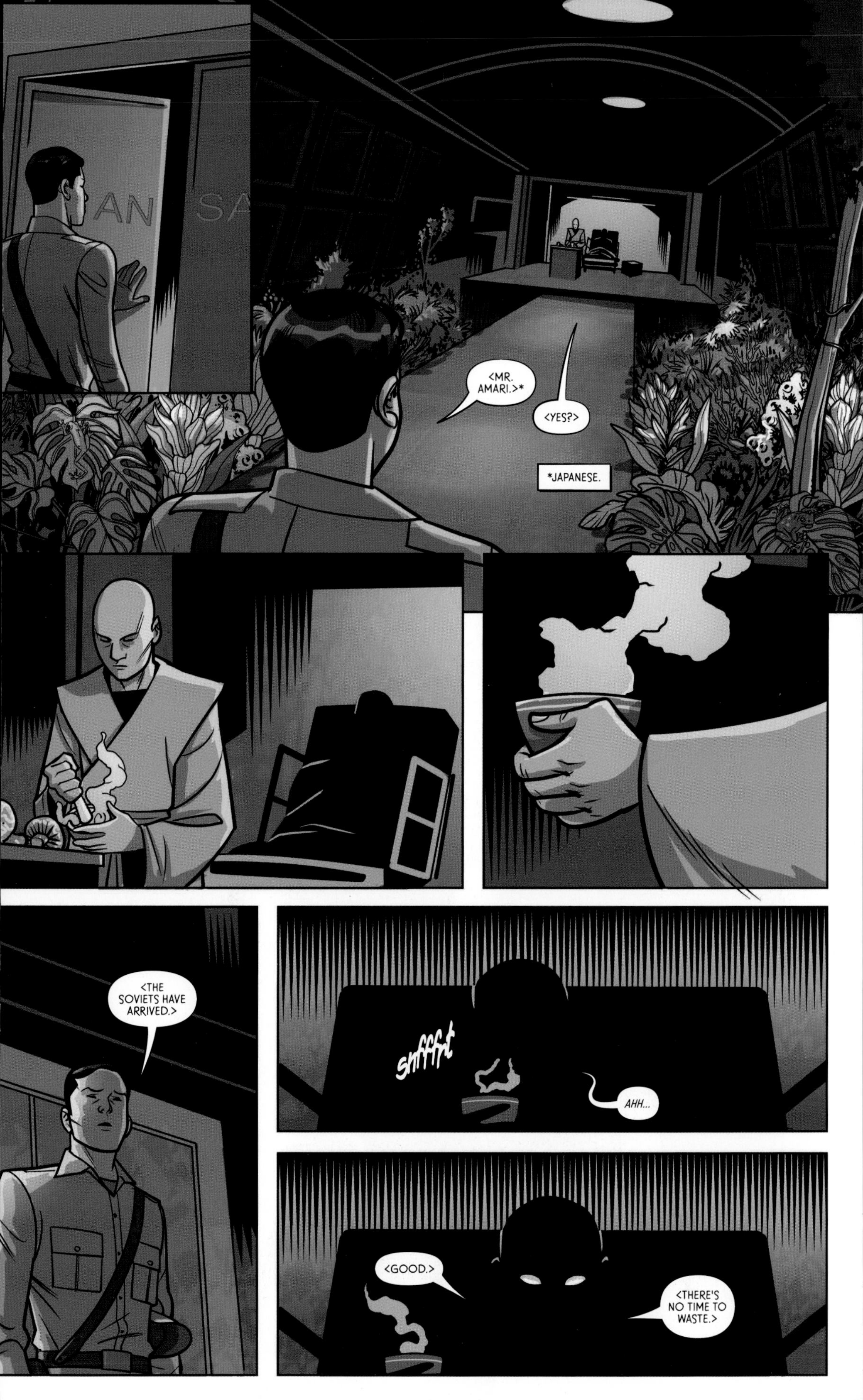
<MR. AMARI.>*
<YES?>
*JAPANESE.
<THE SOVIETS HAVE ARRIVED.>
snfffrt
AHH...
<GOOD.>
<THERE'S NO TIME TO WASTE.>

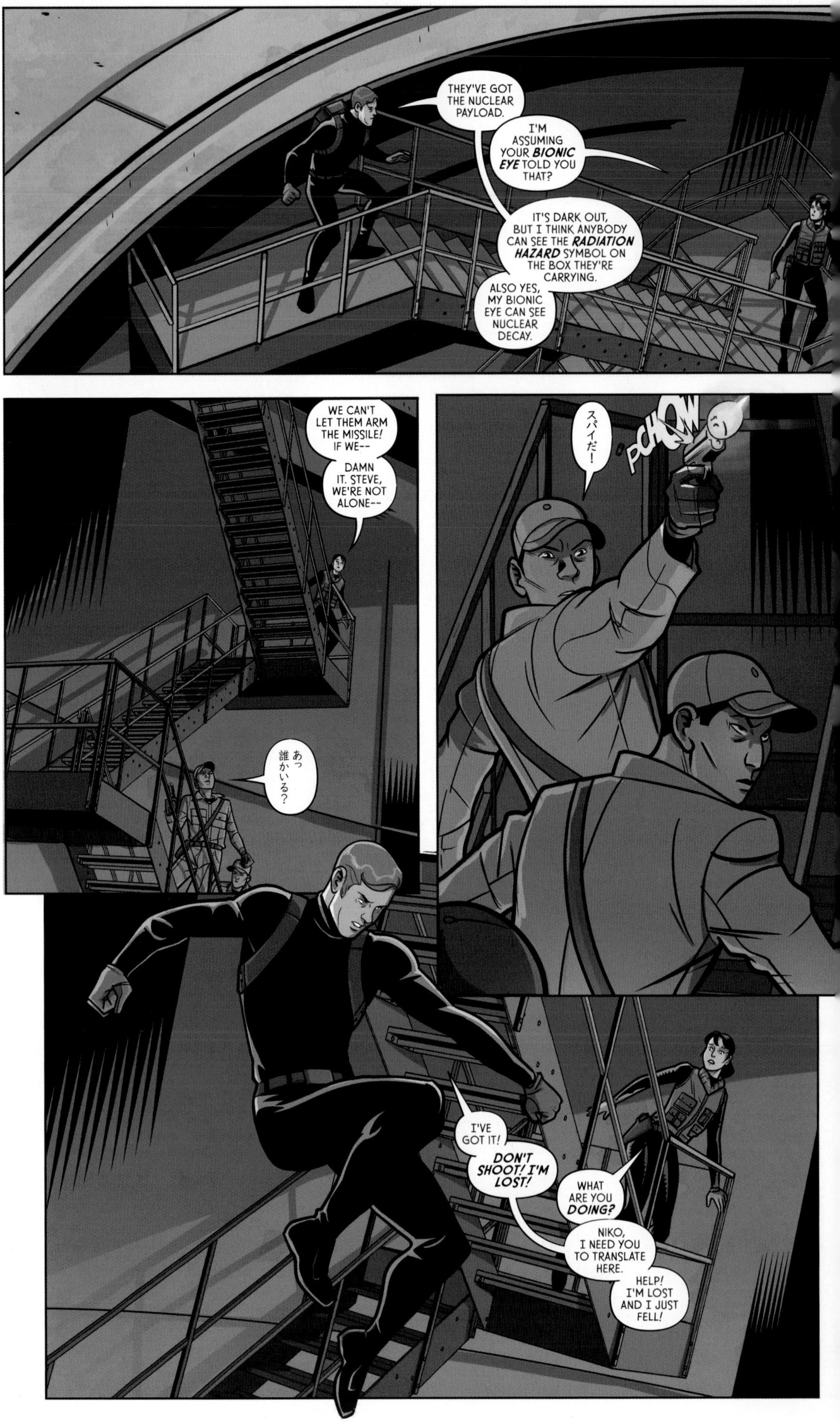
THEY'VE GOT THE NUCLEAR PAYLOAD.
I'M ASSUMING YOUR **BIONIC EYE** TOLD YOU THAT?
IT'S DARK OUT, BUT I THINK ANYBODY CAN SEE THE **RADIATION HAZARD** SYMBOL ON THE BOX THEY'RE CARRYING.
ALSO YES, MY BIONIC EYE CAN SEE NUCLEAR DECAY.
WE CAN'T LET THEM ARM THE MISSILE! IF WE--
DAMN IT. STEVE, WE'RE NOT ALONE--
あっ 誰かいる？
スパイだ！
PCHOW
I'VE GOT IT!
DON'T SHOOT! I'M LOST!
WHAT ARE YOU **DOING?**
NIKO, I NEED YOU TO TRANSLATE HERE.
HELP! I'M LOST AND I JUST FELL!

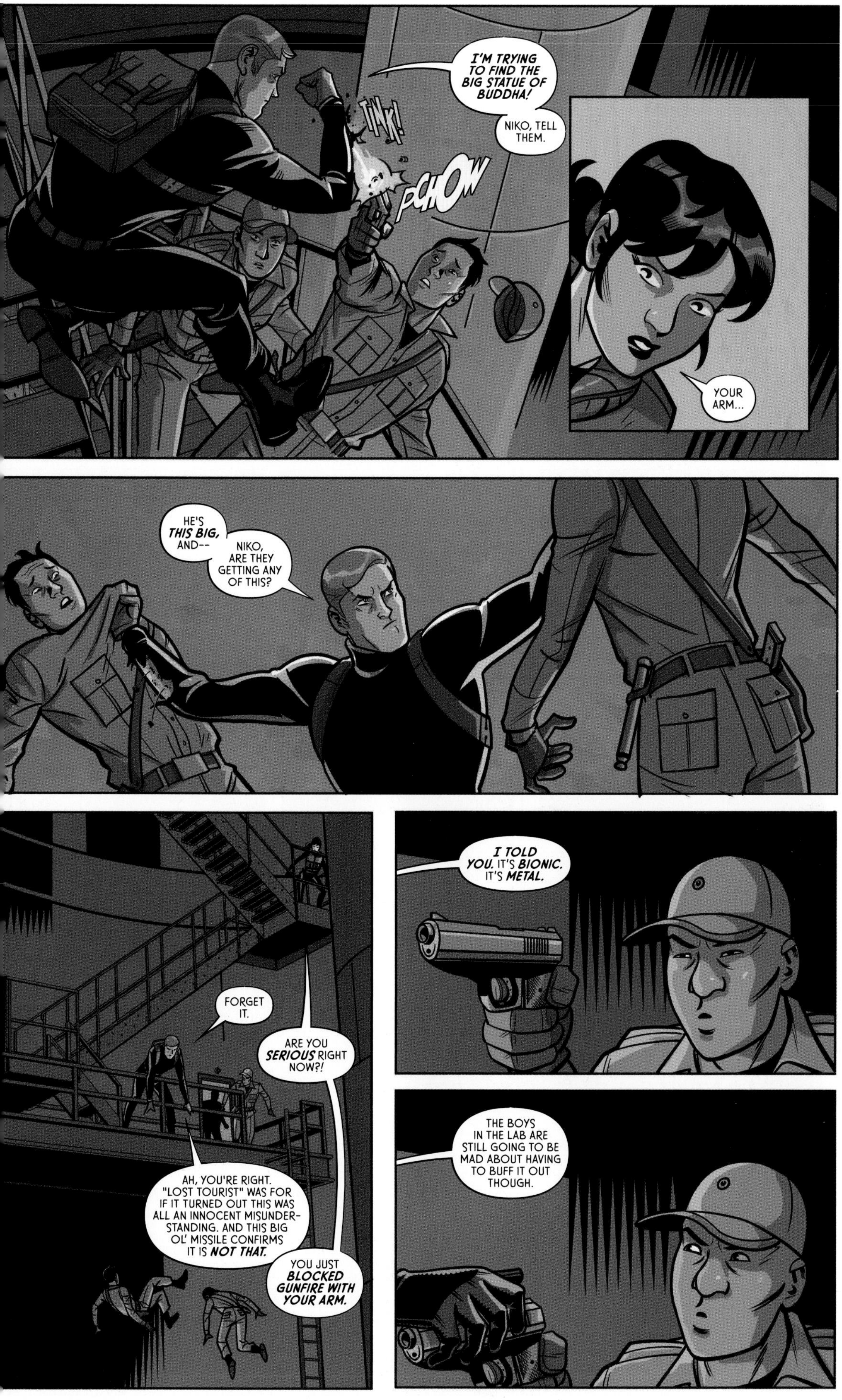
I'M TRYING TO FIND THE BIG STATUE OF BUDDHA!
NIKO, TELL THEM.
TINK!
PCHOW
YOUR ARM...
HE'S THIS BIG, AND--
NIKO, ARE THEY GETTING ANY OF THIS?
FORGET IT.
ARE YOU SERIOUS RIGHT NOW?!
AH, YOU'RE RIGHT. "LOST TOURIST" WAS FOR IF IT TURNED OUT THIS WAS ALL AN INNOCENT MISUNDER-STANDING. AND THIS BIG OL' MISSILE CONFIRMS IT IS NOT THAT.
YOU JUST BLOCKED GUNFIRE WITH YOUR ARM.
I TOLD YOU. IT'S BIONIC. IT'S METAL.
THE BOYS IN THE LAB ARE STILL GOING TO BE MAD ABOUT HAVING TO BUFF IT OUT THOUGH.

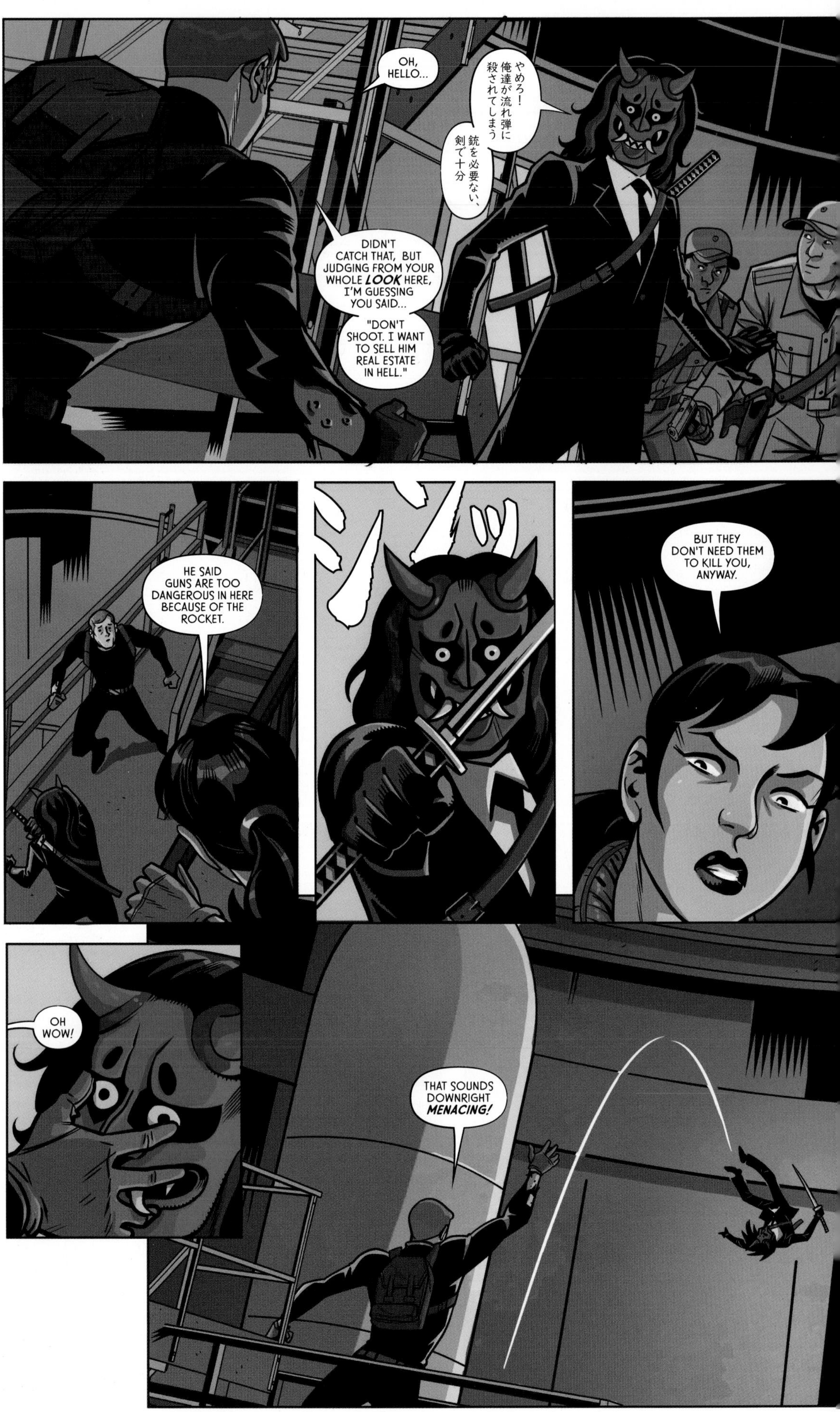

OH, HELLO...
やめろ！
俺達が流れ弾に
殺されてしまう
銃を必要ない、
剣で十分
DIDN'T CATCH THAT, BUT JUDGING FROM YOUR WHOLE ***LOOK*** HERE, I'M GUESSING YOU SAID...
"DON'T SHOOT. I WANT TO SELL HIM REAL ESTATE IN HELL."
HE SAID GUNS ARE TOO DANGEROUS IN HERE BECAUSE OF THE ROCKET.
BUT THEY DON'T NEED THEM TO KILL YOU, ANYWAY.
OH WOW!
THAT SOUNDS DOWNRIGHT ***MENACING!***

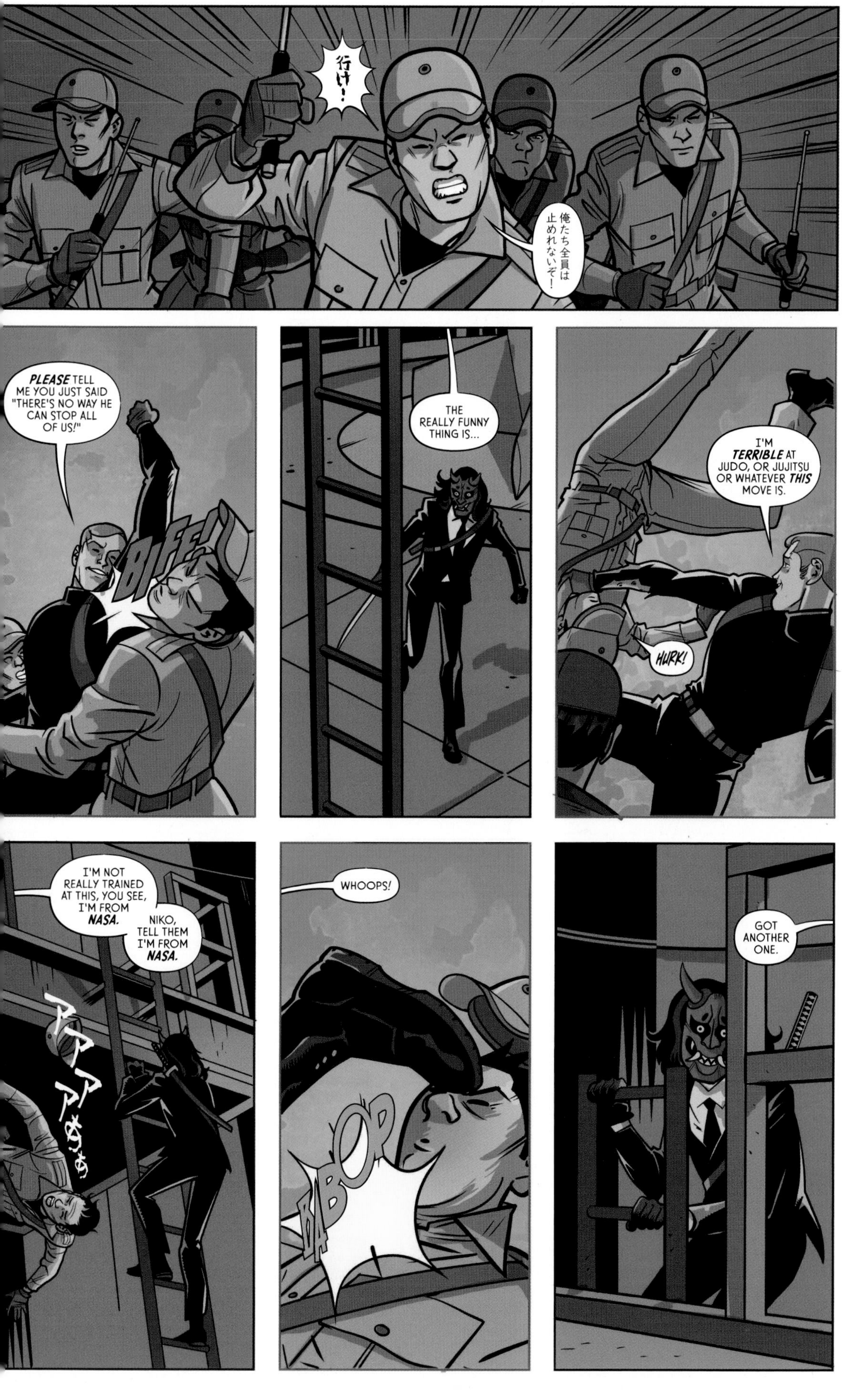

行け！
俺たち全員は止めれないぞ！
PLEASE TELL ME YOU JUST SAID "THERE'S NO WAY HE CAN STOP ALL OF US!"
BIFF!
THE REALLY FUNNY THING IS...
I'M **TERRIBLE** AT JUDO, OR JUJITSU OR WHATEVER **THIS** MOVE IS.
HURK!
I'M NOT REALLY TRAINED AT THIS, YOU SEE, I'M FROM **NASA.**
NIKO, TELL THEM I'M FROM **NASA.**
アアアあぁ
WHOOPS!
BABOP
GOT ANOTHER ONE.

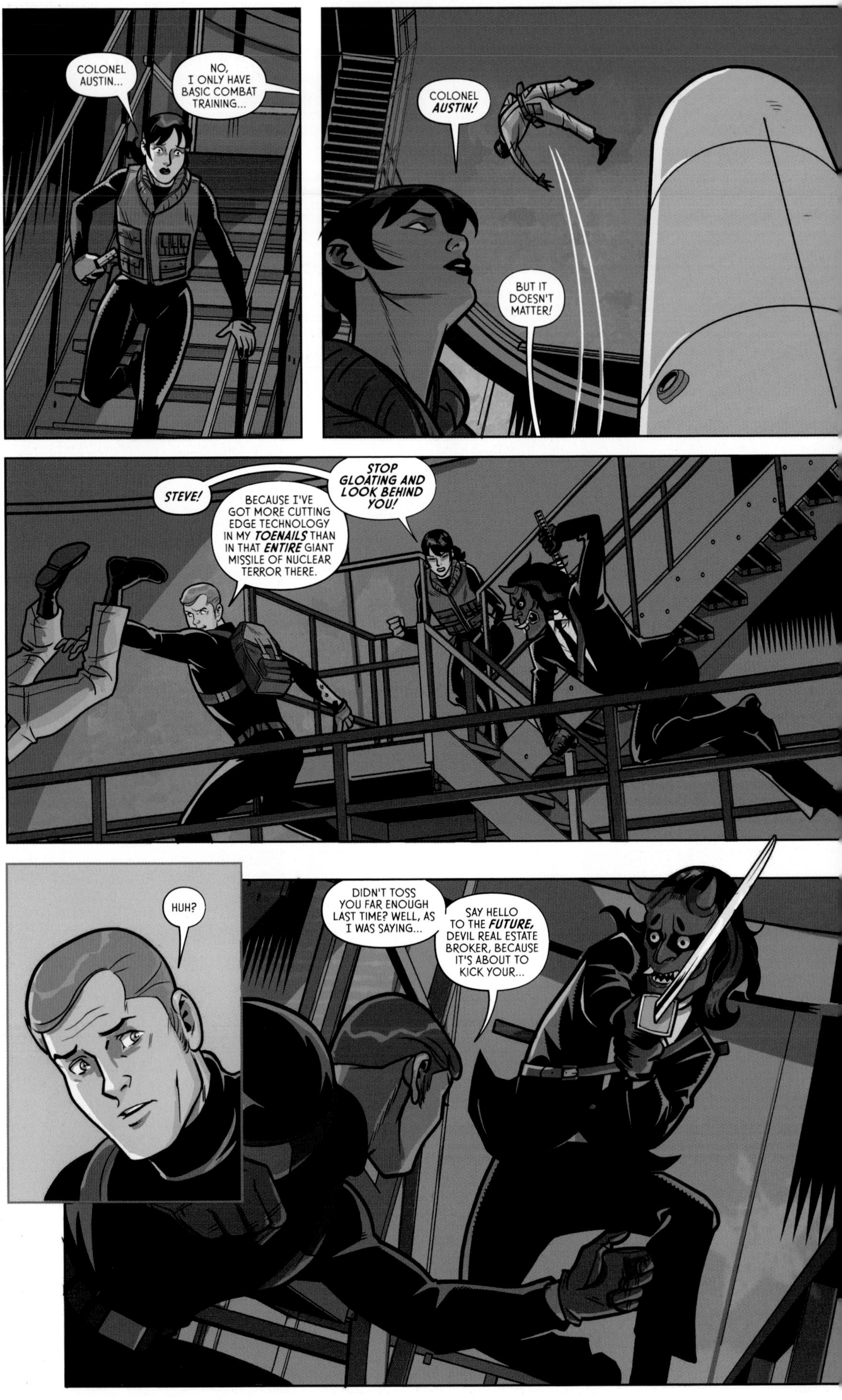

COLONEL AUSTIN...
NO, I ONLY HAVE BASIC COMBAT TRAINING...
COLONEL AUSTIN!
BUT IT DOESN'T MATTER!
STEVE!
STOP GLOATING AND LOOK BEHIND YOU!
BECAUSE I'VE GOT MORE CUTTING EDGE TECHNOLOGY IN MY TOENAILS THAN IN THAT ENTIRE GIANT MISSILE OF NUCLEAR TERROR THERE.
HUH?
DIDN'T TOSS YOU FAR ENOUGH LAST TIME? WELL, AS I WAS SAYING...
SAY HELLO TO THE FUTURE, DEVIL REAL ESTATE BROKER, BECAUSE IT'S ABOUT TO KICK YOUR...

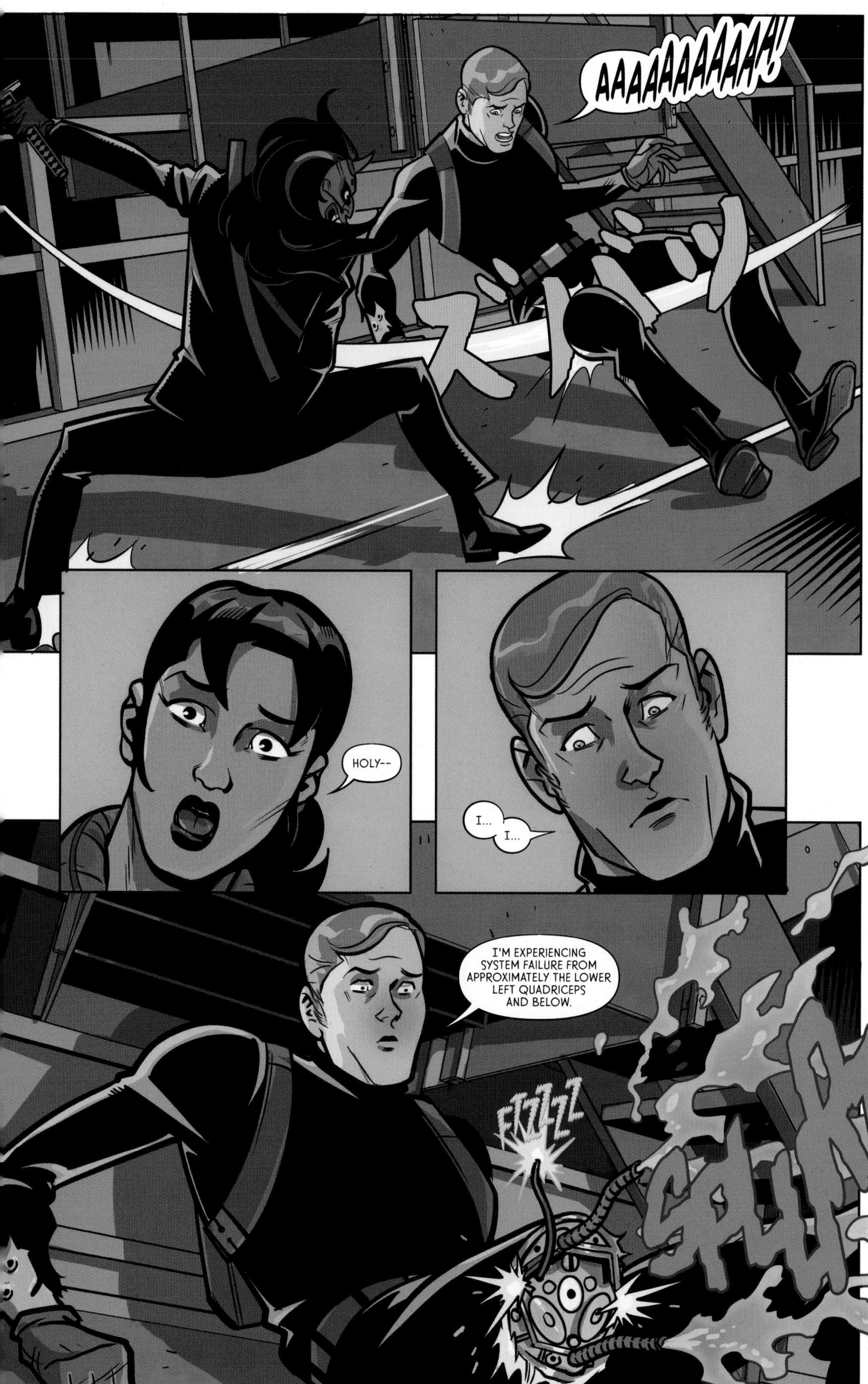
AAAAAAAAAAH!
HOLY--
I... I...
I'M EXPERIENCING SYSTEM FAILURE FROM APPROXIMATELY THE LOWER LEFT QUADRICEPS AND BELOW.
FTZZZZ

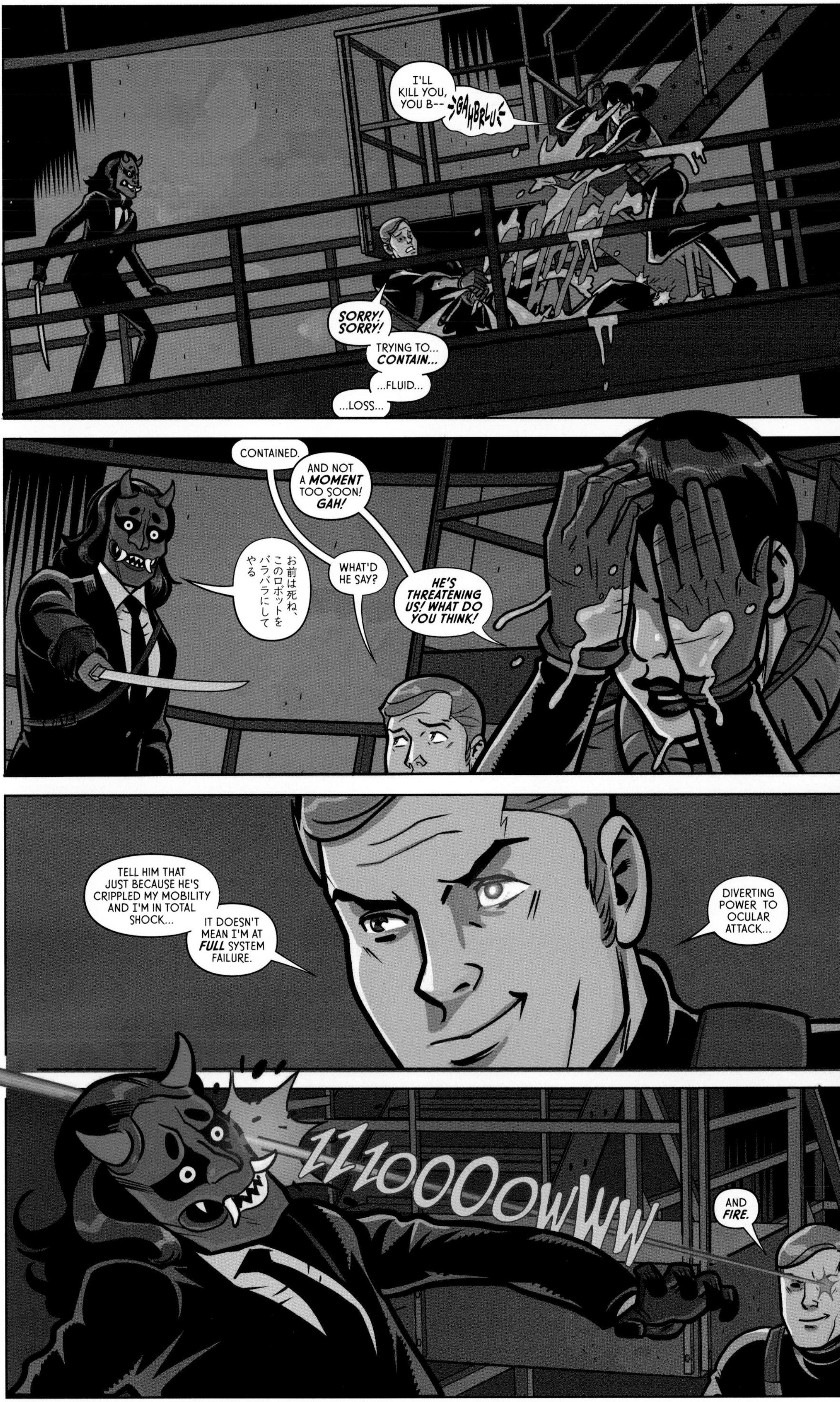

I'LL KILL YOU, YOU B--
GAHBRLU
SORRY! SORRY!
TRYING TO... CONTAIN...
...FLUID...
...LOSS...
CONTAINED.
AND NOT A MOMENT TOO SOON! GAH!
お前は死ね、このロボットをバラバラにしてやる
WHAT'D HE SAY?
HE'S THREATENING US! WHAT DO YOU THINK!
TELL HIM THAT JUST BECAUSE HE'S CRIPPLED MY MOBILITY AND I'M IN TOTAL SHOCK...
IT DOESN'T MEAN I'M AT FULL SYSTEM FAILURE.
DIVERTING POWER TO OCULAR ATTACK...
ZZZOOOOOWWW
AND FIRE.

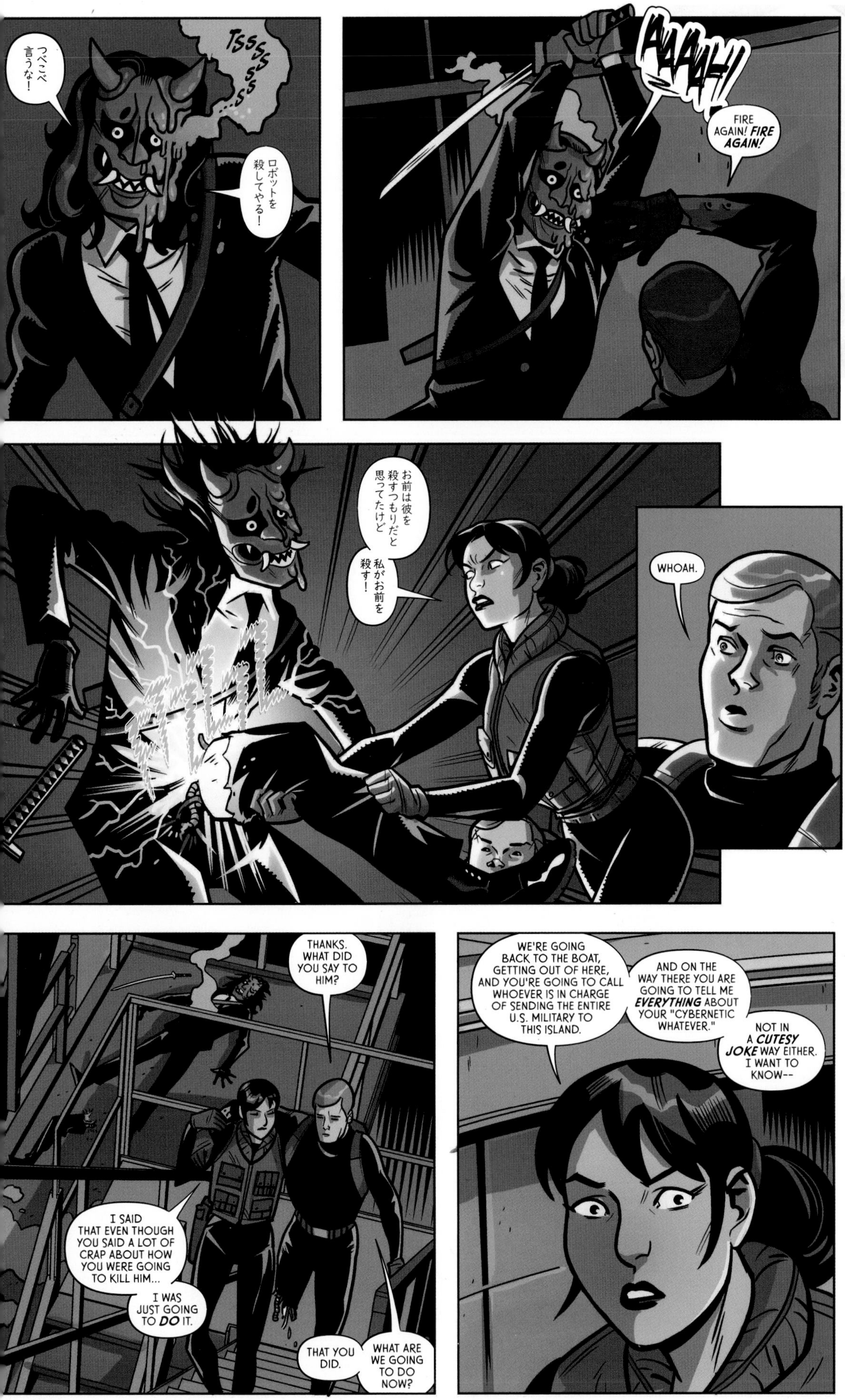

つべこべ言うな！
TSSSSSSS
ロボットを殺してやる！
AAAAAH!!
FIRE AGAIN! ***FIRE AGAIN!***
お前は彼を殺すつもりだと思ってたけど
私がお前を殺す！
WHOAH.
THANKS. WHAT DID YOU SAY TO HIM?
I SAID THAT EVEN THOUGH YOU SAID A LOT OF CRAP ABOUT HOW YOU WERE GOING TO KILL HIM...
I WAS JUST GOING TO ***DO*** IT.
THAT YOU DID.
WHAT ARE WE GOING TO DO NOW?
WE'RE GOING BACK TO THE BOAT, GETTING OUT OF HERE, AND YOU'RE GOING TO CALL WHOEVER IS IN CHARGE OF SENDING THE ENTIRE U.S. MILITARY TO THIS ISLAND.
AND ON THE WAY THERE YOU ARE GOING TO TELL ME ***EVERYTHING*** ABOUT YOUR "CYBERNETIC WHATEVER."
NOT IN A ***CUTESY JOKE*** WAY EITHER. I WANT TO KNOW--

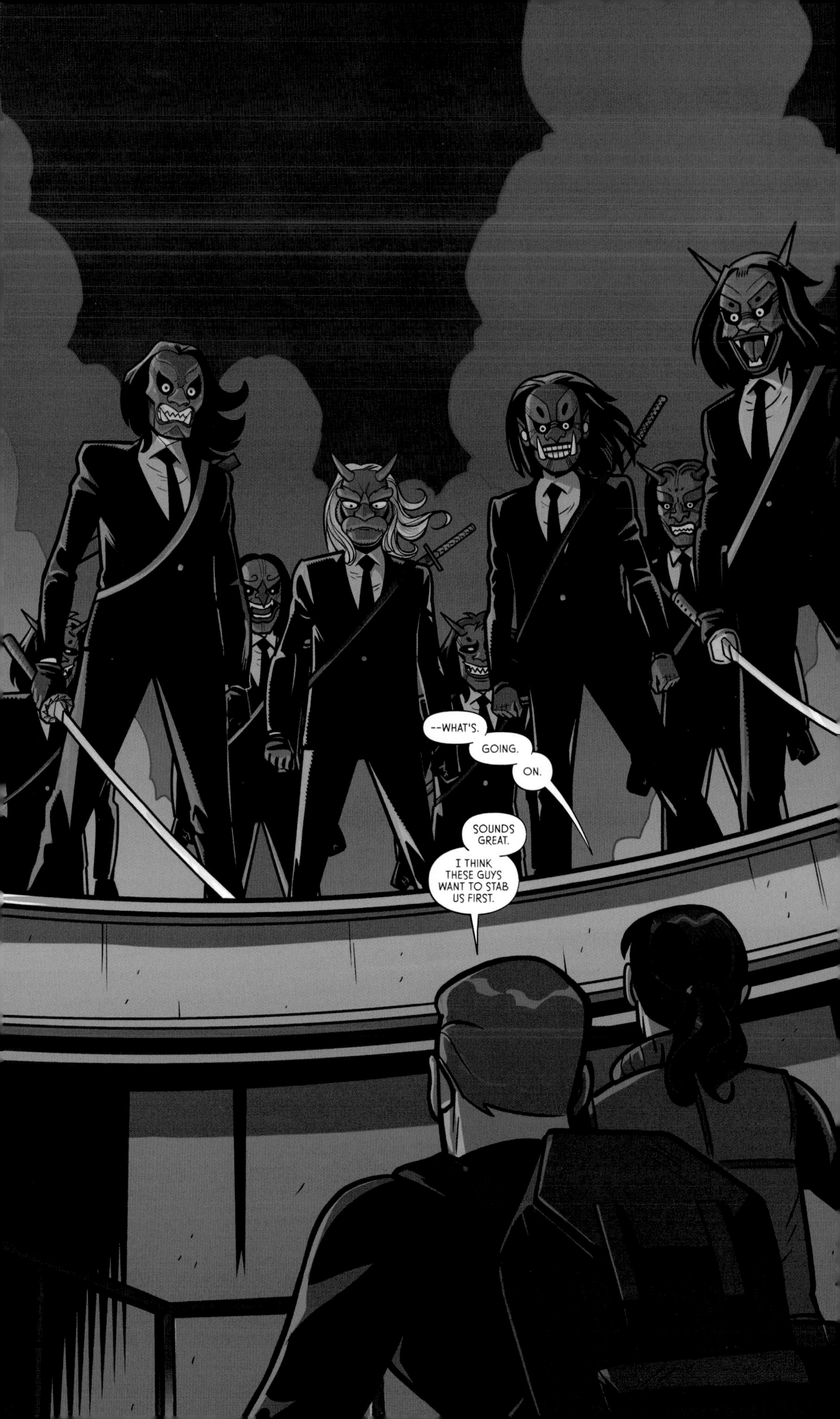
--WHAT'S.
GOING.
ON.
SOUNDS GREAT.
I THINK THESE GUYS WANT TO STAB US FIRST.

TEVE AUSTIN. ASTRONAUT. A MAN BARELY ALIVE AFTER A HORRIBLE ACCIDENT. REBUILT AS THE WORLD'S FIRST BIONIC MAN. BETTER THAN HE WAS BEFORE.

BETTER, STRONGER, FASTER.

THE

3,192,116

DOLLAR

MAN

[...EXCEPT THAT HIS LEG'S BEEN CHOPPED OFF BUT I'M SURE IT'LL BE FINE]

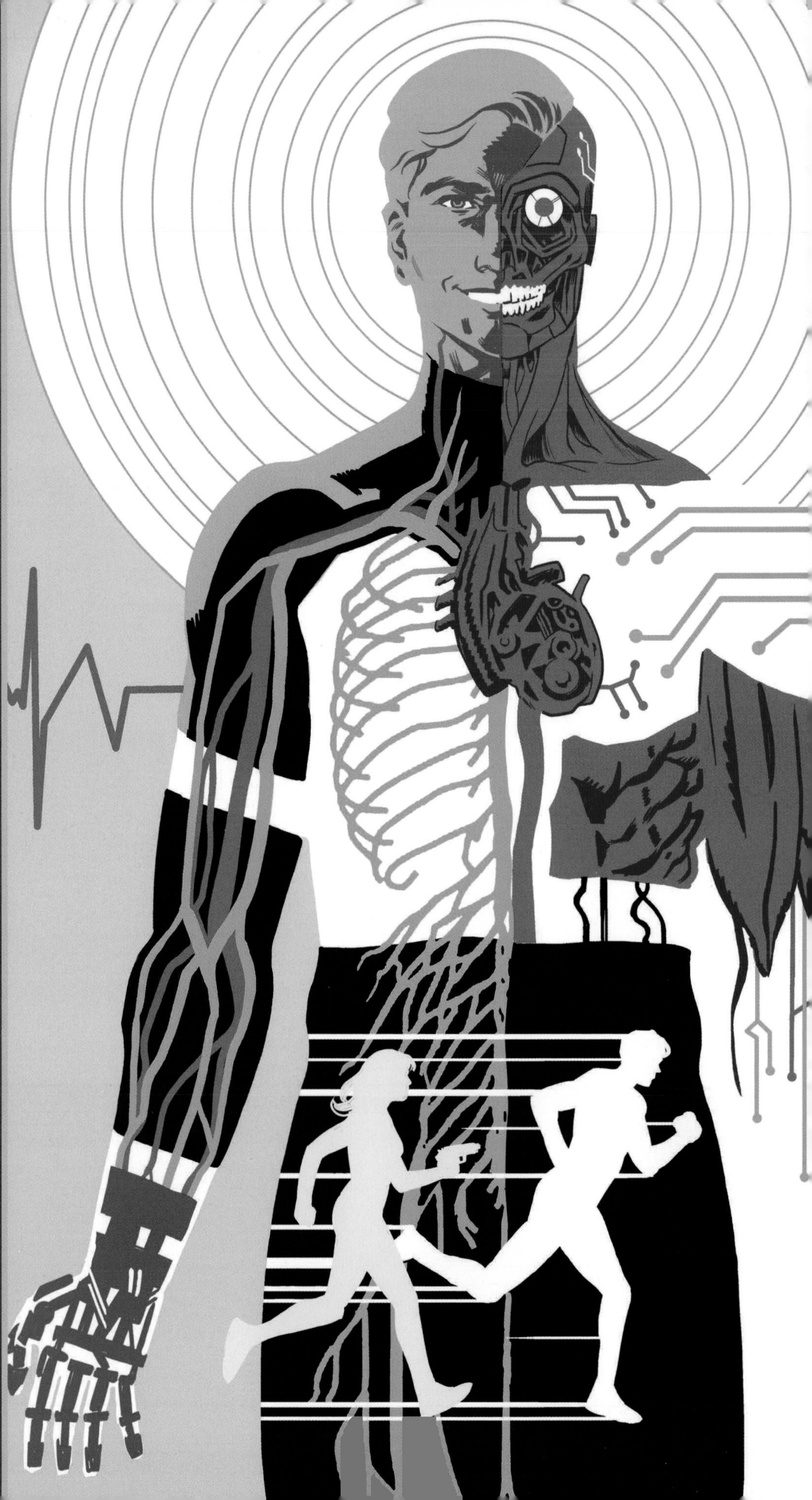

ISSUE 02 COVER ART BY MICHAEL WALSH

<"CONGRATULATIONS ON THE SOON TO BE COMPLETION OF YOUR LONG RANGE MISSILE, MR. AMARI.">*

*RUSSIAN

「ソビエト連邦に大きな恩がある。恩返しできるぐらい生きられないのは残念…」*

*JAPANESE

<"I HOLD A GREAT DEBT TO THE SOVIET UNION FOR ITS OWN CONTRIBUTION...">*

*JAPANESE TO RUSSIAN.

<"...AND I AM ONLY SORRY THAT I WILL NOT BE ALIVE MUCH LONGER TO REPAY.">

<A NUCLEAR EXPLOSION IN HAWAII WILL BE MORE THAN ENOUGH PAYMENT.>

<"BUT AREN'T YOU WORRIED ABOUT MUTUALLY ASSURED DESTRUCTION?">

「相互確証破壊」のこと心配してない?

<YOU ARE NOT THE ONLY PART OF THIS PLAN, MR. AMARI. ALLOW US TO LEAVE IT AT THAT.>

<"THE HOPE OF THIS REVENGE... IT HAS KEPT ME ALIVE FOR NEARLY FORTY YEARS.">

この復讐の希望… それだけで私は40年間…

<YOU WERE AT HIROSHIMA—AAH!

<MR. TAKESHI'S SPIRIT IS ANGRY AND STRONG. BUT IT IS NOT ALL THAT HAS KEPT HIM ALIVE.>

<TO THINK... EVERY AMERICAN WHO BUYS ONE OF YOUR RADIOS OR TELEVISIONS IS PLACING A DOWN PAYMENT ON THEIR OWN DEMISE—>

BLAM BLAM

<IS THAT GUNFIRE?>

セキュリティビデオ!今ぞ!

<"PULL UP THE SECURITY FEEDS.">

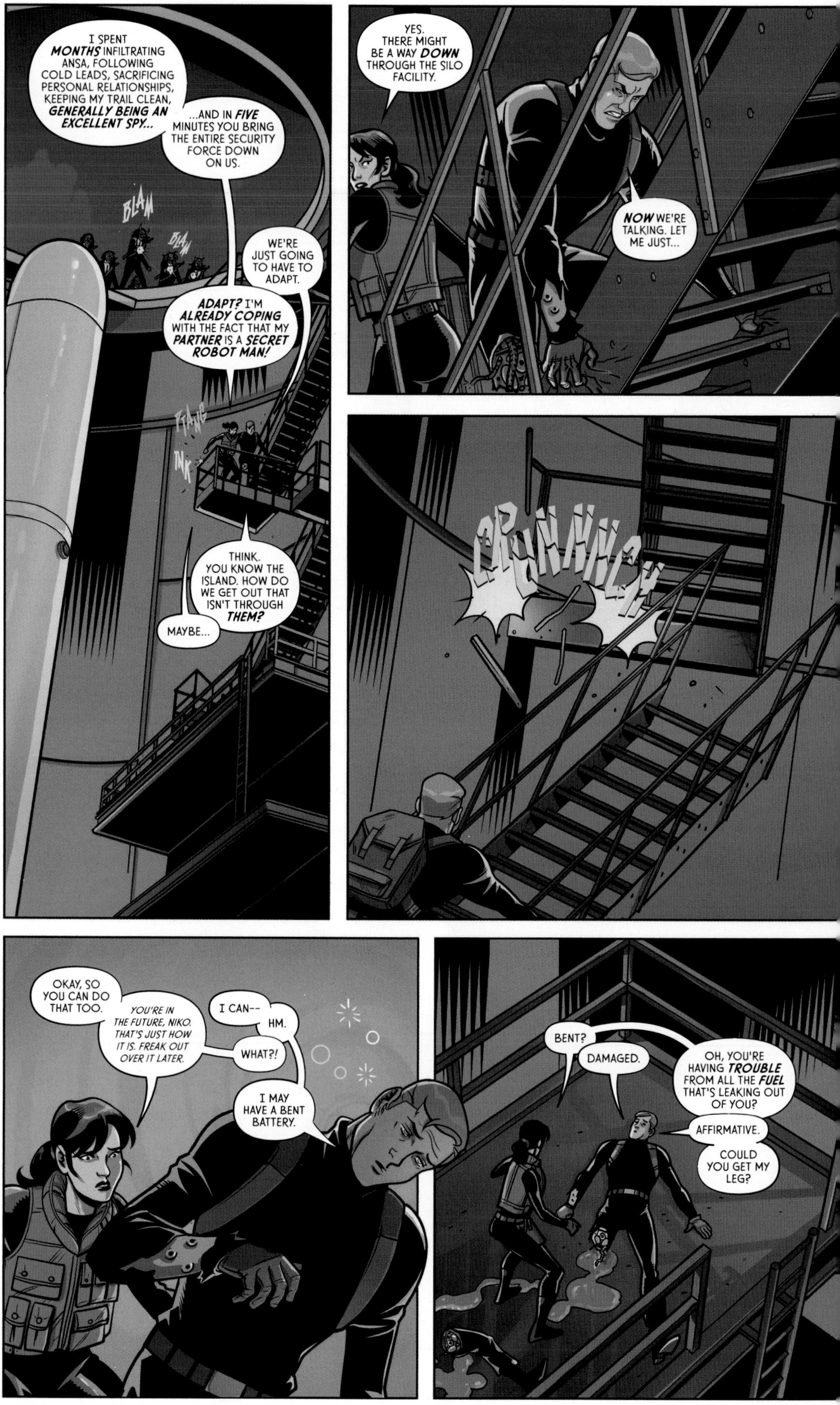

I SPENT MONTHS INFILTRATING ANSA, FOLLOWING COLD LEADS, SACRIFICING PERSONAL RELATIONSHIPS, KEEPING MY TRAIL CLEAN, GENERALLY BEING AN EXCELLENT SPY...
...AND IN FIVE MINUTES YOU BRING THE ENTIRE SECURITY FORCE DOWN ON US.
BLAM
BLAM
WE'RE JUST GOING TO HAVE TO ADAPT.
ADAPT? I'M ALREADY COPING WITH THE FACT THAT MY PARTNER IS A SECRET ROBOT MAN!
TINK
THINK. YOU KNOW THE ISLAND. HOW DO WE GET OUT THAT ISN'T THROUGH THEM?
MAYBE...
YES. THERE MIGHT BE A WAY DOWN THROUGH THE SILO FACILITY.
NOW WE'RE TALKING. LET ME JUST...
OKAY, SO YOU CAN DO THAT TOO.
YOU'RE IN THE FUTURE, NIKO. THAT'S JUST HOW IT IS. FREAK OUT OVER IT LATER.
I CAN--
HM.
WHAT?!
I MAY HAVE A BENT BATTERY.
BENT?
DAMAGED.
OH, YOU'RE HAVING TROUBLE FROM ALL THE FUEL THAT'S LEAKING OUT OF YOU?
AFFIRMATIVE.
COULD YOU GET MY LEG?

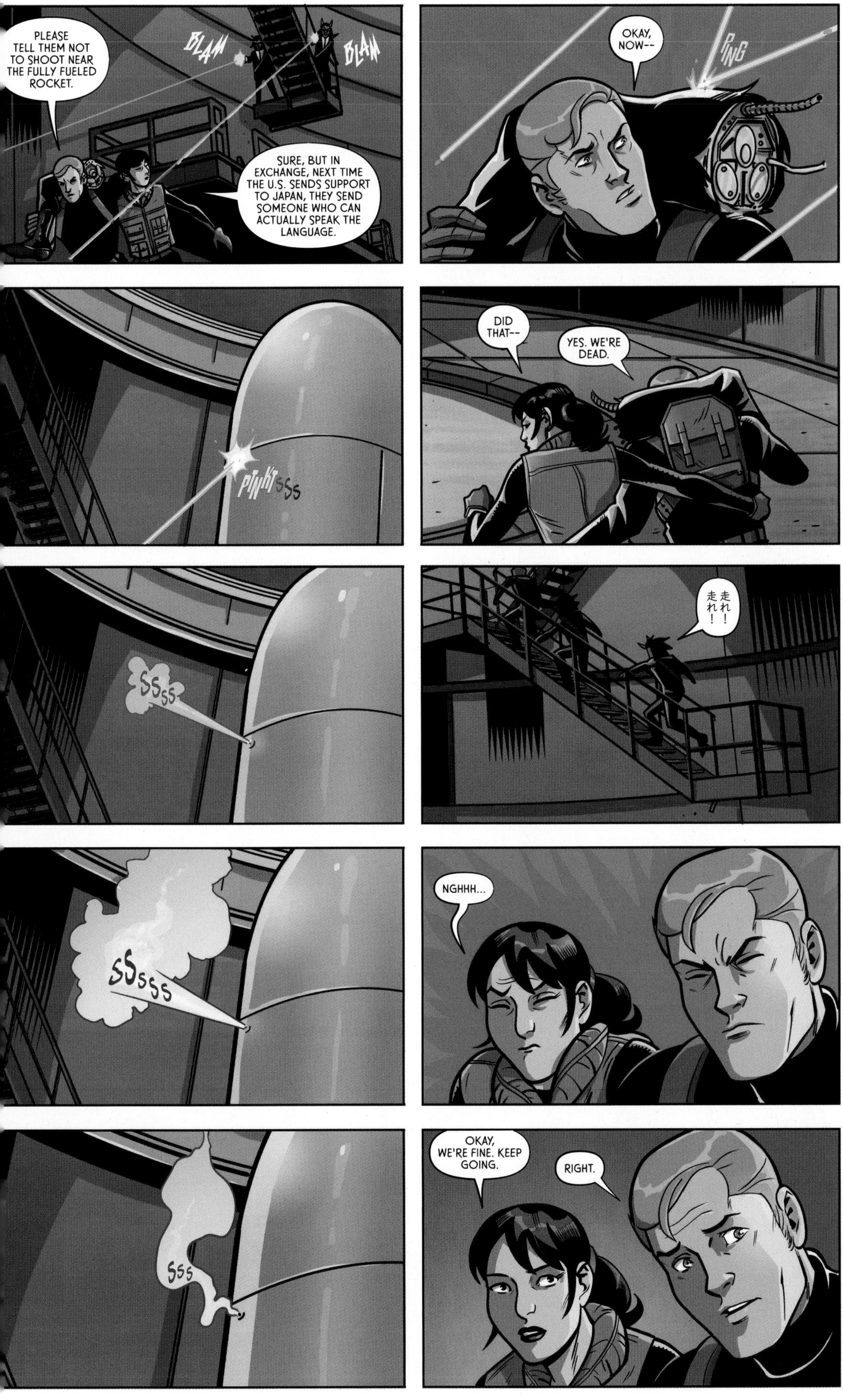
PLEASE TELL THEM NOT TO SHOOT NEAR THE FULLY FUELED ROCKET.
BLAM
BLAM
SURE, BUT IN EXCHANGE, NEXT TIME THE U.S. SENDS SUPPORT TO JAPAN, THEY SEND SOMEONE WHO CAN ACTUALLY SPEAK THE LANGUAGE.
OKAY, NOW--
PING
PINKTsss
DID THAT--
YES. WE'RE DEAD.
SSss
走れ！走れ！
SSssss
NGHHH...
Sss
OKAY, WE'RE FINE. KEEP GOING.
RIGHT.

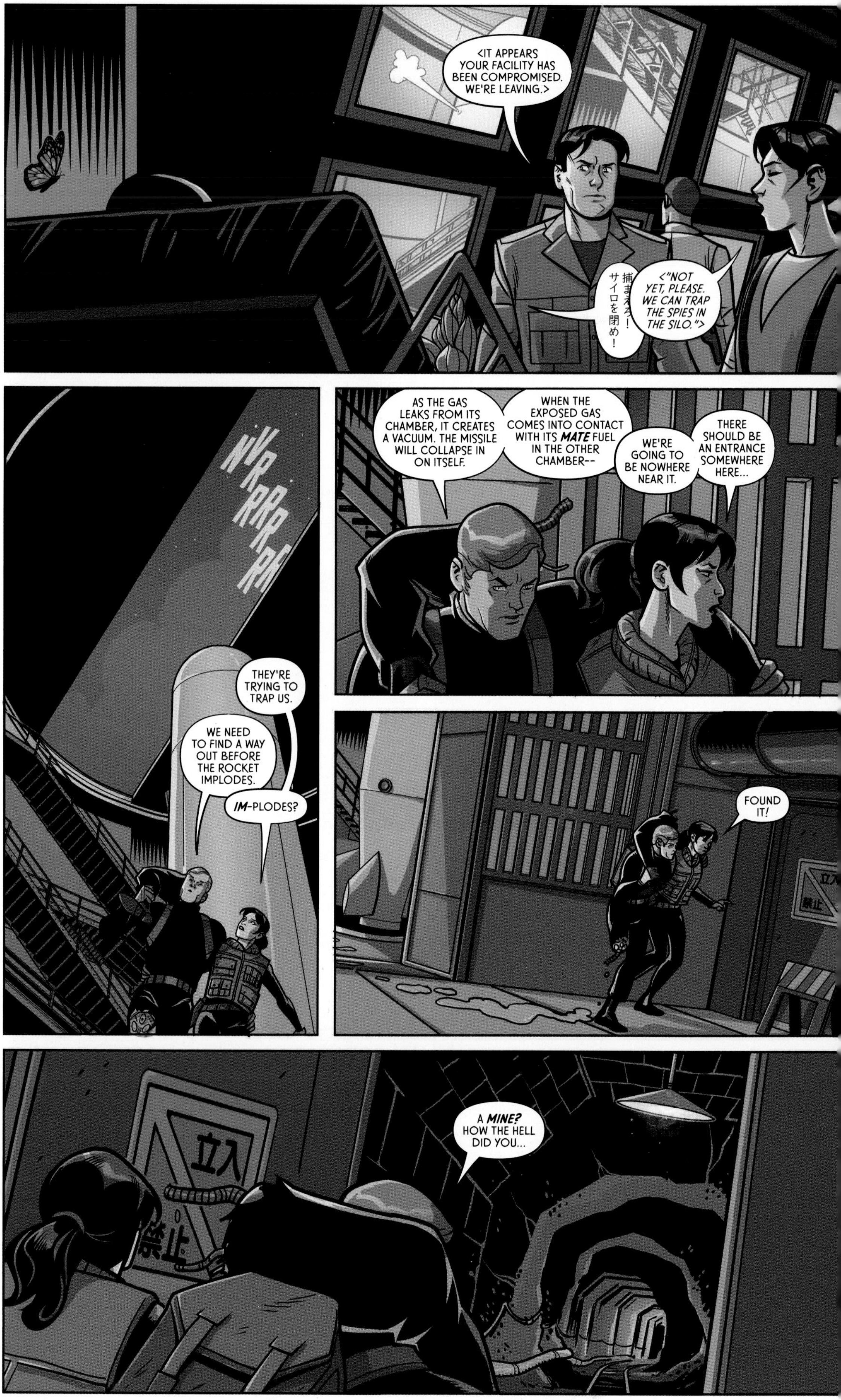

<IT APPEARS YOUR FACILITY HAS BEEN COMPROMISED. WE'RE LEAVING.>
捕まえろ！サイロを閉め！
<"NOT YET, PLEASE. WE CAN TRAP THE SPIES IN THE SILO.">
NVRRRRR
THEY'RE TRYING TO TRAP US.
WE NEED TO FIND A WAY OUT BEFORE THE ROCKET IMPLODES.
IM-PLODES?
AS THE GAS LEAKS FROM ITS CHAMBER, IT CREATES A VACUUM. THE MISSILE WILL COLLAPSE IN ON ITSELF.
WHEN THE EXPOSED GAS COMES INTO CONTACT WITH ITS ***MATE*** FUEL IN THE OTHER CHAMBER--
WE'RE GOING TO BE NOWHERE NEAR IT.
THERE SHOULD BE AN ENTRANCE SOMEWHERE HERE...
FOUND IT!
立入 禁止
A ***MINE?*** HOW THE HELL DID YOU...

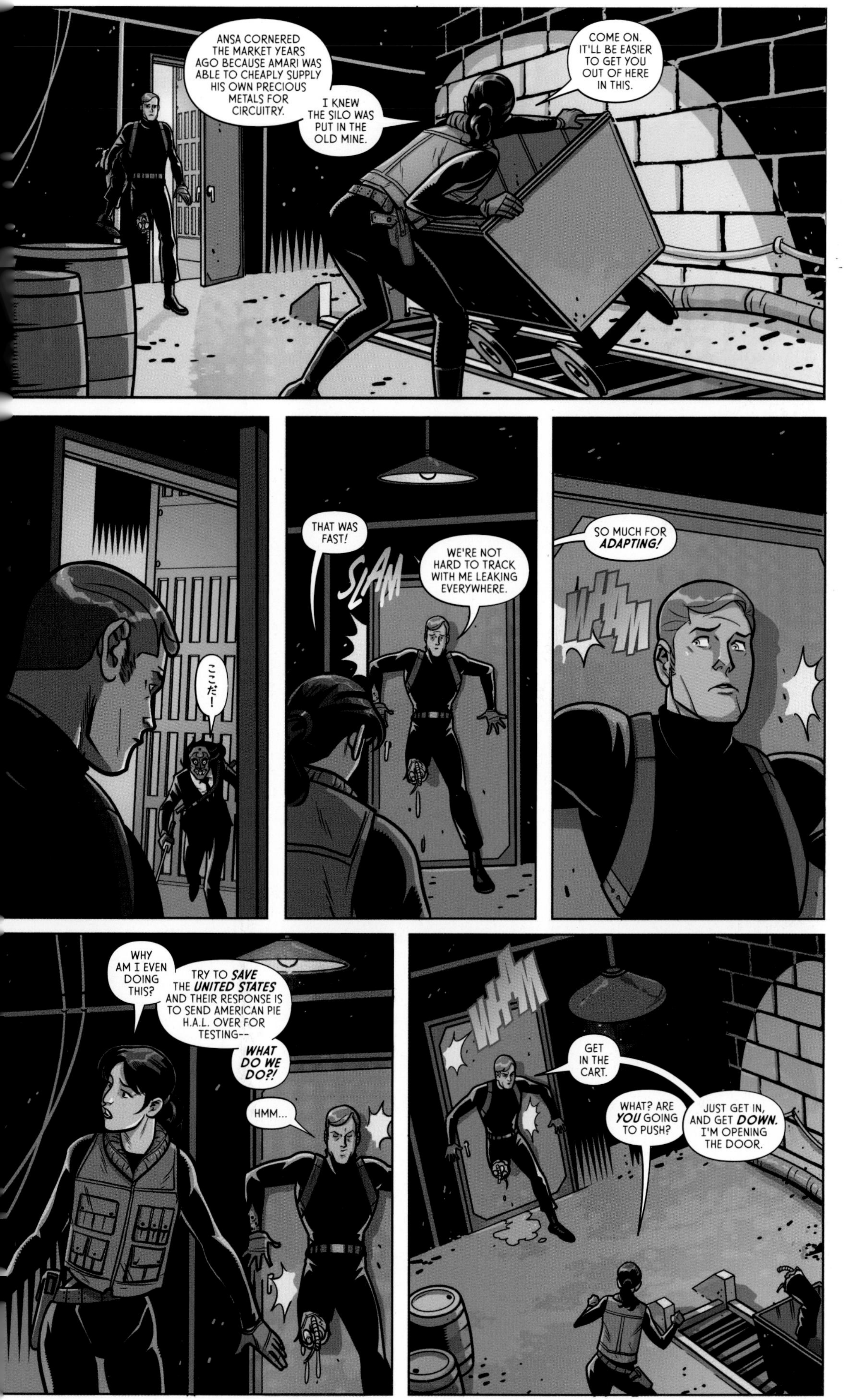
ANSA CORNERED THE MARKET YEARS AGO BECAUSE AMARI WAS ABLE TO CHEAPLY SUPPLY HIS OWN PRECIOUS METALS FOR CIRCUITRY.
I KNEW THE SILO WAS PUT IN THE OLD MINE.
COME ON. IT'LL BE EASIER TO GET YOU OUT OF HERE IN THIS.
ここだ！
THAT WAS FAST!
SLAM
WE'RE NOT HARD TO TRACK WITH ME LEAKING EVERYWHERE.
SO MUCH FOR *ADAPTING!*
WHAM
WHY AM I EVEN DOING THIS?
TRY TO *SAVE* THE *UNITED STATES* AND THEIR RESPONSE IS TO SEND AMERICAN PIE H.A.L. OVER FOR TESTING--
WHAT DO WE DO?!
HMM...
WHAM
GET IN THE CART.
WHAT? ARE *YOU* GOING TO PUSH?
JUST GET IN, AND GET *DOWN.* I'M OPENING THE DOOR.

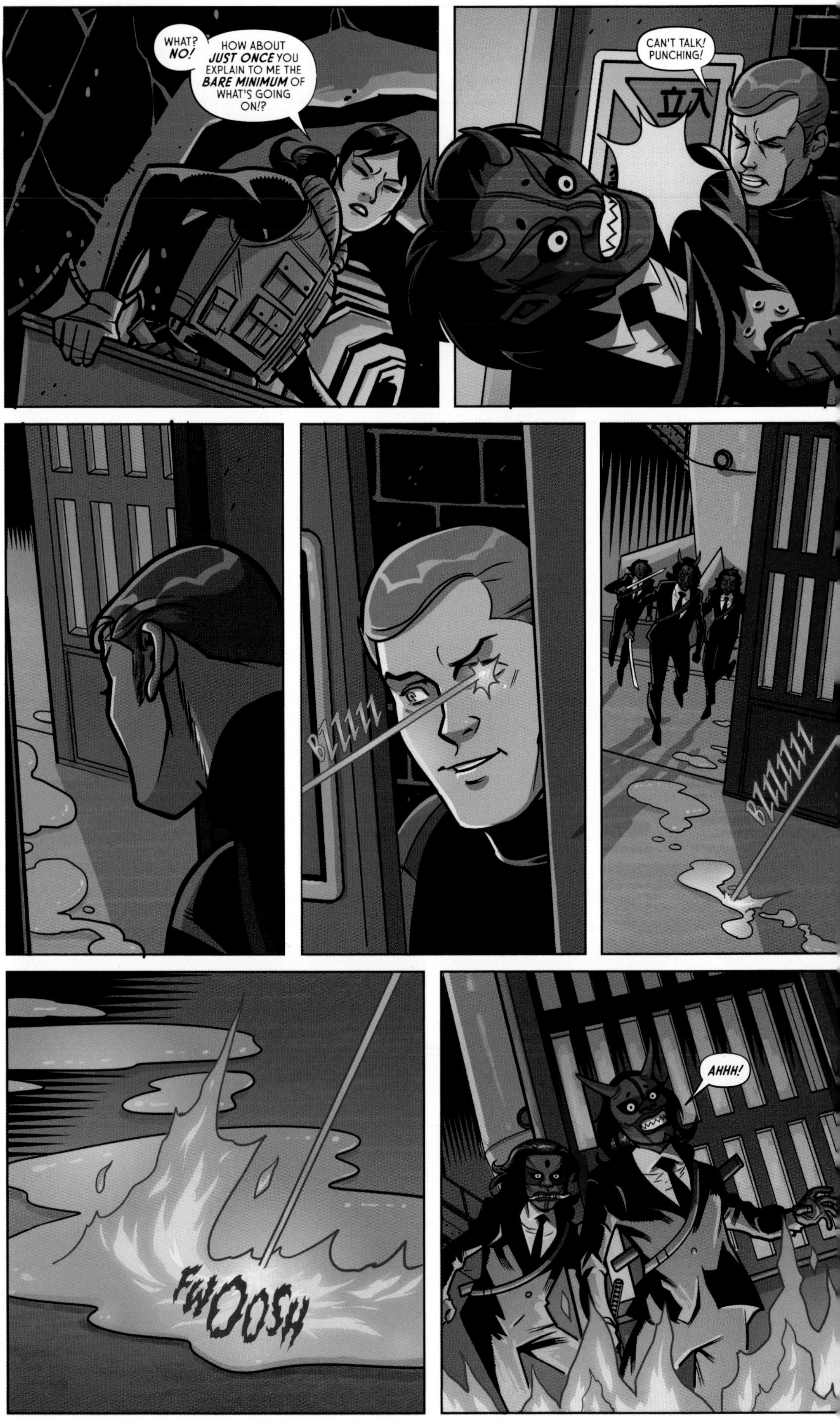
WHAT? NO!
HOW ABOUT JUST ONCE YOU EXPLAIN TO ME THE BARE MINIMUM OF WHAT'S GOING ON!?
CAN'T TALK! PUNCHING!
立入
BZZZZZ
BZZZZZZ
FWOOSH
AHHH!

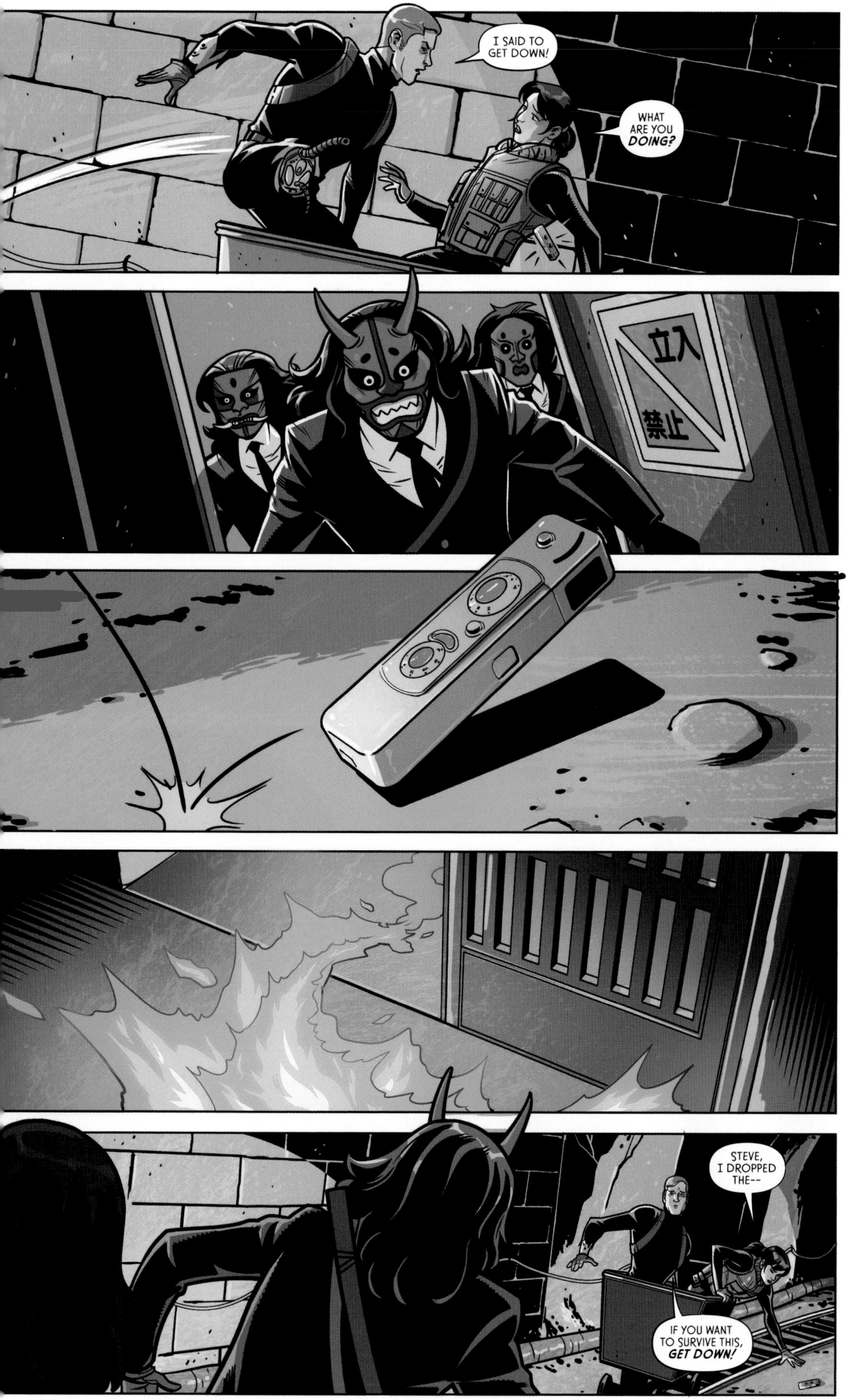
I SAID TO GET DOWN!
WHAT ARE YOU DOING?
立入
禁止
STEVE, I DROPPED THE--
IF YOU WANT TO SURVIVE THIS, GET DOWN!

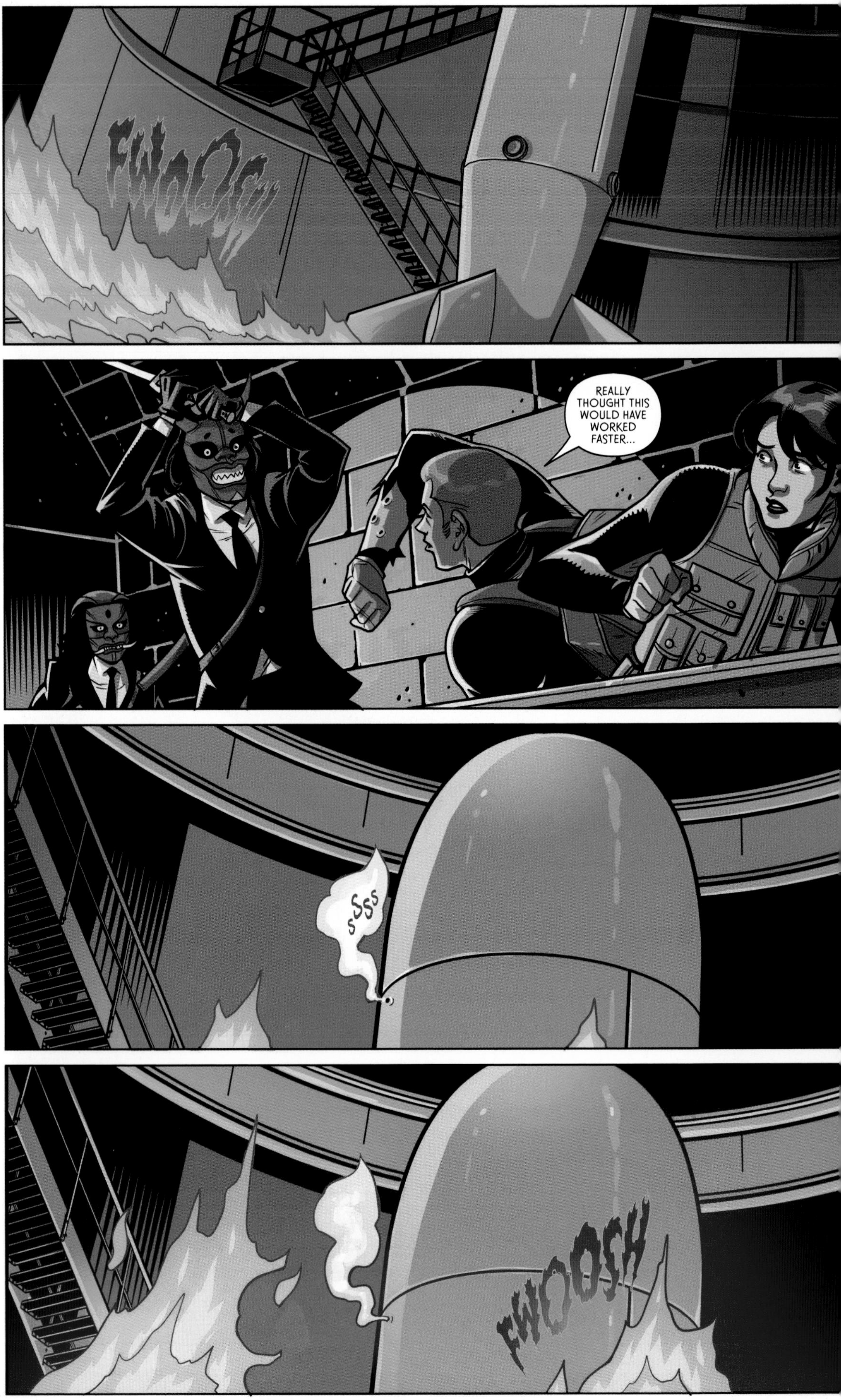
FWOOSH
REALLY THOUGHT THIS WOULD HAVE WORKED FASTER...
SSSS
FWOOSH

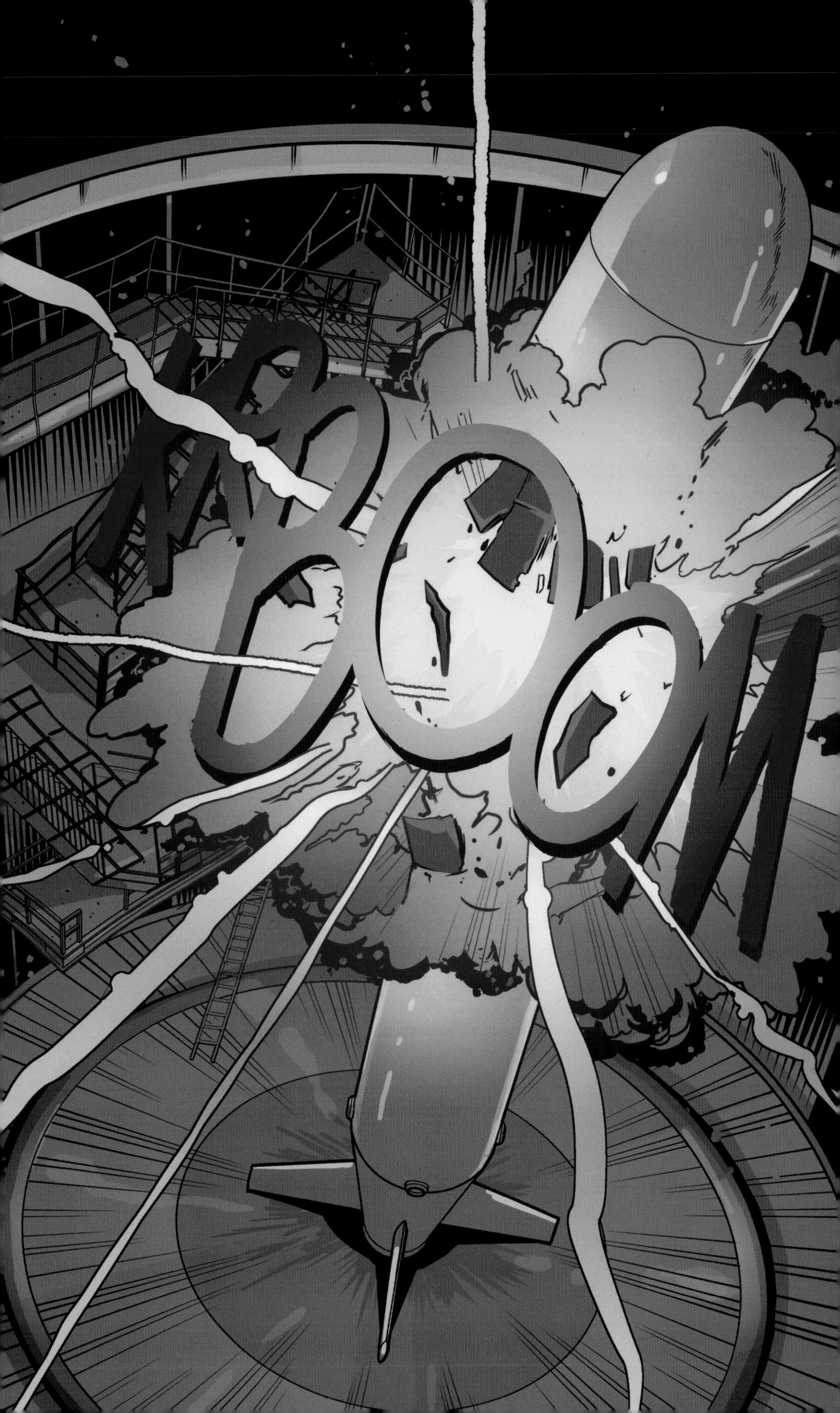
KABOOM

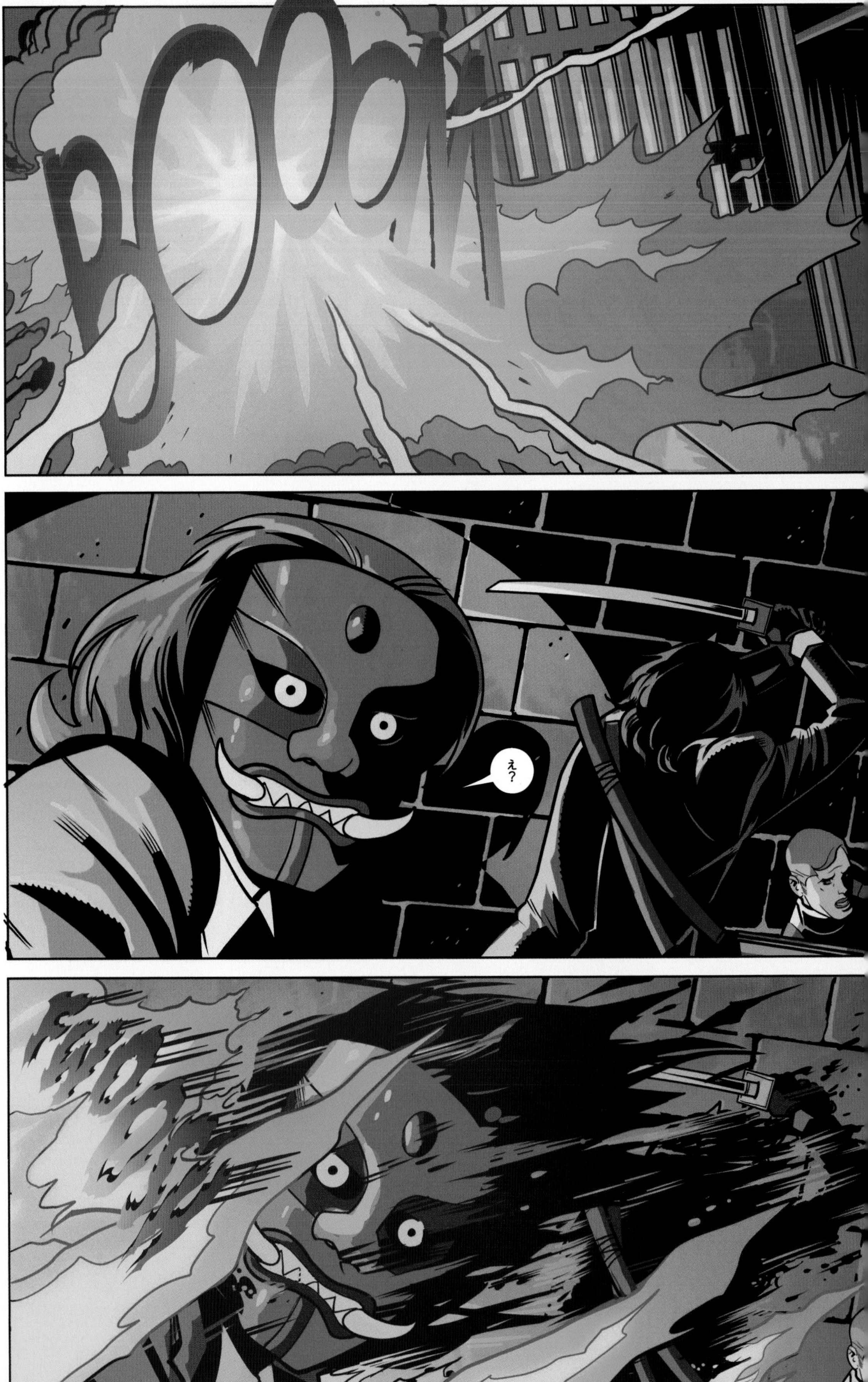
BOOOM
え?

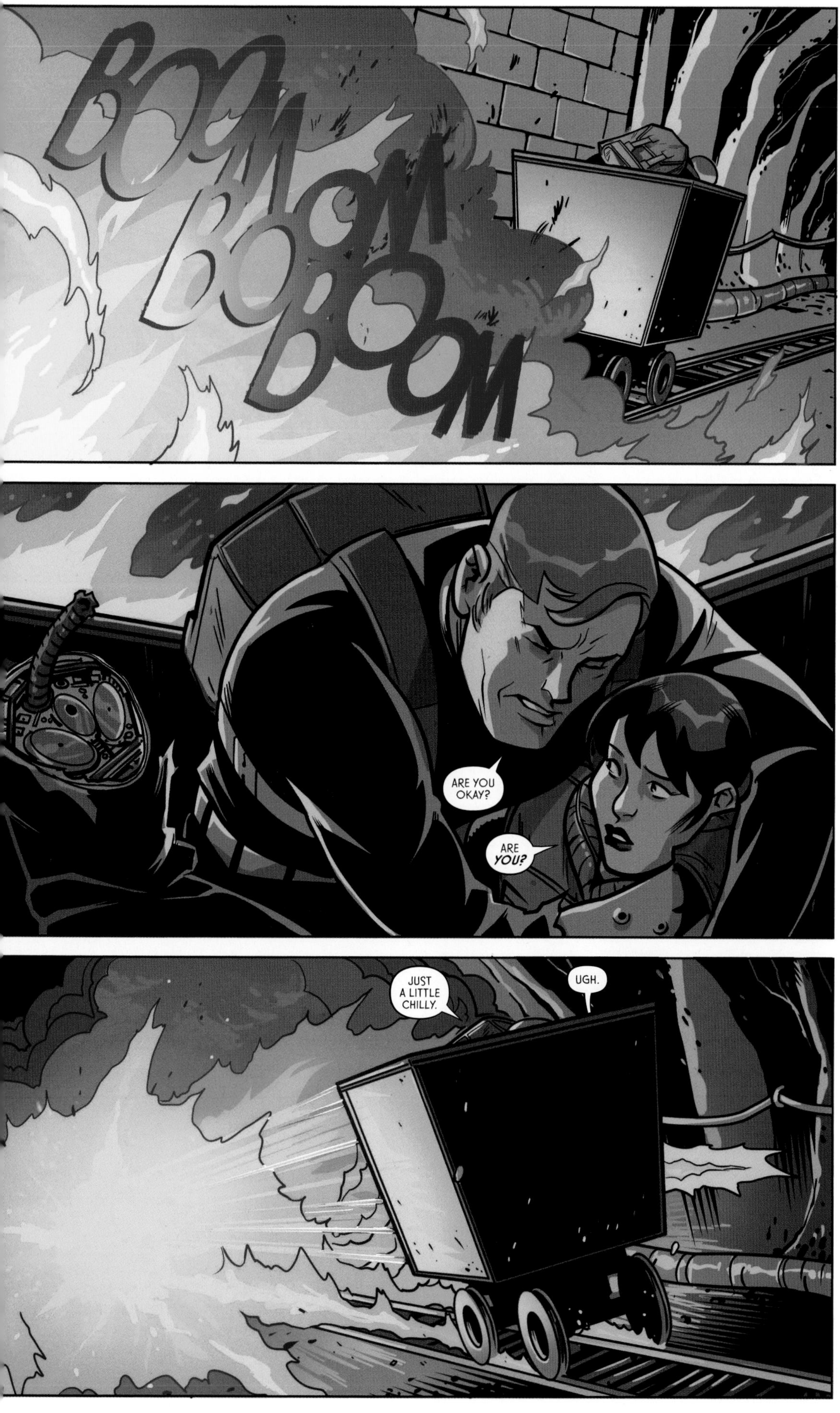
BOOM
BOOM
BOOM
ARE YOU OKAY?
ARE *YOU?*
JUST A LITTLE CHILLY.
UGH.

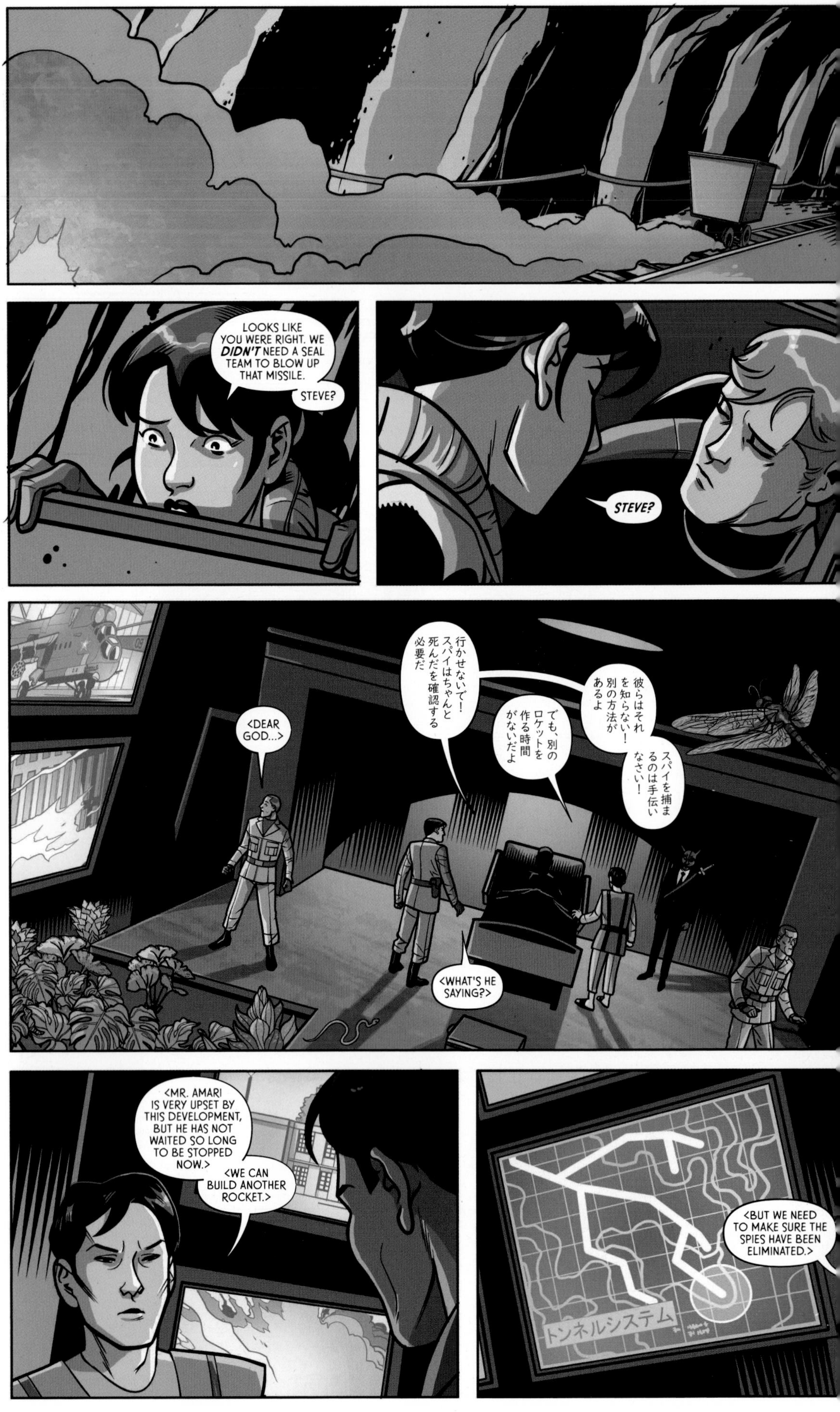
LOOKS LIKE YOU WERE RIGHT. WE DIDN'T NEED A SEAL TEAM TO BLOW UP THAT MISSILE.
STEVE?
STEVE?
<DEAR GOD...>
スパイを捕まるのは手伝いなさい！
彼らはそれを知らない！別の方法があるよ
でも、別のロケットを作る時間がないだよ
行かせないで！スパイはちゃんと死んだを確認する必要だ
<WHAT'S HE SAYING?>
<MR. AMARI IS VERY UPSET BY THIS DEVELOPMENT, BUT HE HAS NOT WAITED SO LONG TO BE STOPPED NOW.>
<WE CAN BUILD ANOTHER ROCKET.>
<BUT WE NEED TO MAKE SURE THE SPIES HAVE BEEN ELIMINATED.>
トンネルシステム

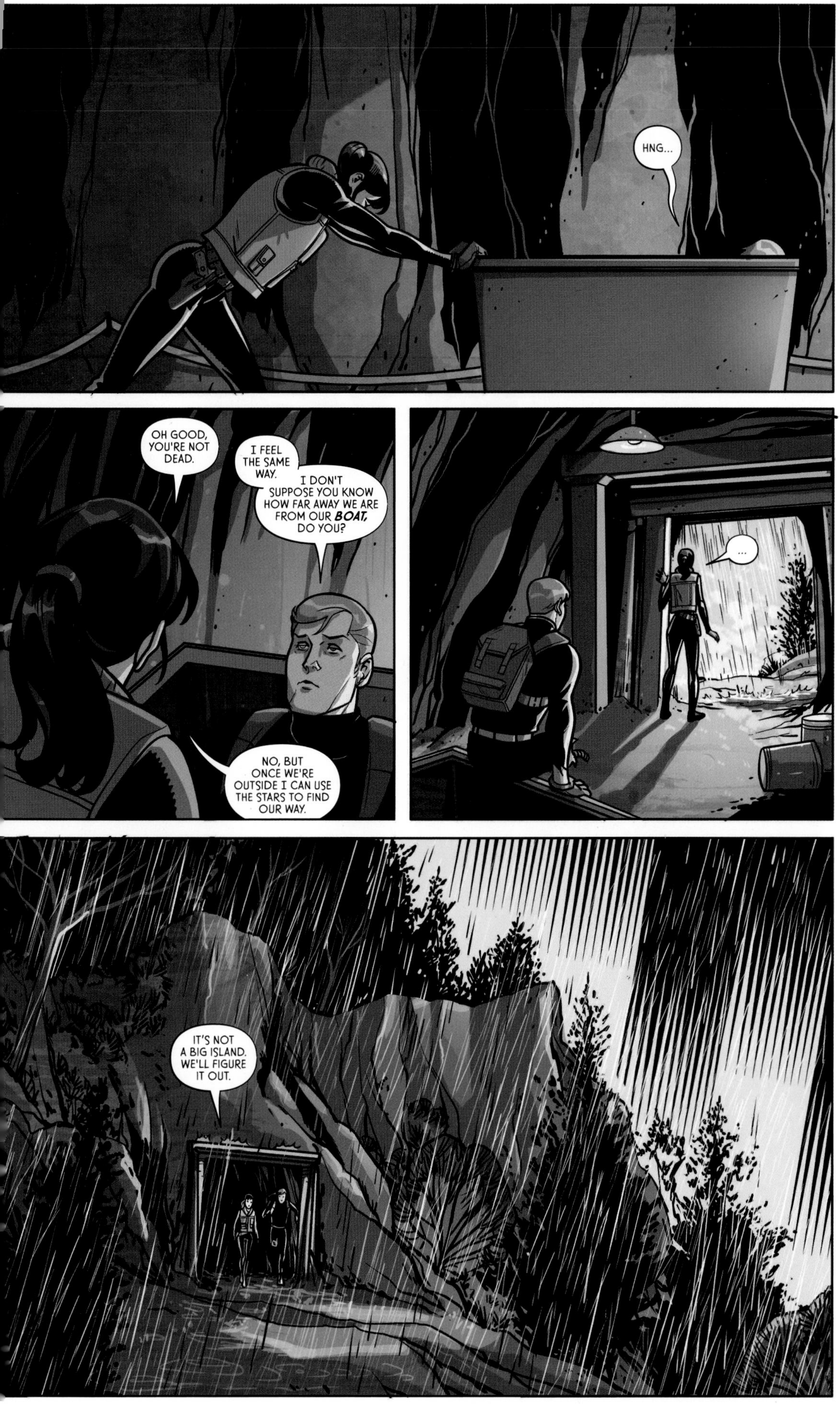
HNG...
OH GOOD, YOU'RE NOT DEAD.
I FEEL THE SAME WAY.
I DON'T SUPPOSE YOU KNOW HOW FAR AWAY WE ARE FROM OUR **BOAT,** DO YOU?
NO, BUT ONCE WE'RE OUTSIDE I CAN USE THE STARS TO FIND OUR WAY.
...
IT'S NOT A BIG ISLAND. WE'LL FIGURE IT OUT.

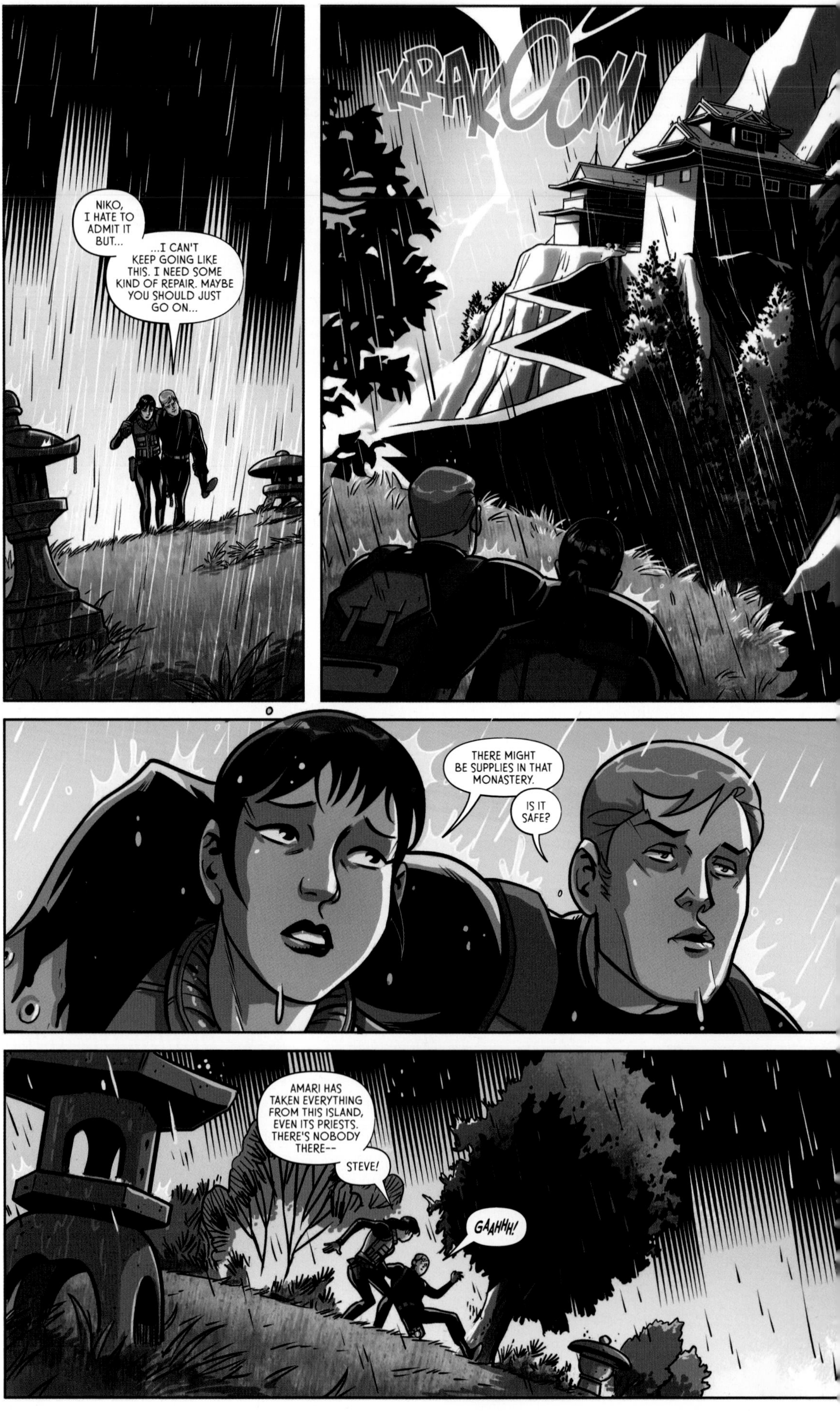
NIKO, I HATE TO ADMIT IT BUT...
...I CAN'T KEEP GOING LIKE THIS. I NEED SOME KIND OF REPAIR. MAYBE YOU SHOULD JUST GO ON...
KRAKOOM
THERE MIGHT BE SUPPLIES IN THAT MONASTERY.
IS IT SAFE?
AMARI HAS TAKEN EVERYTHING FROM THIS ISLAND, EVEN ITS PRIESTS. THERE'S NOBODY THERE--
STEVE!
GAAHHH!

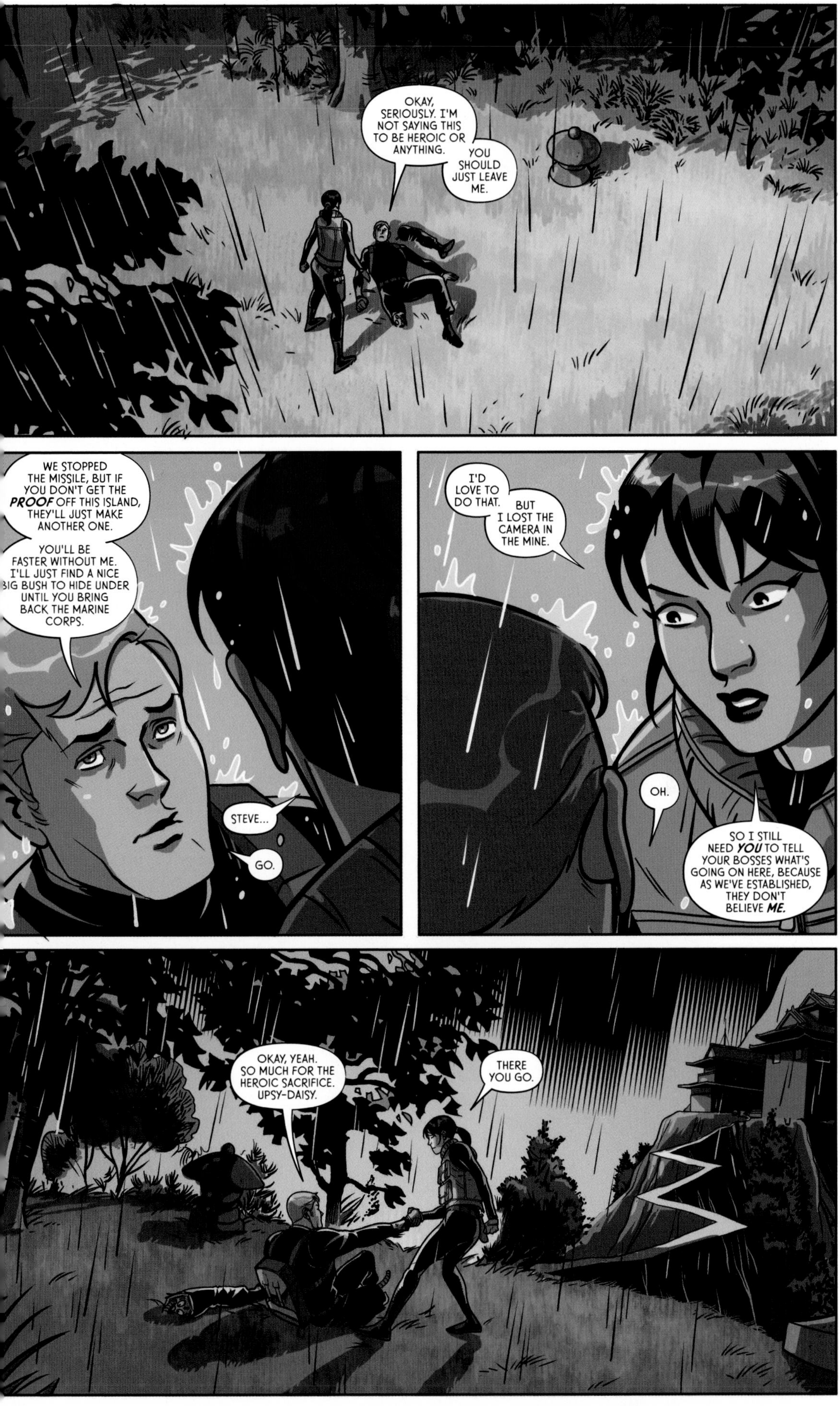
OKAY, SERIOUSLY. I'M NOT SAYING THIS TO BE HEROIC OR ANYTHING.
YOU SHOULD JUST LEAVE ME.
WE STOPPED THE MISSILE, BUT IF YOU DON'T GET THE PROOF OFF THIS ISLAND, THEY'LL JUST MAKE ANOTHER ONE.
YOU'LL BE FASTER WITHOUT ME. I'LL JUST FIND A NICE BIG BUSH TO HIDE UNDER UNTIL YOU BRING BACK THE MARINE CORPS.
STEVE...
GO.
I'D LOVE TO DO THAT.
BUT I LOST THE CAMERA IN THE MINE.
OH.
SO I STILL NEED YOU TO TELL YOUR BOSSES WHAT'S GOING ON HERE, BECAUSE AS WE'VE ESTABLISHED, THEY DON'T BELIEVE ME.
OKAY, YEAH. SO MUCH FOR THE HEROIC SACRIFICE. UPSY-DAISY.
THERE YOU GO.

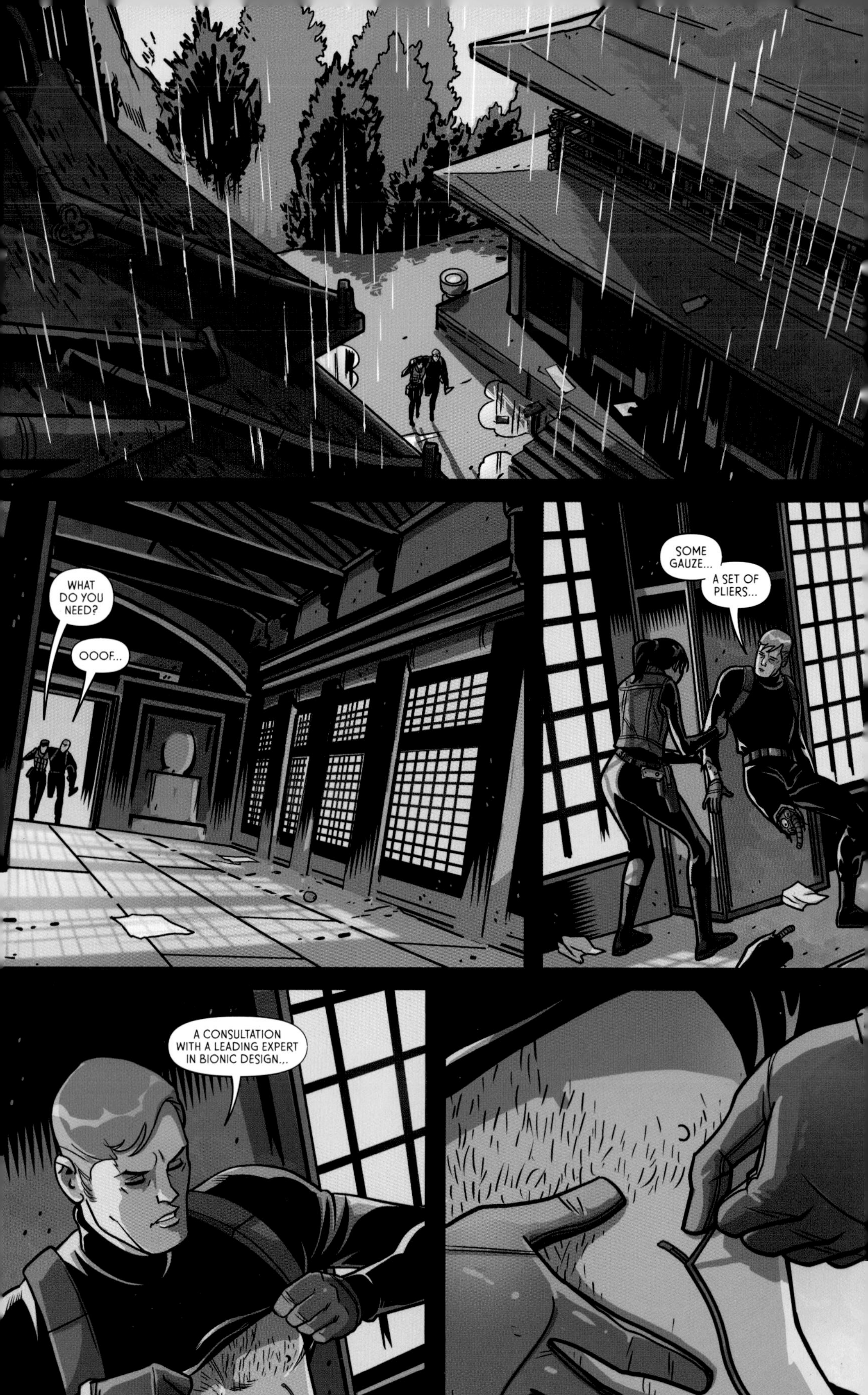
WHAT DO YOU NEED?
OOOF...
SOME GAUZE...
A SET OF PLIERS...
A CONSULTATION WITH A LEADING EXPERT IN BIONIC DESIGN...

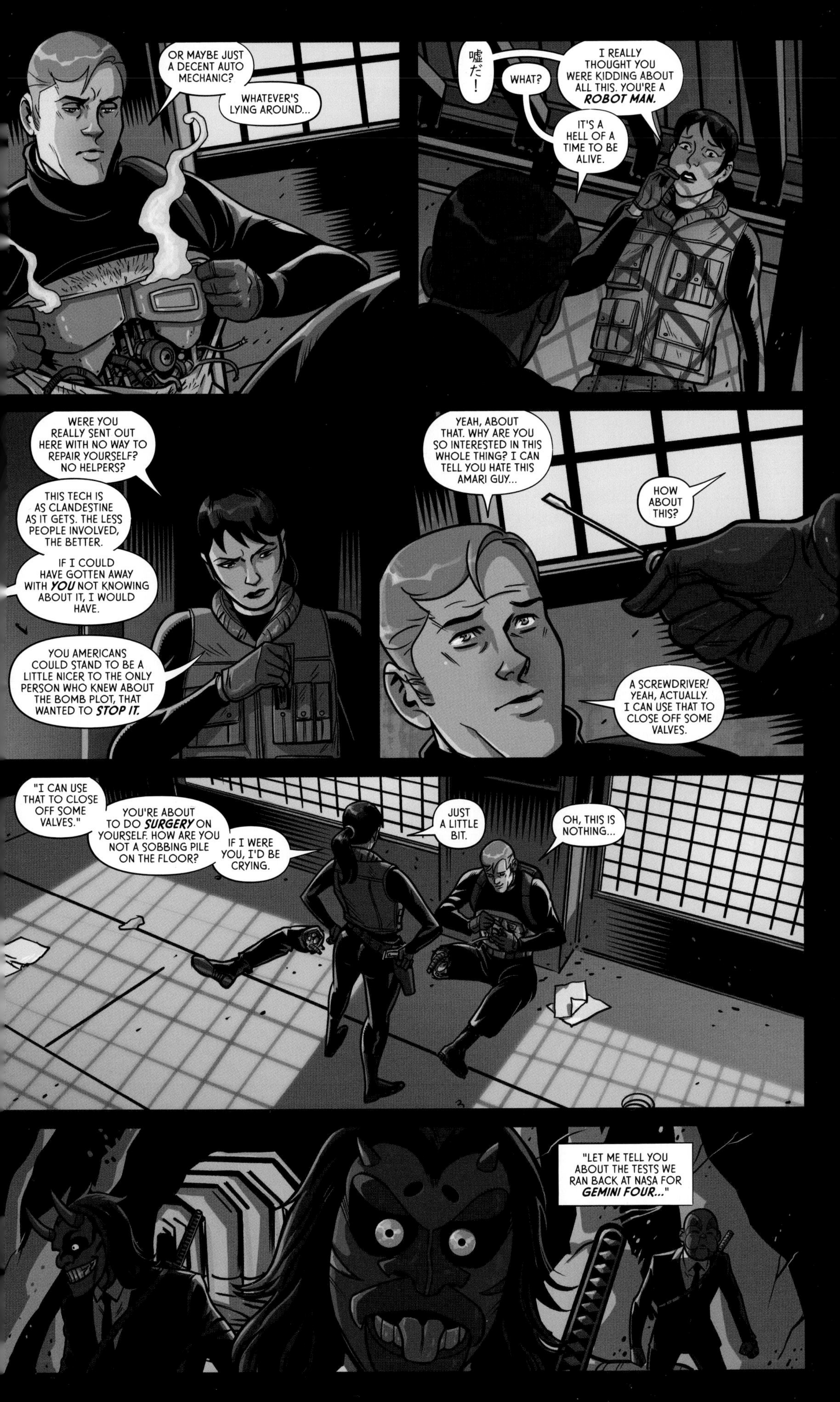
OR MAYBE JUST A DECENT AUTO MECHANIC?
WHATEVER'S LYING AROUND...
嘘だ！
I REALLY THOUGHT YOU WERE KIDDING ABOUT ALL THIS. YOU'RE A **ROBOT MAN.**
WHAT?
IT'S A HELL OF A TIME TO BE ALIVE.
WERE YOU REALLY SENT OUT HERE WITH NO WAY TO REPAIR YOURSELF? NO HELPERS?
THIS TECH IS AS CLANDESTINE AS IT GETS. THE LESS PEOPLE INVOLVED, THE BETTER.
IF I COULD HAVE GOTTEN AWAY WITH ***YOU*** NOT KNOWING ABOUT IT, I WOULD HAVE.
YOU AMERICANS COULD STAND TO BE A LITTLE NICER TO THE ONLY PERSON WHO KNEW ABOUT THE BOMB PLOT, THAT WANTED TO ***STOP IT.***
YEAH, ABOUT THAT. WHY ARE YOU SO INTERESTED IN THIS WHOLE THING? I CAN TELL YOU HATE THIS AMARI GUY...
HOW ABOUT THIS?
A SCREWDRIVER! YEAH, ACTUALLY. I CAN USE THAT TO CLOSE OFF SOME VALVES.
"I CAN USE THAT TO CLOSE OFF SOME VALVES."
YOU'RE ABOUT TO DO ***SURGERY*** ON YOURSELF. HOW ARE YOU NOT A SOBBING PILE ON THE FLOOR?
IF I WERE YOU, I'D BE CRYING.
JUST A LITTLE BIT.
OH, THIS IS NOTHING...
"LET ME TELL YOU ABOUT THE TESTS WE RAN BACK AT NASA FOR ***GEMINI FOUR...***"

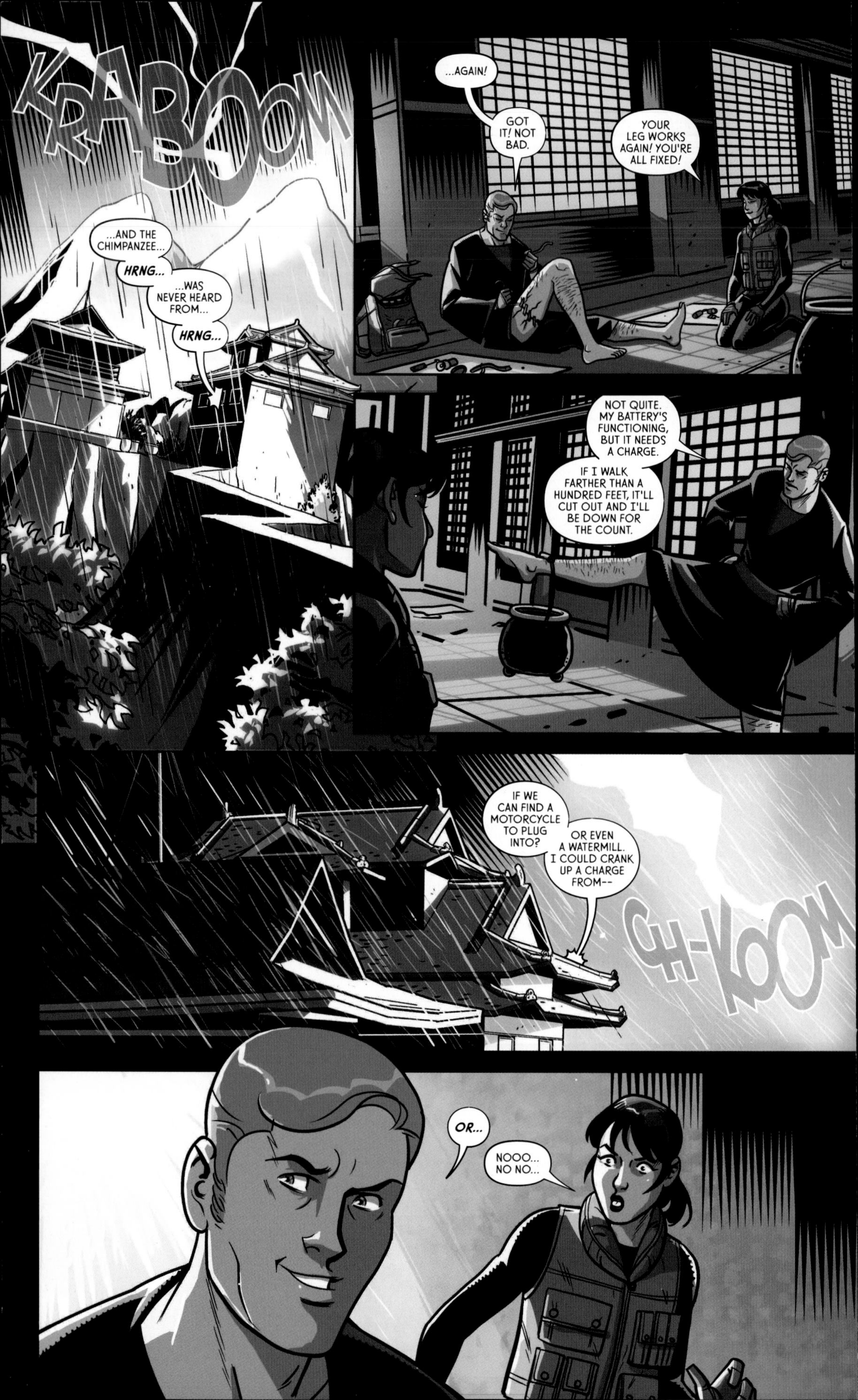
KRABOOM
...AND THE CHIMPANZEE...
HRNG...
...WAS NEVER HEARD FROM...
HRNG...
...AGAIN!
GOT IT! NOT BAD.
YOUR LEG WORKS AGAIN! YOU'RE ALL FIXED!
NOT QUITE. MY BATTERY'S FUNCTIONING, BUT IT NEEDS A CHARGE.
IF I WALK FARTHER THAN A HUNDRED FEET, IT'LL CUT OUT AND I'LL BE DOWN FOR THE COUNT.
IF WE CAN FIND A MOTORCYCLE TO PLUG INTO?
OR EVEN A WATERMILL. I COULD CRANK UP A CHARGE FROM--
CH-KOOM
OR...
NOOO... NO NO...

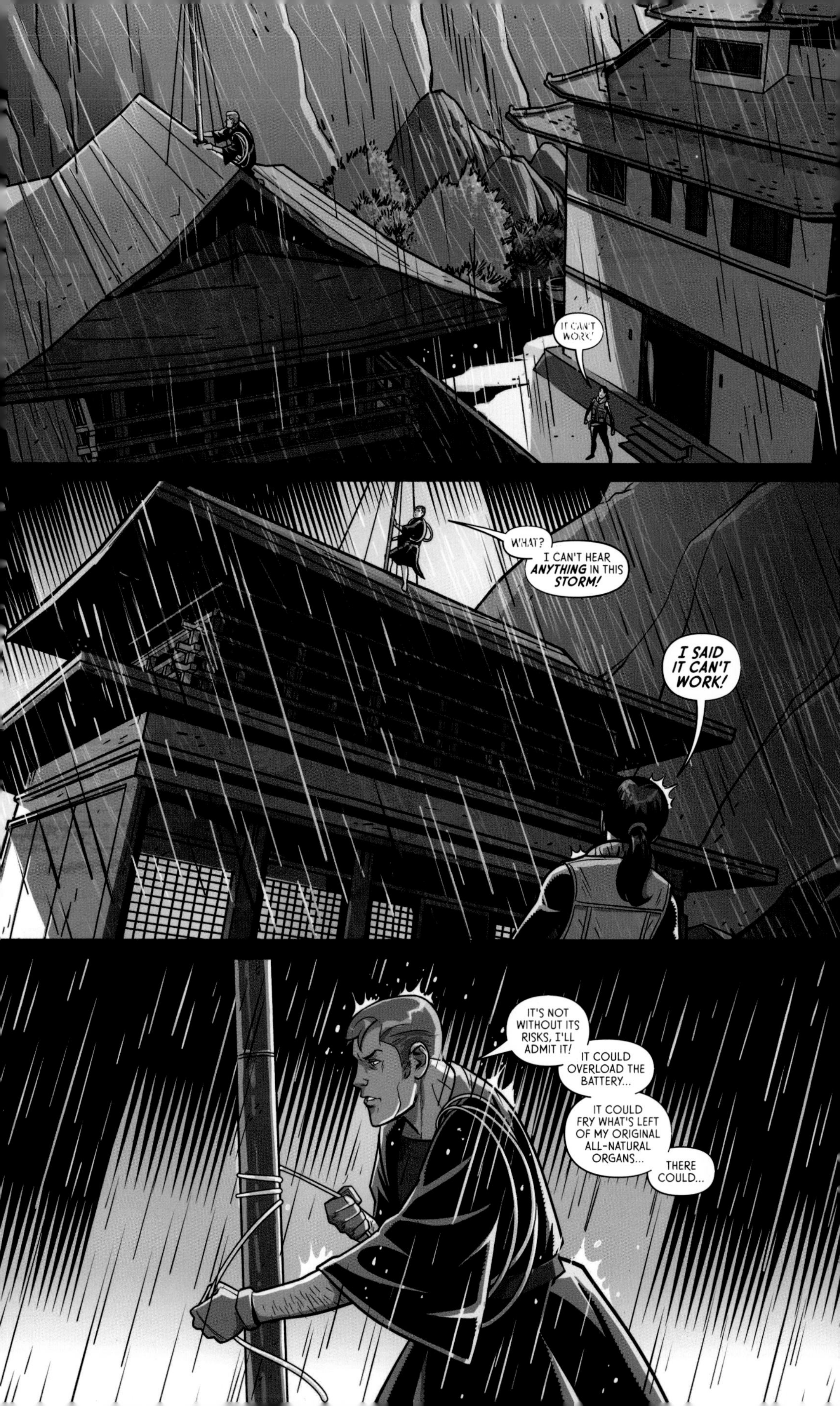
IT CAN'T WORK!
WHAT?
I CAN'T HEAR ANYTHING IN THIS STORM!
I SAID IT CAN'T WORK!
IT'S NOT WITHOUT ITS RISKS, I'LL ADMIT IT!
IT COULD OVERLOAD THE BATTERY...
IT COULD FRY WHAT'S LEFT OF MY ORIGINAL ALL-NATURAL ORGANS...
THERE COULD...

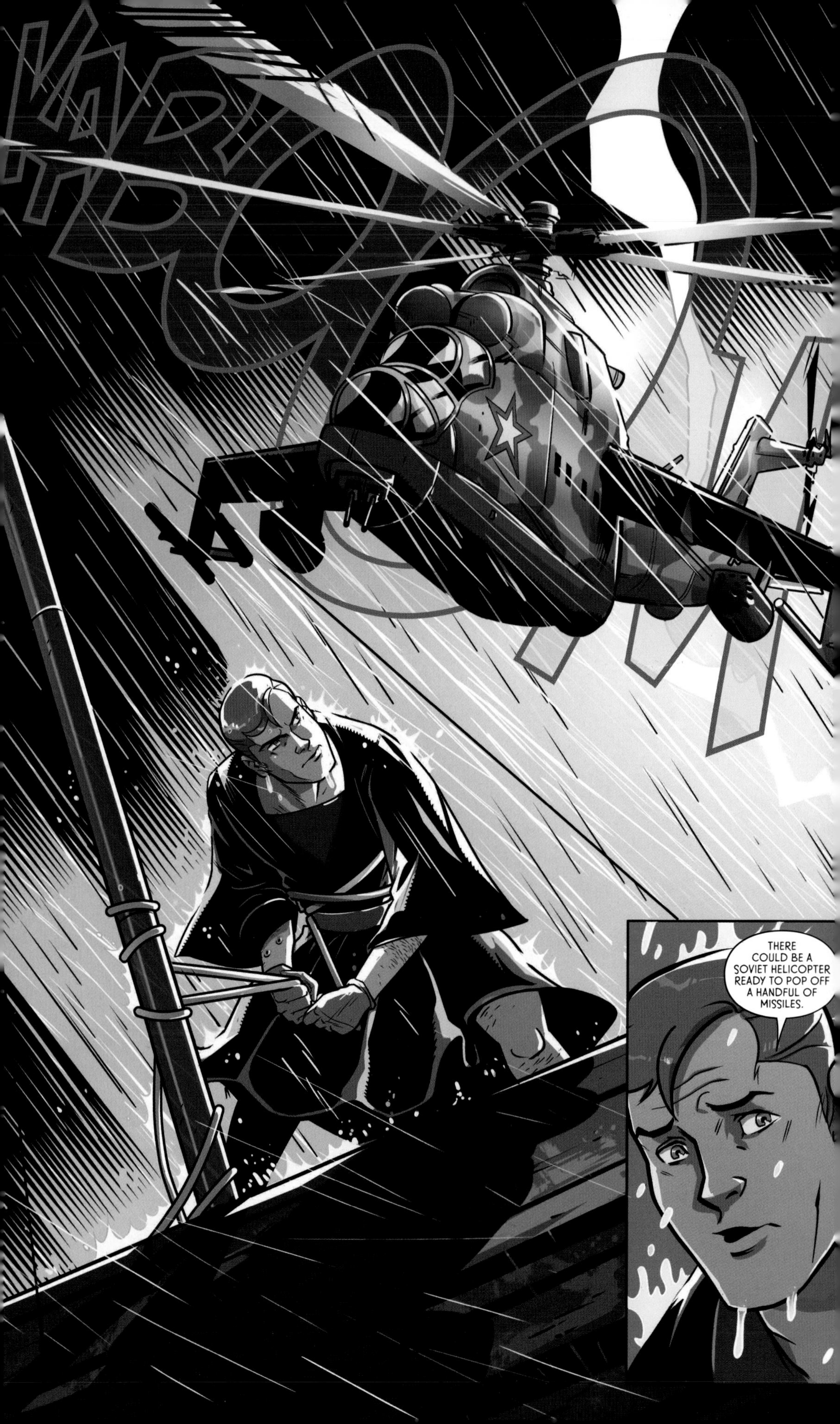
THERE COULD BE A SOVIET HELICOPTER READY TO POP OFF A HANDFUL OF MISSILES.

TEVE AUSTIN. ASTRONAUT. A MAN BARELY ALIVE AFTER A HORRIBLE ACCIDENT.
REBUILT AS THE WORLD'S FIRST BIONIC MAN. BETTER THAN HE WAS BEFORE.

BETTER, STRONGER, FASTER.

THE

0,276,497

DOLLAR
MAN

[...EXCEPT HE'S IN JAPAN RUNNING FROM KGB AGENTS AND HIS
BODY'S BATTERY'S DEAD, BUT THAT'S JUST A MINOR SETBACK]

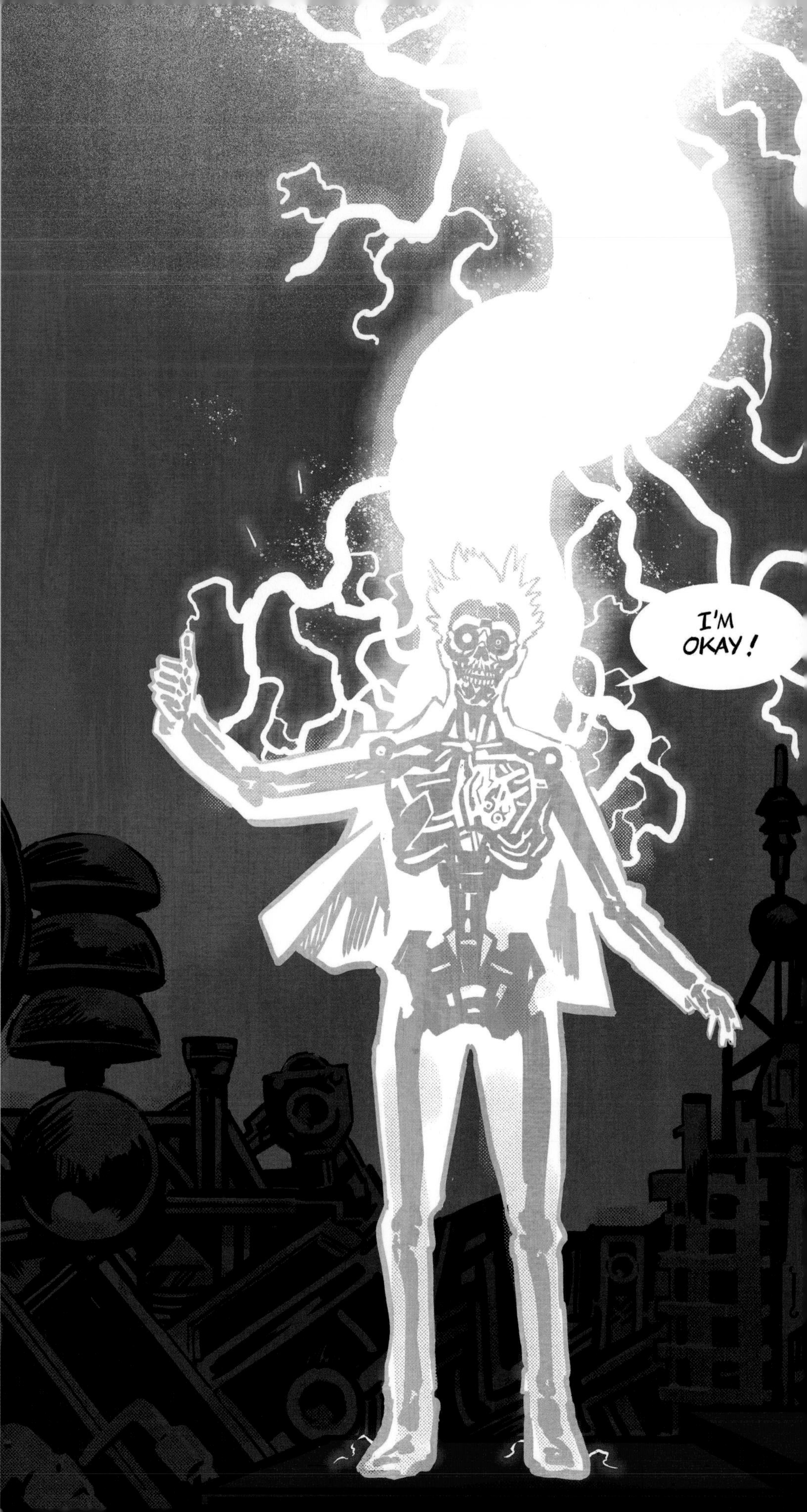
I'M OKAY!

ISSUE 03 COVER ART BY MICHAEL WALSH

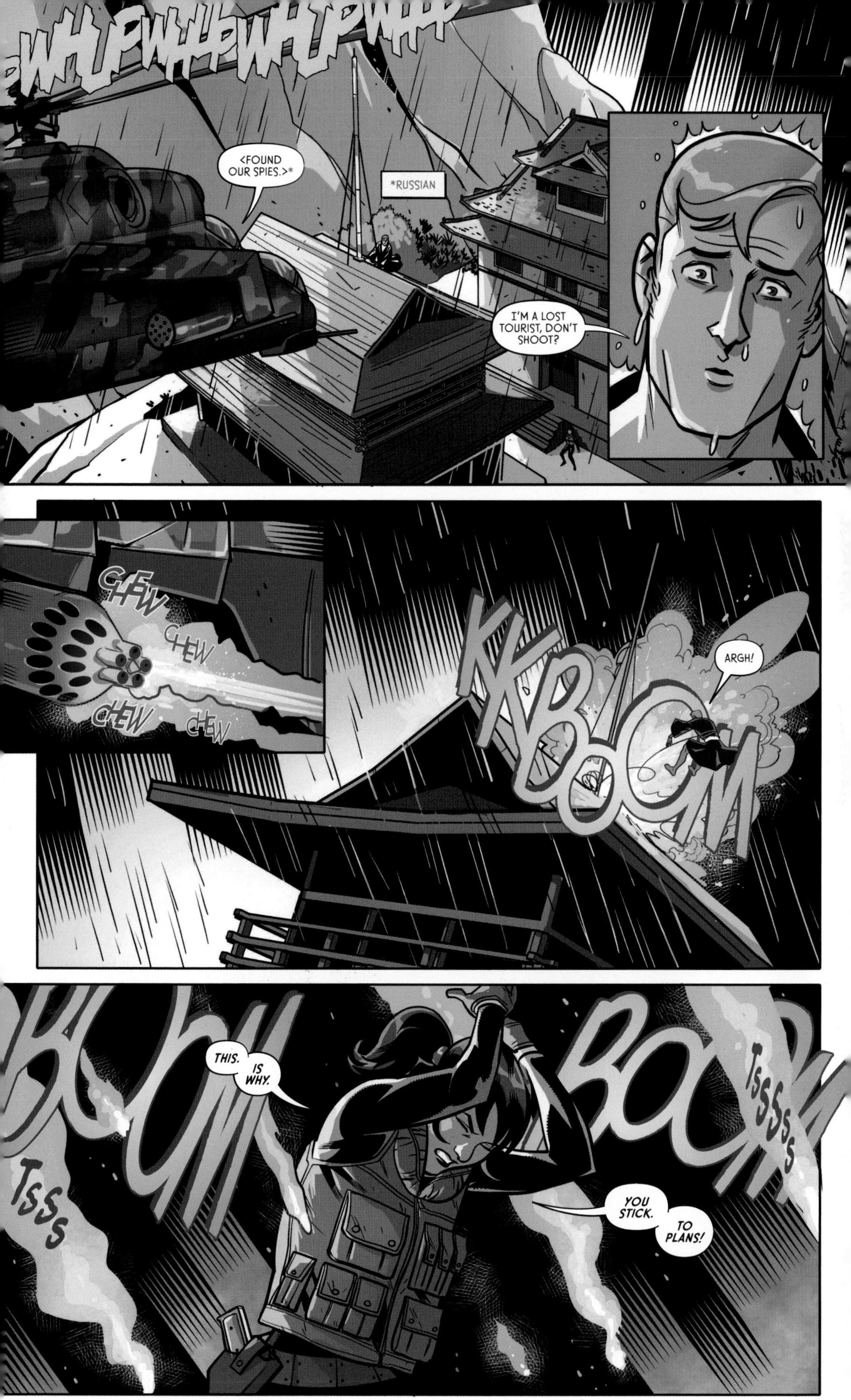
WHUPWHUPWHUPWHUP
<FOUND OUR SPIES.>*
*RUSSIAN
I'M A LOST TOURIST, DON'T SHOOT?
CHEW
CHEW
CHEW
CHEW
KKBOOM
ARGH!
BOOM
THIS.
IS WHY.
BOOM
TsSSs
TsSs
YOU STICK.
TO PLANS!

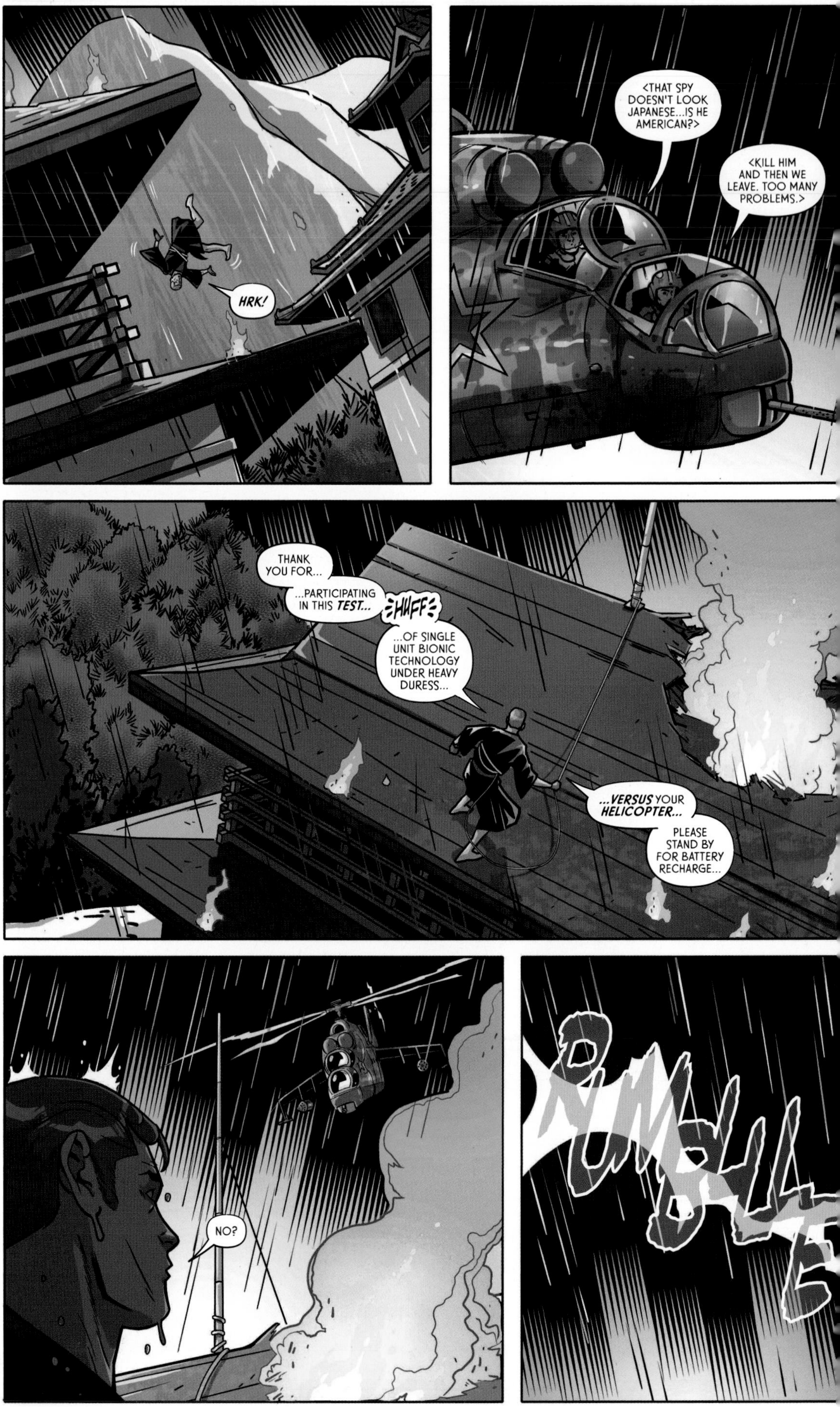
HRK!
<THAT SPY DOESN'T LOOK JAPANESE...IS HE AMERICAN?>
<KILL HIM AND THEN WE LEAVE. TOO MANY PROBLEMS.>
THANK YOU FOR...
...PARTICIPATING IN THIS TEST...
HUFF
...OF SINGLE UNIT BIONIC TECHNOLOGY UNDER HEAVY DURESS...
...VERSUS YOUR HELICOPTER...
PLEASE STAND BY FOR BATTERY RECHARGE...
NO?

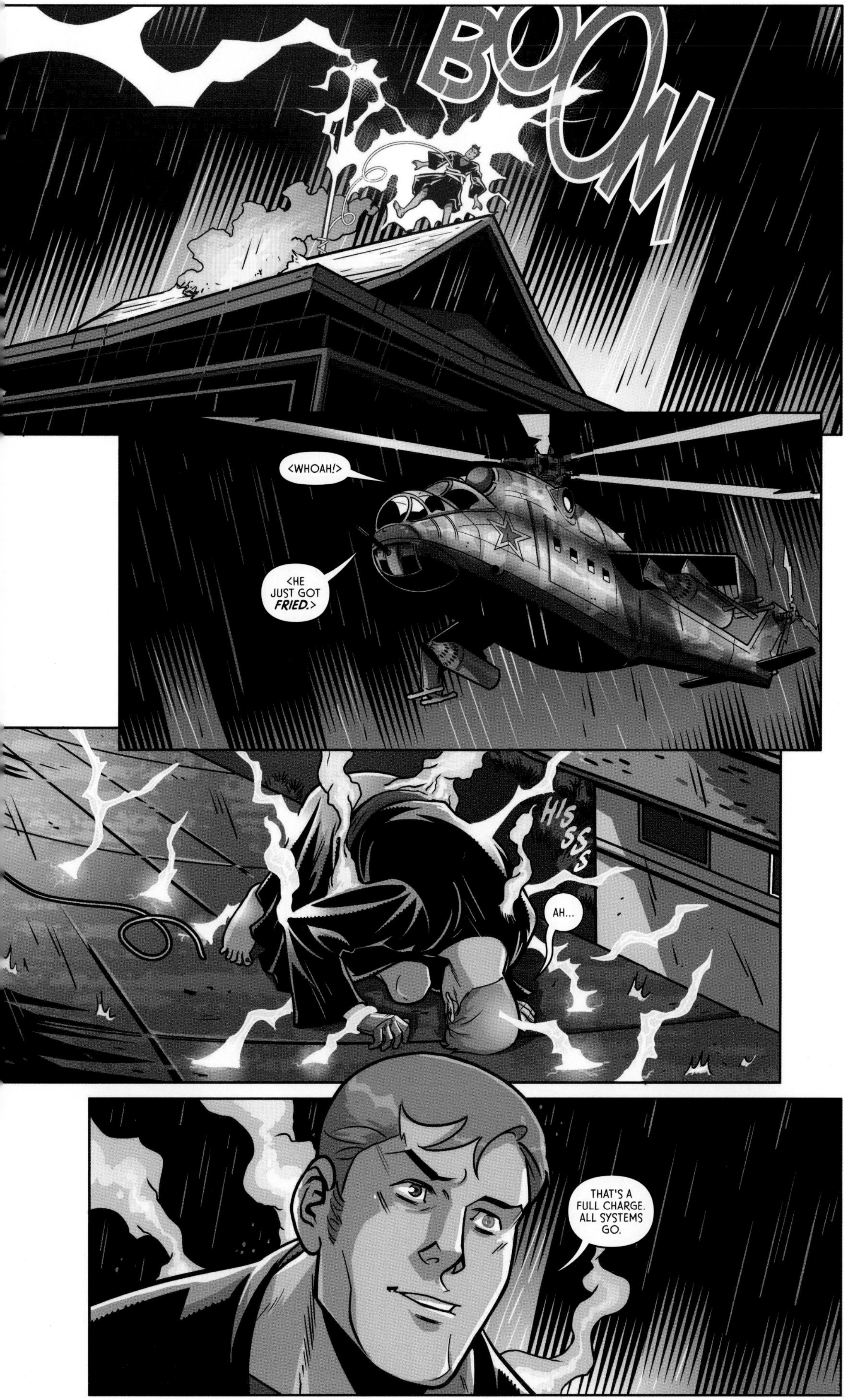
BOOM
<WHOAH!>
<HE JUST GOT *FRIED.*>
HISSSS
AH...
THAT'S A FULL CHARGE. ALL SYSTEMS GO.

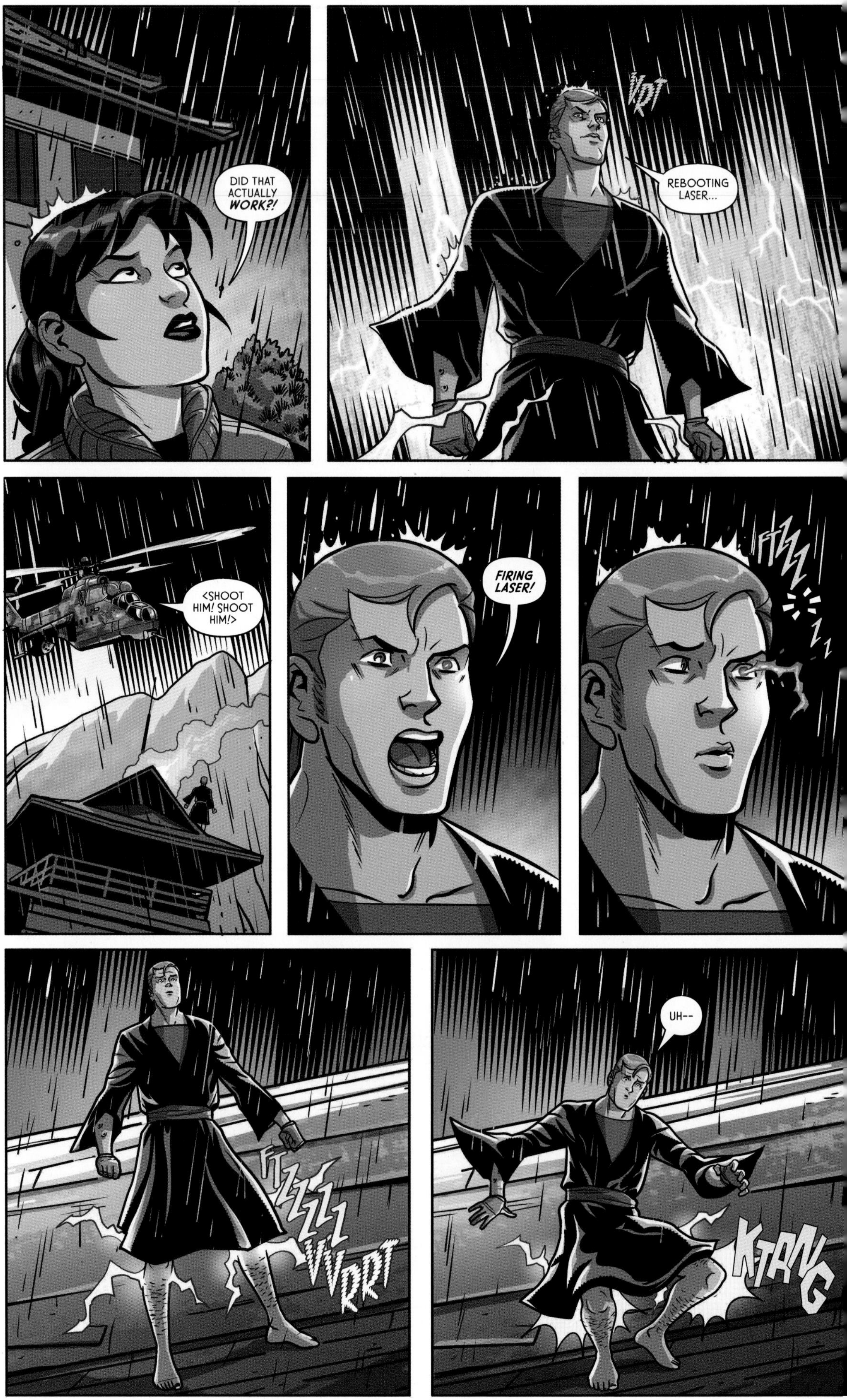
DID THAT ACTUALLY WORK?!
VRT
REBOOTING LASER...
<SHOOT HIM! SHOOT HIM!>
FIRING LASER!
FTZZZ
FTZZZZZ
VVRRT
UH--
K-TANG

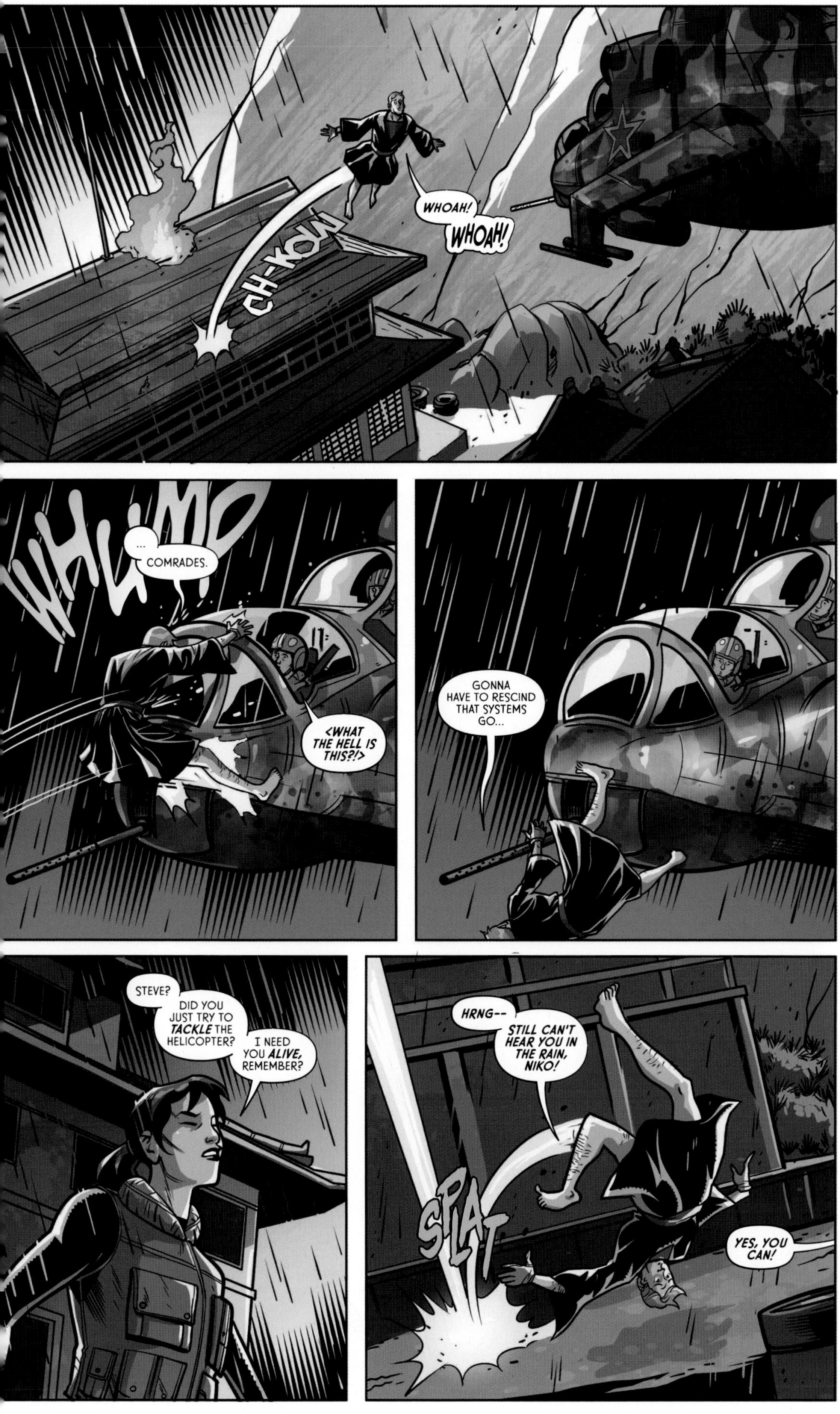

CH-KOW
WHOAH!
WHOAH!
WHUMP
... COMRADES.
<WHAT THE HELL IS THIS?!>
GONNA HAVE TO RESCIND THAT SYSTEMS GO...
STEVE?
DID YOU JUST TRY TO *TACKLE* THE HELICOPTER?
I NEED YOU *ALIVE,* REMEMBER?
HRNG--
STILL CAN'T HEAR YOU IN THE RAIN, NIKO!
SPLAT
YES, YOU CAN!

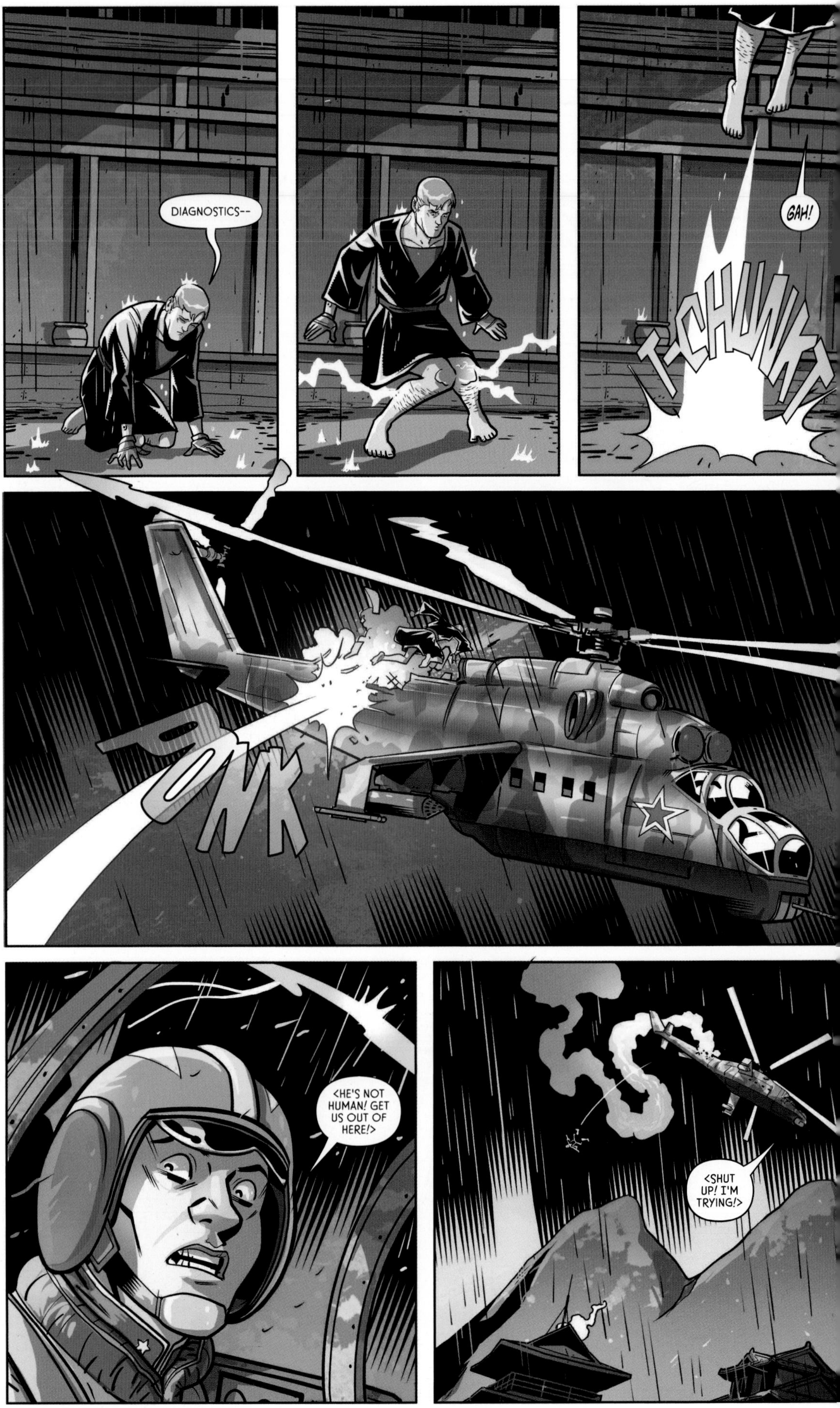

DIAGNOSTICS--
GAH!
T-CHUNK!
PONK
<HE'S NOT HUMAN! GET US OUT OF HERE!>
<SHUT UP! I'M TRYING!>

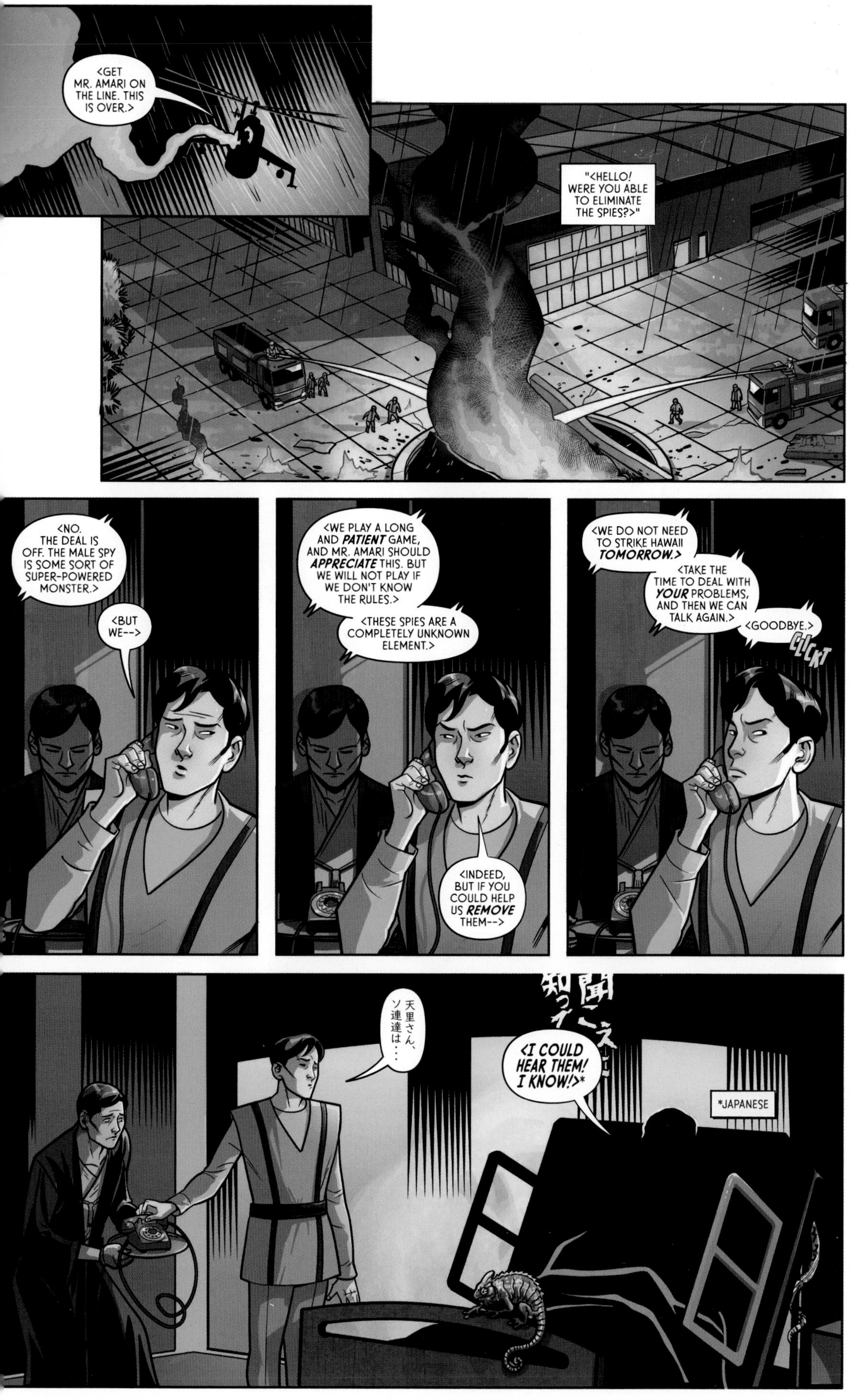
<GET MR. AMARI ON THE LINE. THIS IS OVER.>
"<HELLO! WERE YOU ABLE TO ELIMINATE THE SPIES?>"
<NO. THE DEAL IS OFF. THE MALE SPY IS SOME SORT OF SUPER-POWERED MONSTER.>
<BUT WE-->
<WE PLAY A LONG AND *PATIENT* GAME, AND MR. AMARI SHOULD *APPRECIATE* THIS. BUT WE WILL NOT PLAY IF WE DON'T KNOW THE RULES.>
<THESE SPIES ARE A COMPLETELY UNKNOWN ELEMENT.>
<INDEED, BUT IF YOU COULD HELP US *REMOVE* THEM-->
<WE DO NOT NEED TO STRIKE HAWAII *TOMORROW*.>
<TAKE THE TIME TO DEAL WITH *YOUR* PROBLEMS, AND THEN WE CAN TALK AGAIN.>
<GOODBYE.>
CLICK!
天里さん、ソ連達は・・・
聞こえ
知って
*<I COULD HEAR THEM! I KNOW!>**
*JAPANESE

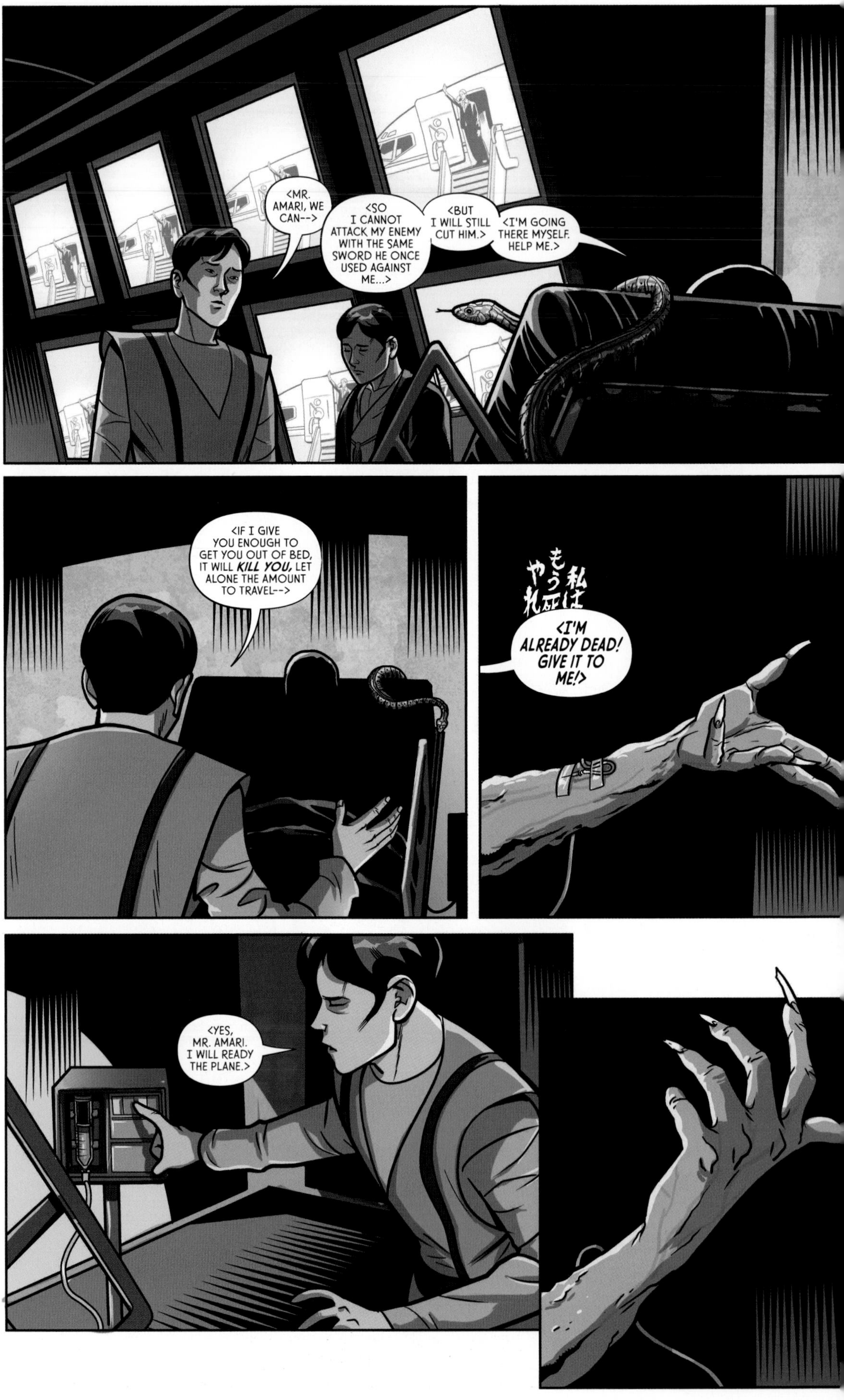
<MR. AMARI, WE CAN-->
<SO I CANNOT ATTACK MY ENEMY WITH THE SAME SWORD HE ONCE USED AGAINST ME...>
<BUT I WILL STILL CUT HIM.>
<I'M GOING THERE MYSELF. HELP ME.>
<IF I GIVE YOU ENOUGH TO GET YOU OUT OF BED, IT WILL KILL YOU, LET ALONE THE AMOUNT TO TRAVEL-->
私は
もう死
やれ
<I'M ALREADY DEAD! GIVE IT TO ME!>
<YES, MR. AMARI. I WILL READY THE PLANE.>

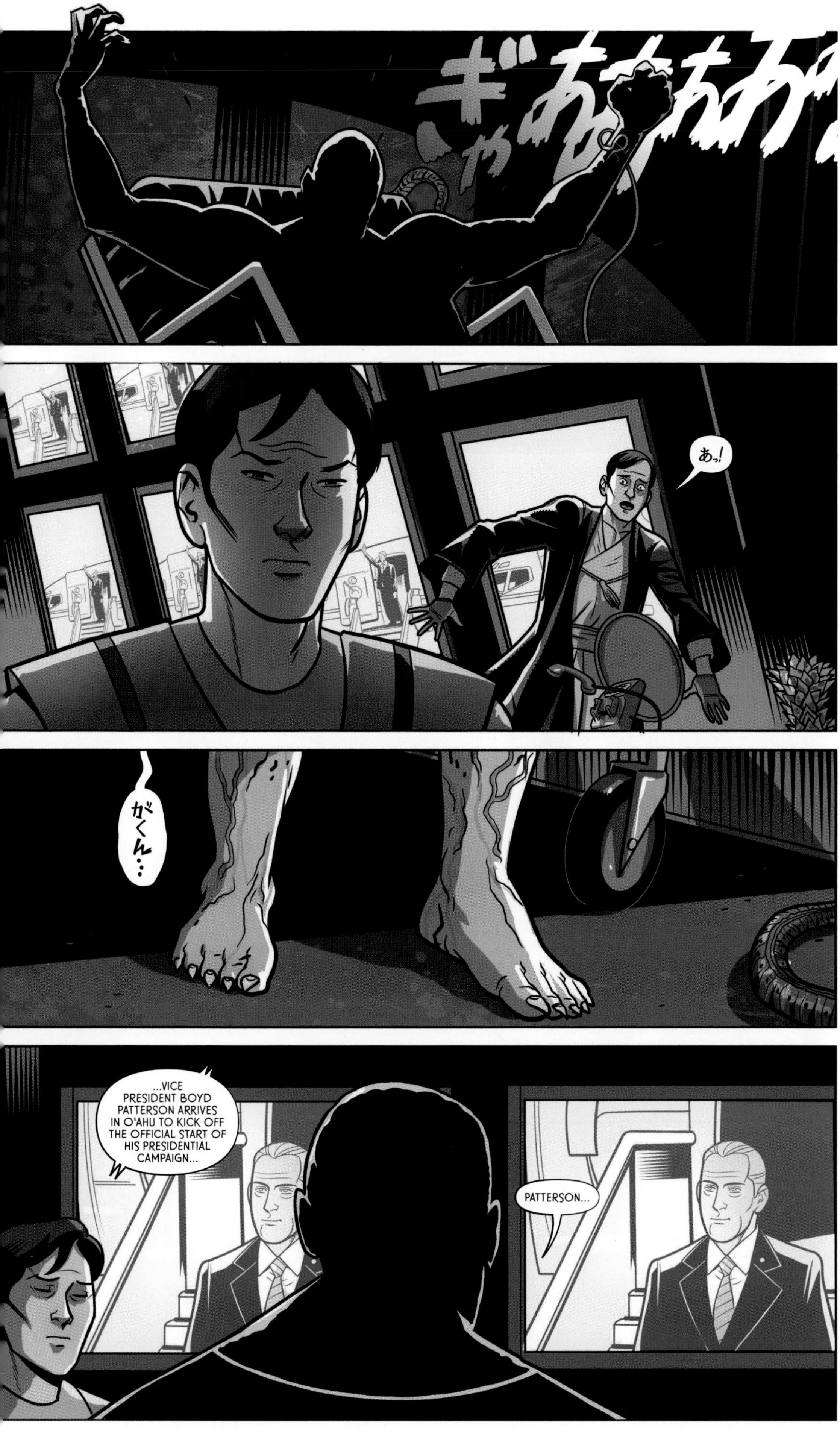
ぎゃあああ
あっ!
がくん…
...VICE PRESIDENT BOYD PATTERSON ARRIVES IN O'AHU TO KICK OFF THE OFFICIAL START OF HIS PRESIDENTIAL CAMPAIGN...
PATTERSON...

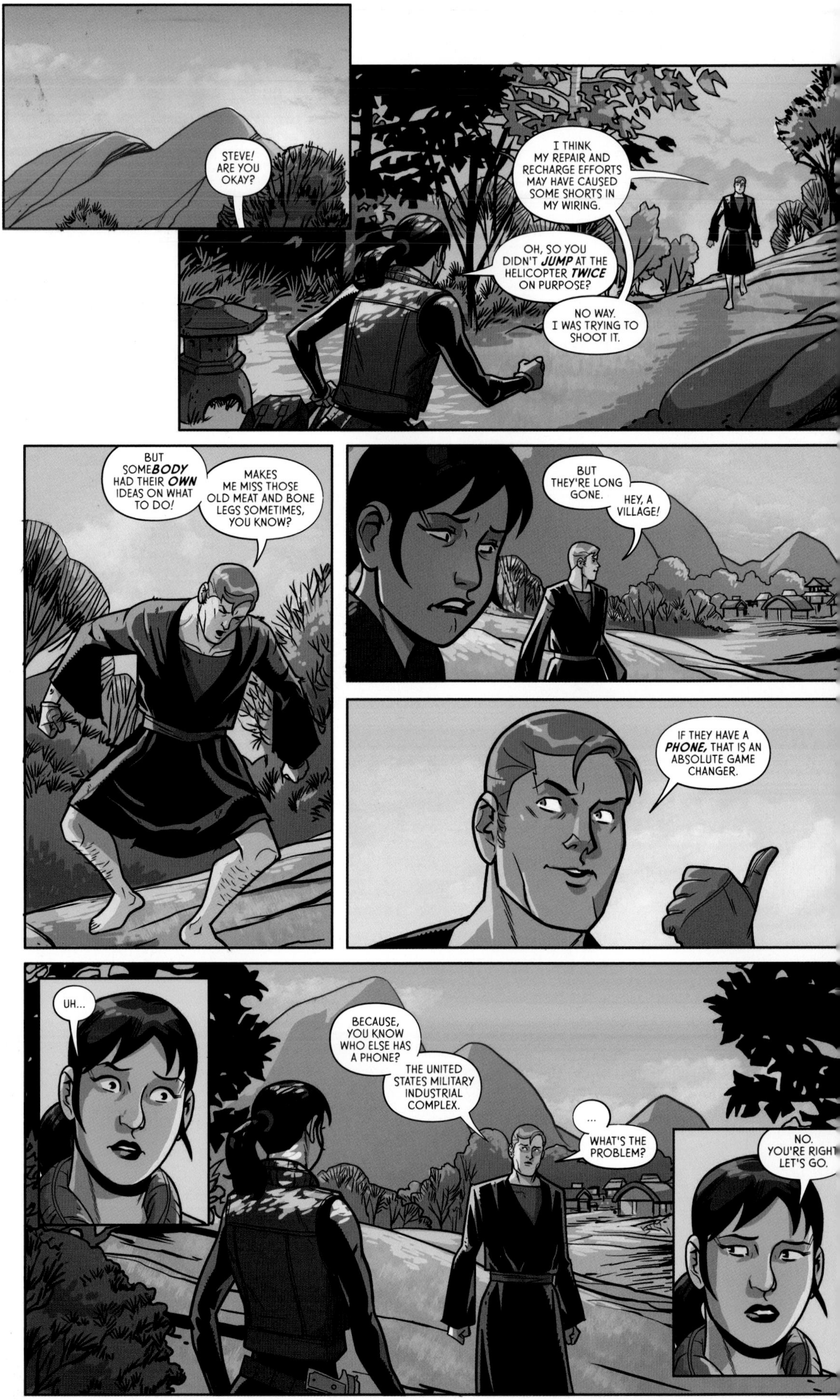
STEVE! ARE YOU OKAY?
I THINK MY REPAIR AND RECHARGE EFFORTS MAY HAVE CAUSED SOME SHORTS IN MY WIRING.
OH, SO YOU DIDN'T **JUMP** AT THE HELICOPTER **TWICE** ON PURPOSE?
NO WAY. I WAS TRYING TO SHOOT IT.
BUT SOME**BODY** HAD THEIR **OWN** IDEAS ON WHAT TO DO!
MAKES ME MISS THOSE OLD MEAT AND BONE LEGS SOMETIMES, YOU KNOW?
BUT THEY'RE LONG GONE.
HEY, A VILLAGE!
IF THEY HAVE A **PHONE,** THAT IS AN ABSOLUTE GAME CHANGER.
UH...
BECAUSE, YOU KNOW WHO ELSE HAS A PHONE?
THE UNITED STATES MILITARY INDUSTRIAL COMPLEX.
...
WHAT'S THE PROBLEM?
NO. YOU'RE RIGHT. LET'S GO.

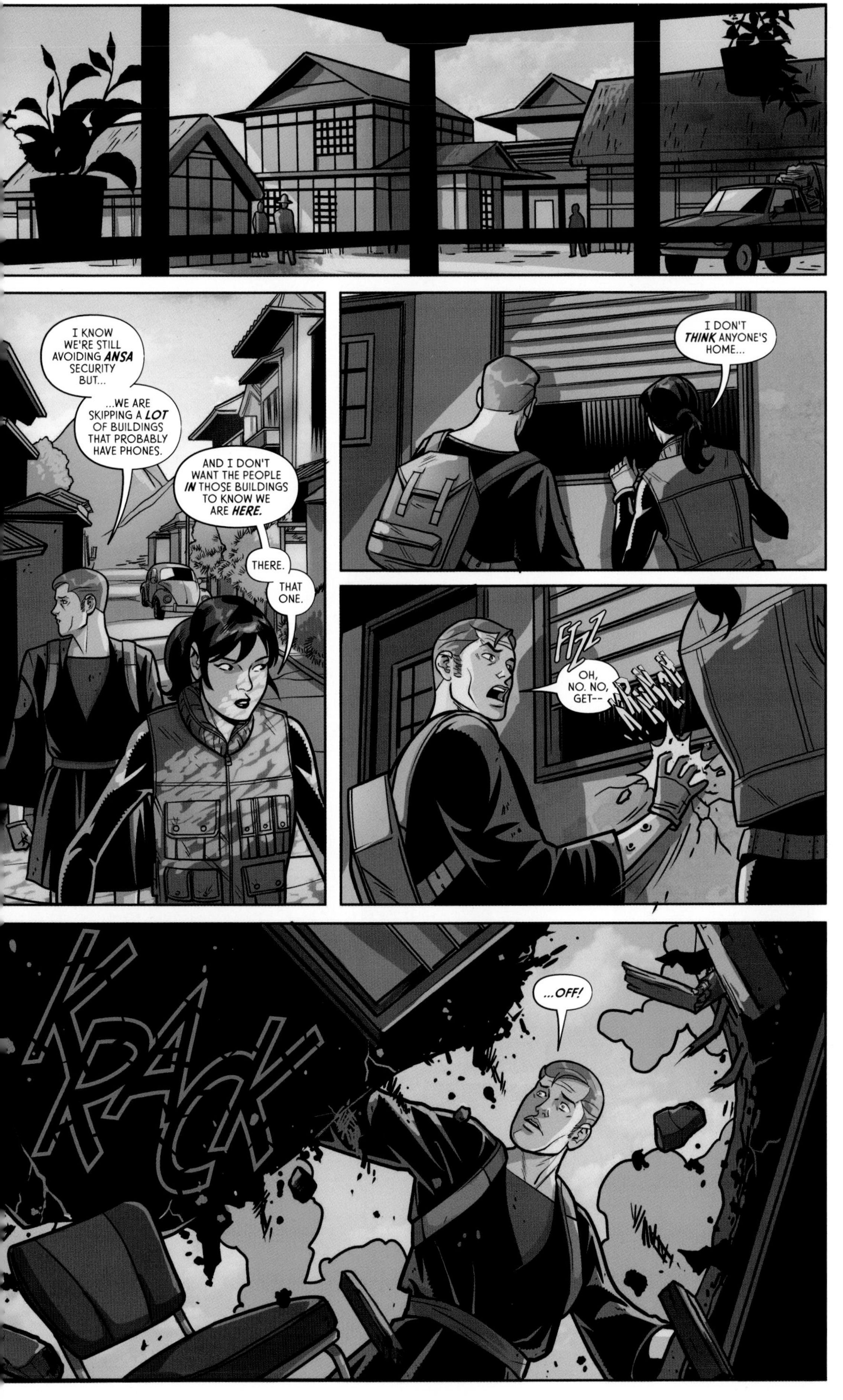
I KNOW WE'RE STILL AVOIDING ***ANSA*** SECURITY BUT...
...WE ARE SKIPPING A ***LOT*** OF BUILDINGS THAT PROBABLY HAVE PHONES.
AND I DON'T WANT THE PEOPLE ***IN*** THOSE BUILDINGS TO KNOW WE ARE ***HERE.***
THERE.
THAT ONE.
I DON'T ***THINK*** ANYONE'S HOME...
FIZZ
OH, NO. NO, GET--
KRACK
...OFF!

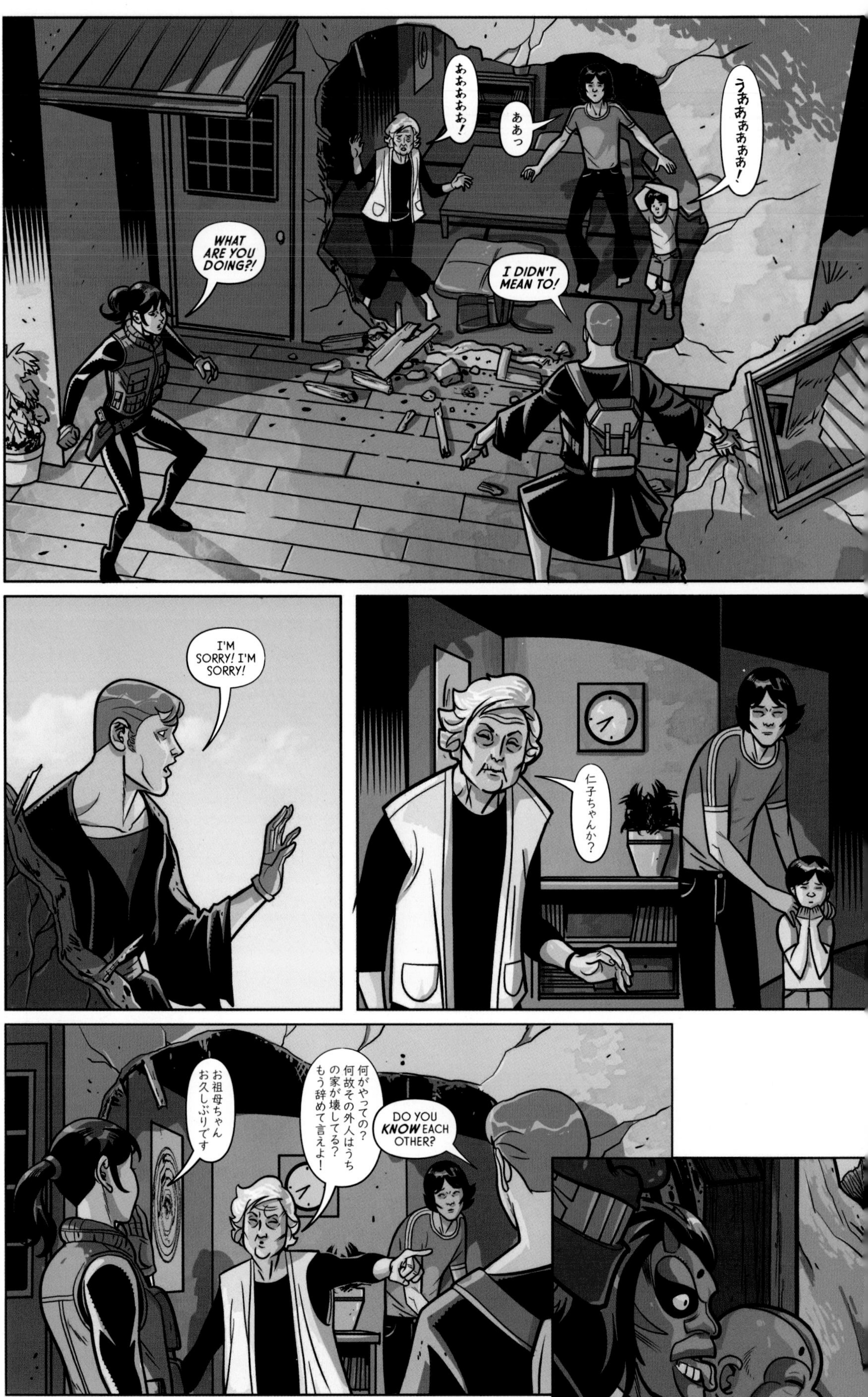
ああああああ！
ああっ
うああああああ！
WHAT ARE YOU DOING?!
I DIDN'T MEAN TO!
I'M SORRY! I'M SORRY!
仁子ちゃんか？
何がやっての？何故その外人はうちの家が壊してる？もう辞めて言えよ！
お祖母ちゃんお久しぶりです
DO YOU KNOW EACH OTHER?

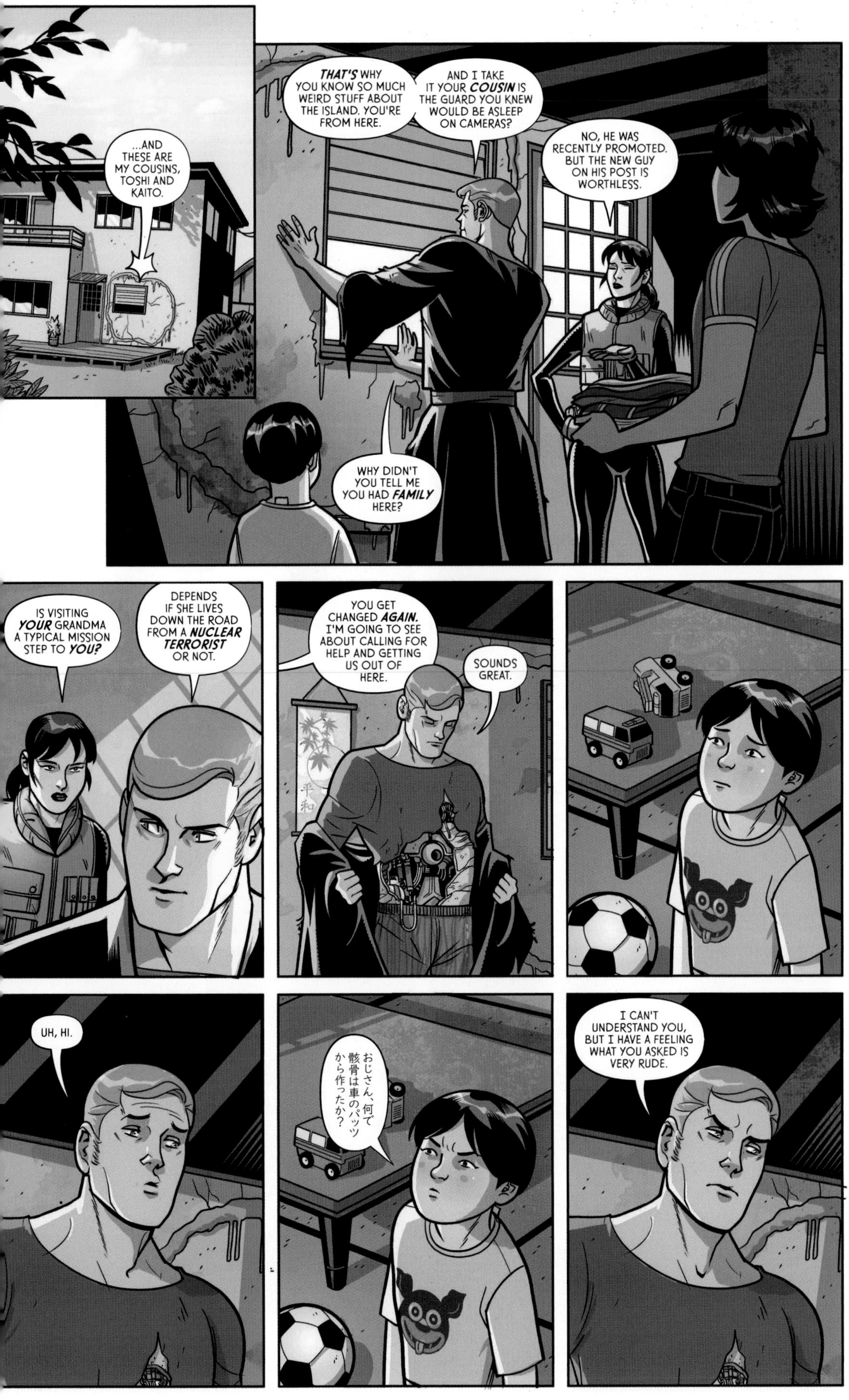
...AND THESE ARE MY COUSINS, TOSHI AND KAITO.
THAT'S WHY YOU KNOW SO MUCH WEIRD STUFF ABOUT THE ISLAND. YOU'RE FROM HERE.
AND I TAKE IT YOUR COUSIN IS THE GUARD YOU KNEW WOULD BE ASLEEP ON CAMERAS?
NO, HE WAS RECENTLY PROMOTED. BUT THE NEW GUY ON HIS POST IS WORTHLESS.
WHY DIDN'T YOU TELL ME YOU HAD FAMILY HERE?
IS VISITING YOUR GRANDMA A TYPICAL MISSION STEP TO YOU?
DEPENDS IF SHE LIVES DOWN THE ROAD FROM A NUCLEAR TERRORIST OR NOT.
YOU GET CHANGED AGAIN. I'M GOING TO SEE ABOUT CALLING FOR HELP AND GETTING US OUT OF HERE.
SOUNDS GREAT.
平和
UH, HI.
おじさん、何で骸骨は車のパッツから作ったか？
I CAN'T UNDERSTAND YOU, BUT I HAVE A FEELING WHAT YOU ASKED IS VERY RUDE.

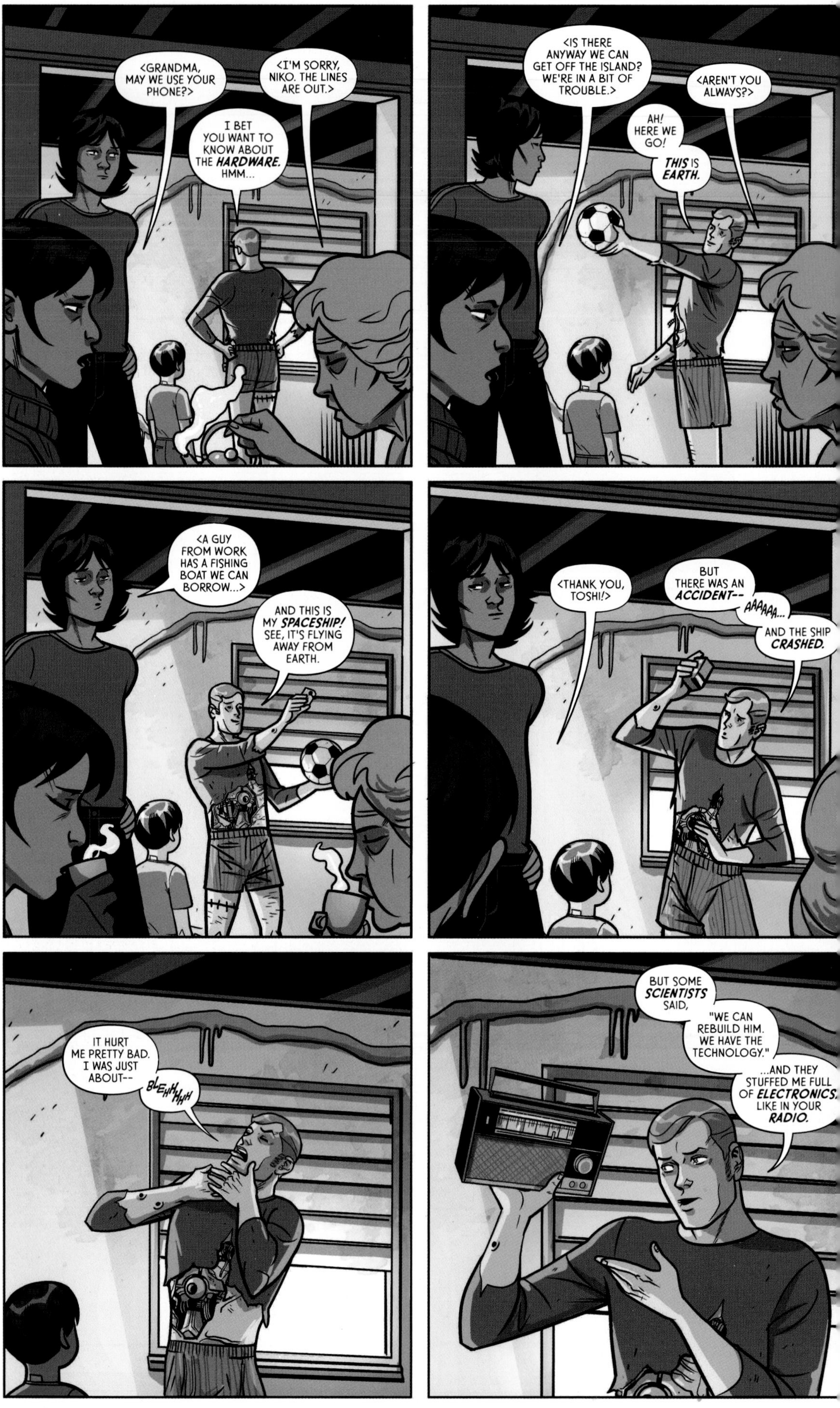
<GRANDMA, MAY WE USE YOUR PHONE?>
<I'M SORRY, NIKO. THE LINES ARE OUT.>
I BET YOU WANT TO KNOW ABOUT THE **HARDWARE.** HMM...
<IS THERE ANYWAY WE CAN GET OFF THE ISLAND? WE'RE IN A BIT OF TROUBLE.>
<AREN'T YOU ALWAYS?>
AH! HERE WE GO!
THIS IS **EARTH.**
<A GUY FROM WORK HAS A FISHING BOAT WE CAN BORROW...>
AND THIS IS MY **SPACESHIP!** SEE, IT'S FLYING AWAY FROM EARTH.
<THANK YOU, TOSHI!>
BUT THERE WAS AN **ACCIDENT--**
AAAAAA...
AND THE SHIP **CRASHED.**
IT HURT ME PRETTY BAD. I WAS JUST ABOUT--
BLEHHHHH
BUT SOME **SCIENTISTS** SAID,
"WE CAN REBUILD HIM. WE HAVE THE TECHNOLOGY."
...AND THEY STUFFED ME FULL OF **ELECTRONICS,** LIKE IN YOUR **RADIO.**

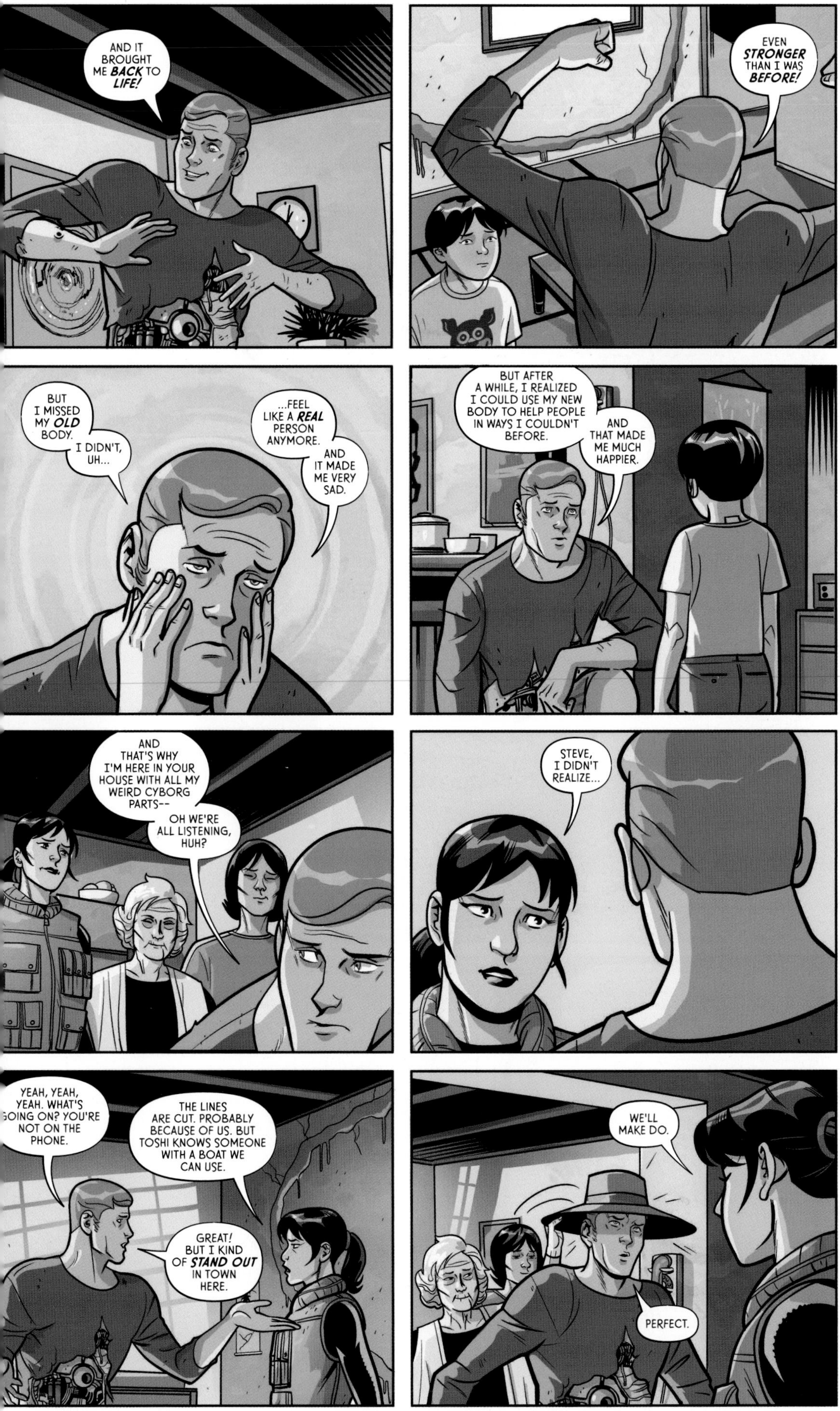
AND IT BROUGHT ME BACK TO LIFE!
EVEN STRONGER THAN I WAS BEFORE!
BUT I MISSED MY OLD BODY.
I DIDN'T, UH...
...FEEL LIKE A REAL PERSON ANYMORE.
AND IT MADE ME VERY SAD.
BUT AFTER A WHILE, I REALIZED I COULD USE MY NEW BODY TO HELP PEOPLE IN WAYS I COULDN'T BEFORE.
AND THAT MADE ME MUCH HAPPIER.
AND THAT'S WHY I'M HERE IN YOUR HOUSE WITH ALL MY WEIRD CYBORG PARTS--
OH WE'RE ALL LISTENING, HUH?
STEVE, I DIDN'T REALIZE...
YEAH, YEAH, YEAH. WHAT'S GOING ON? YOU'RE NOT ON THE PHONE.
THE LINES ARE CUT. PROBABLY BECAUSE OF US. BUT TOSHI KNOWS SOMEONE WITH A BOAT WE CAN USE.
GREAT! BUT I KIND OF STAND OUT IN TOWN HERE.
WE'LL MAKE DO.
PERFECT.

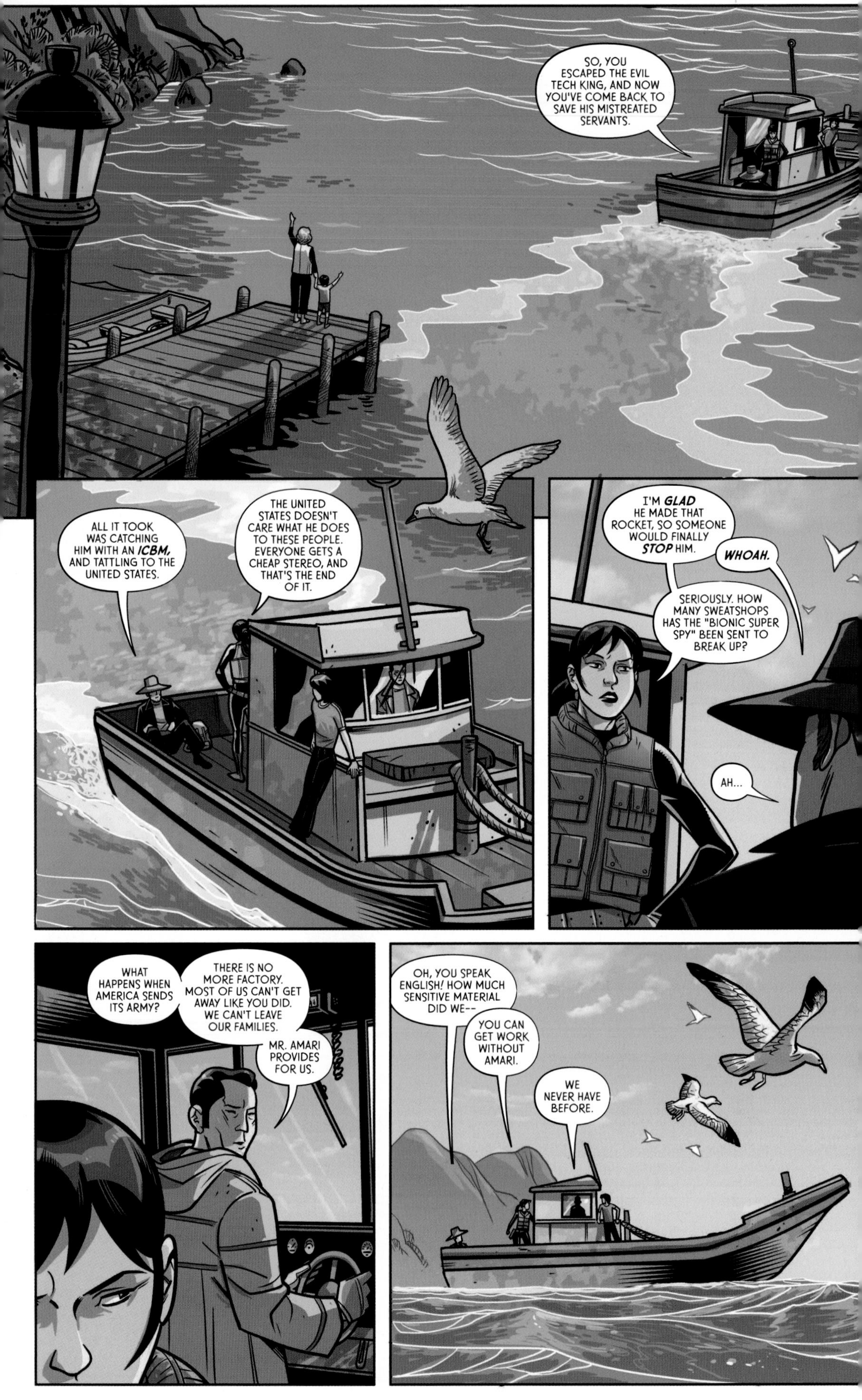
SO, YOU ESCAPED THE EVIL TECH KING, AND NOW YOU'VE COME BACK TO SAVE HIS MISTREATED SERVANTS.
ALL IT TOOK WAS CATCHING HIM WITH AN *ICBM,* AND TATTLING TO THE UNITED STATES.
THE UNITED STATES DOESN'T CARE WHAT HE DOES TO THESE PEOPLE. EVERYONE GETS A CHEAP STEREO, AND THAT'S THE END OF IT.
I'M *GLAD* HE MADE THAT ROCKET, SO SOMEONE WOULD FINALLY *STOP* HIM.
WHOAH.
SERIOUSLY. HOW MANY SWEATSHOPS HAS THE "BIONIC SUPER SPY" BEEN SENT TO BREAK UP?
AH...
WHAT HAPPENS WHEN AMERICA SENDS ITS ARMY?
THERE IS NO MORE FACTORY. MOST OF US CAN'T GET AWAY LIKE YOU DID. WE CAN'T LEAVE OUR FAMILIES.
MR. AMARI PROVIDES FOR US.
OH, YOU SPEAK ENGLISH! HOW MUCH SENSITIVE MATERIAL DID WE--
YOU CAN GET WORK WITHOUT AMARI.
WE NEVER HAVE BEFORE.

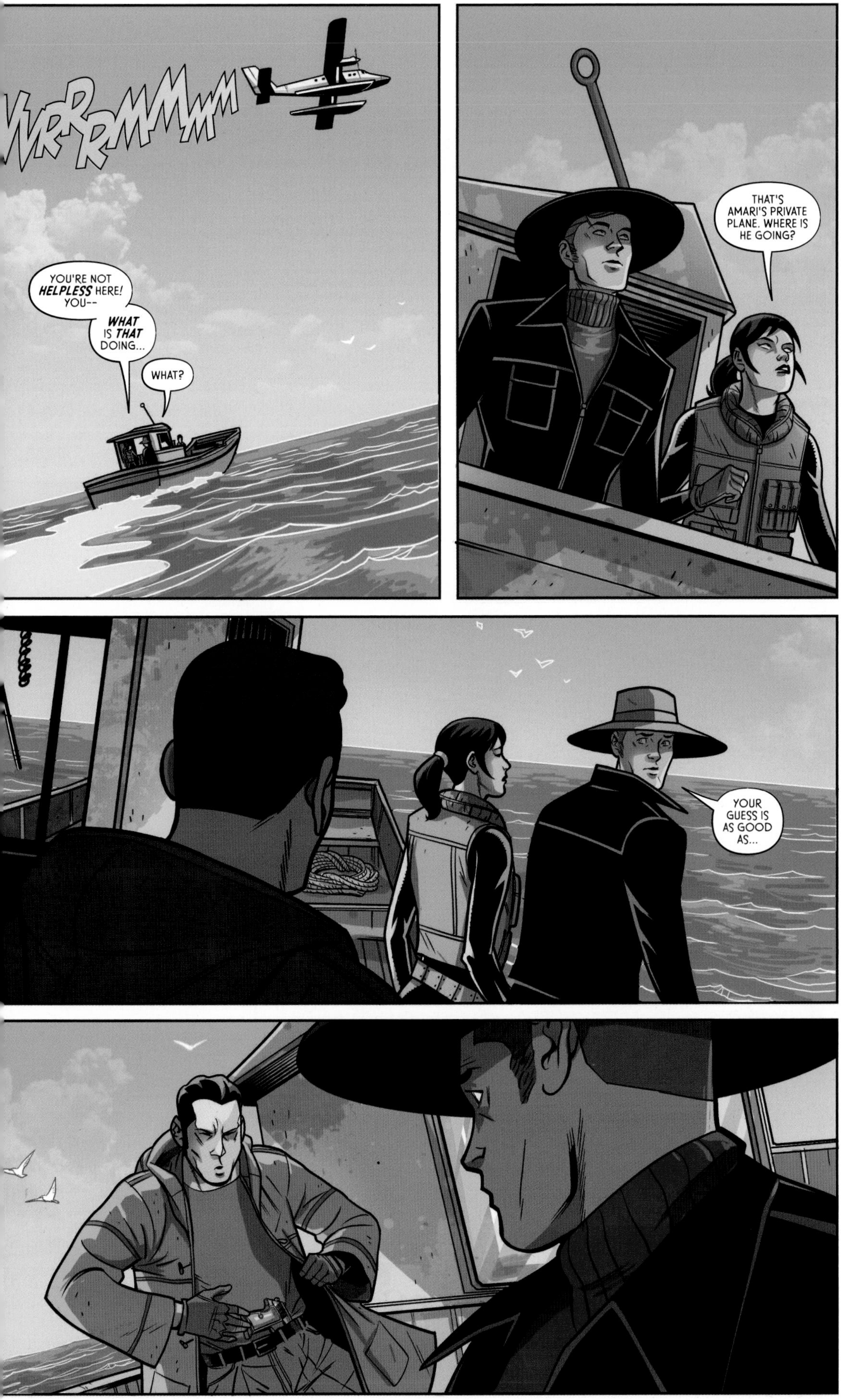
VRRRMMMMM
YOU'RE NOT HELPLESS HERE! YOU--
WHAT IS THAT DOING...
WHAT?
THAT'S AMARI'S PRIVATE PLANE. WHERE IS HE GOING?
YOUR GUESS IS AS GOOD AS...

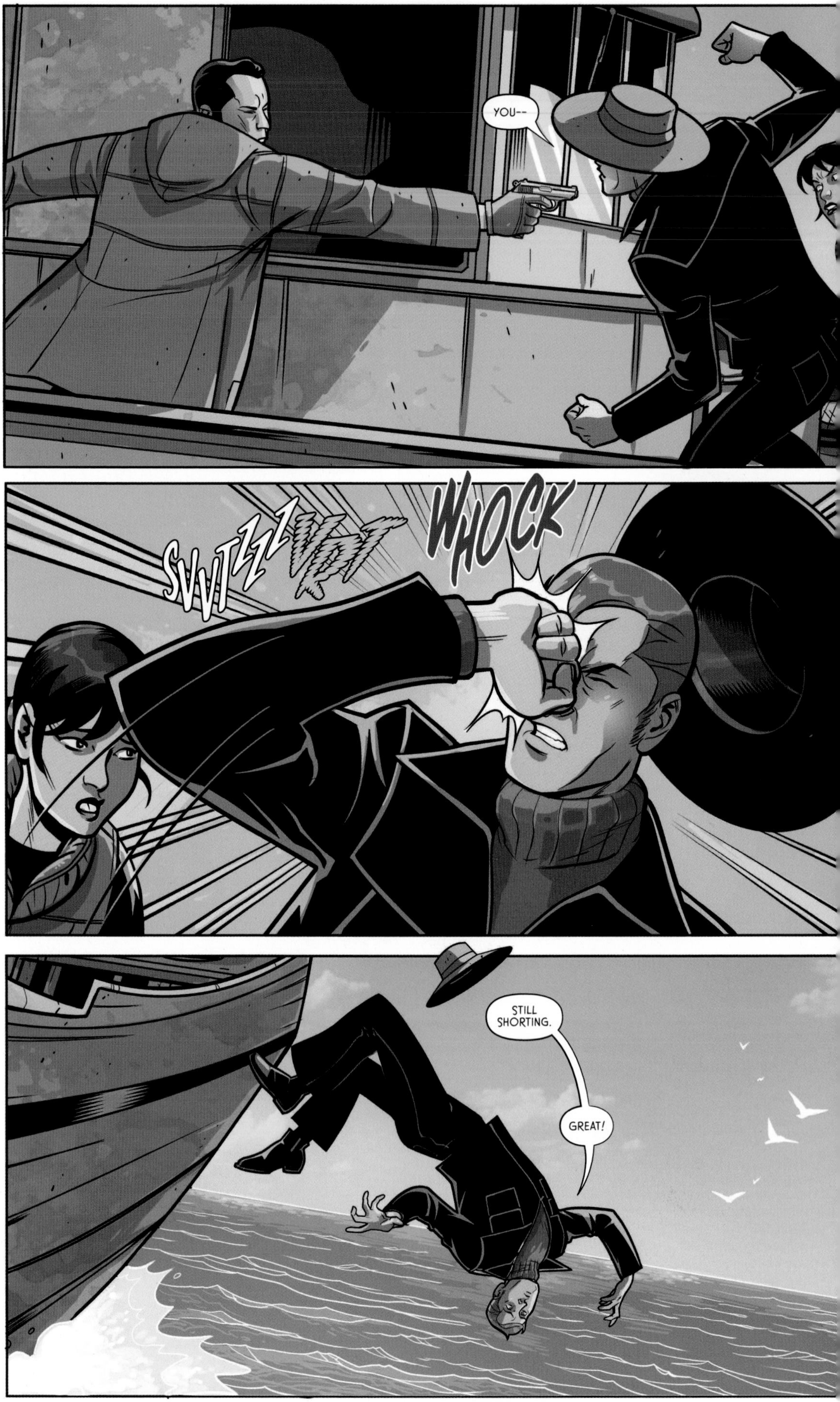
YOU--
SVVTZZZZVRT
WHOCK
STILL SHORTING.
GREAT!

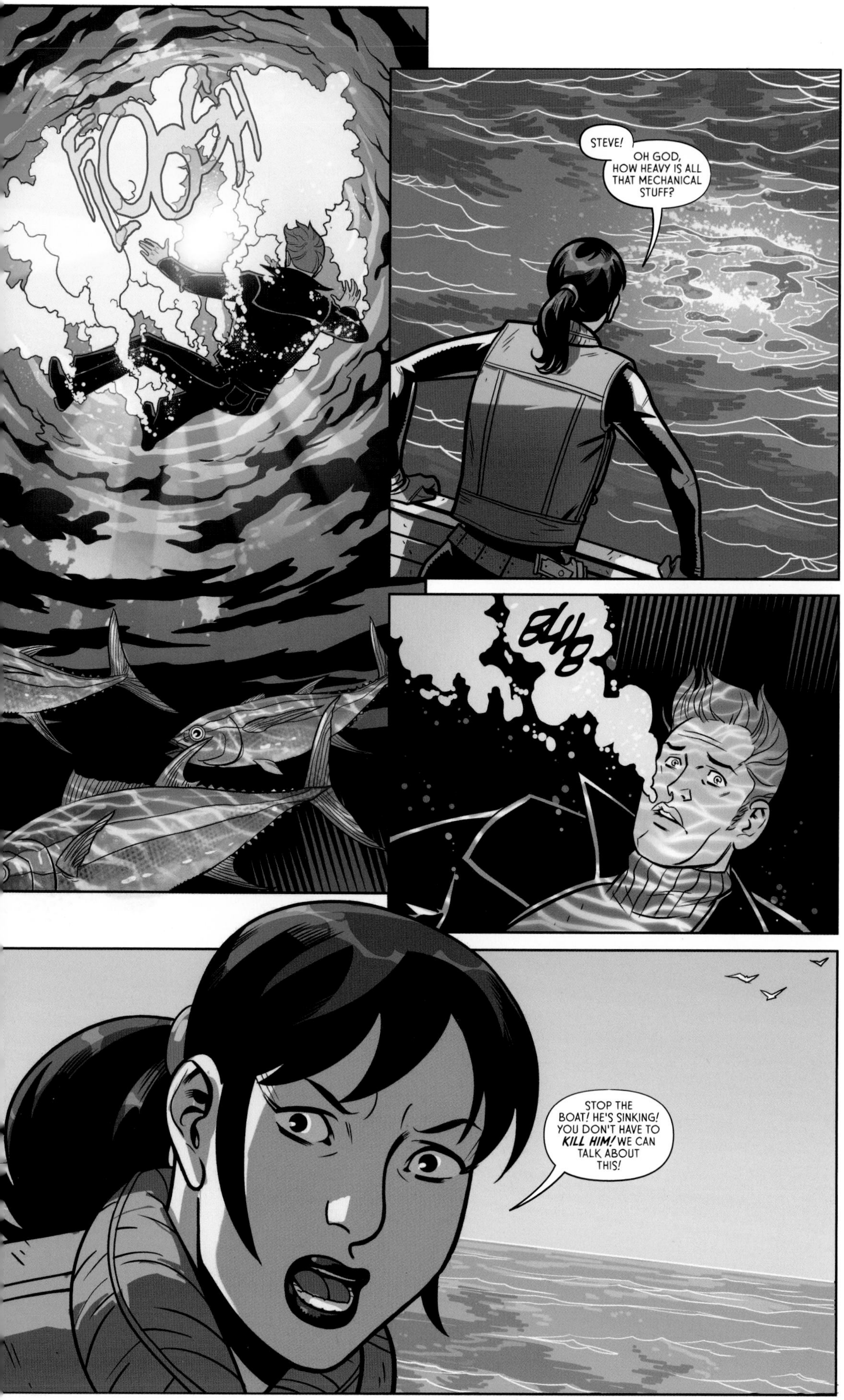
FOOSH
STEVE!
OH GOD, HOW HEAVY IS ALL THAT MECHANICAL STUFF?
BLUB
STOP THE BOAT! HE'S SINKING! YOU DON'T HAVE TO *KILL HIM!* WE CAN TALK ABOUT THIS!

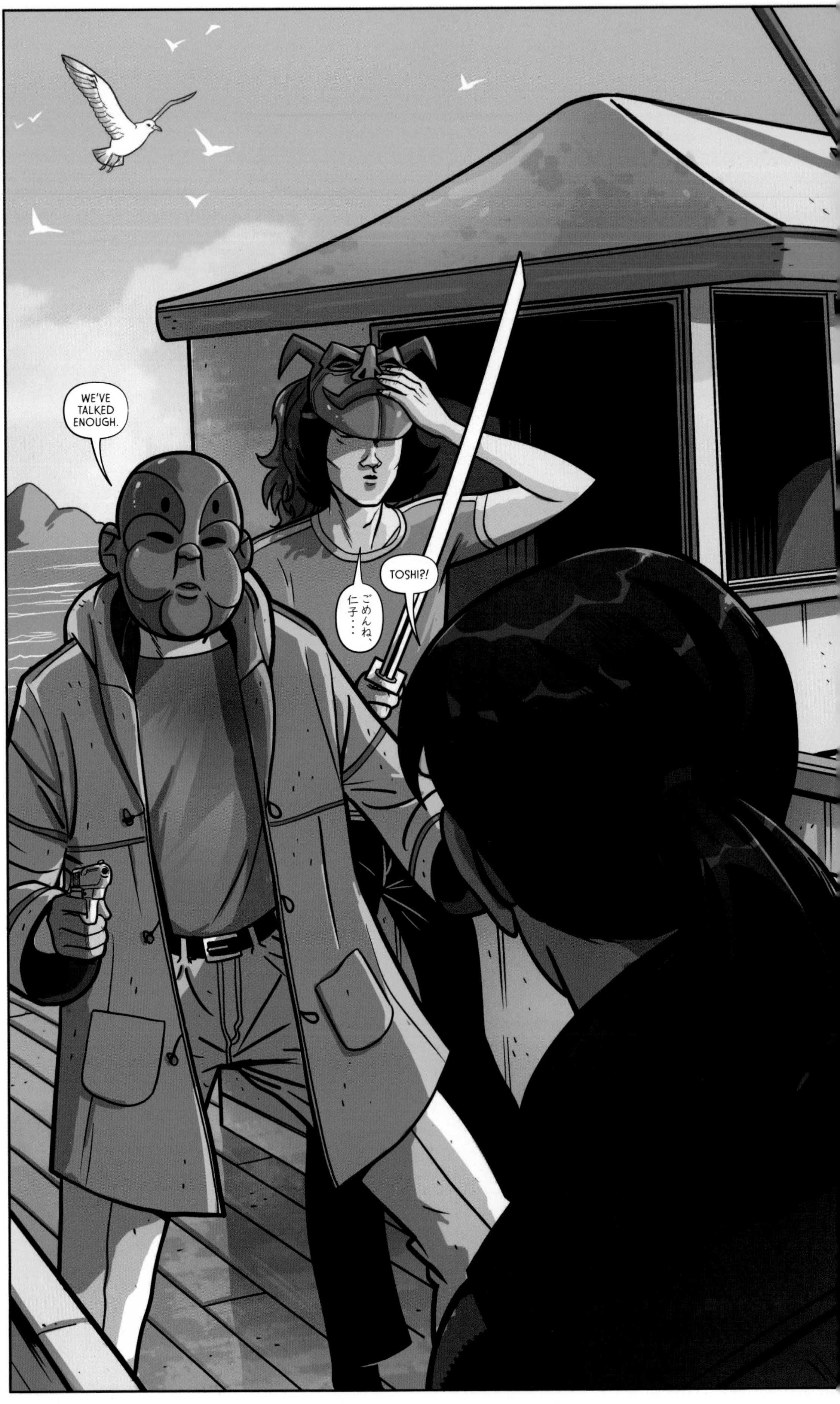
WE'VE TALKED ENOUGH.
ごめんね、仁子・・・
TOSHI?!

STEVE AUSTIN. ASTRONAUT. A MAN BARELY ALIVE AFTER A HORRIBLE ACCIDENT. REBUILT AS THE WORLD'S FIRST BIONIC MAN. BETTER THAN HE WAS BEFORE.

BETTER, STRONGER, FASTER.

THE

0,006,004

DOLLAR

MAN

[...AND CURRENTLY MALFUNCTIONING AS HE SINKS TO THE BOTTOM OF THE OCEAN. BUT THINGS COULD BE SO MUCH WORSE.]

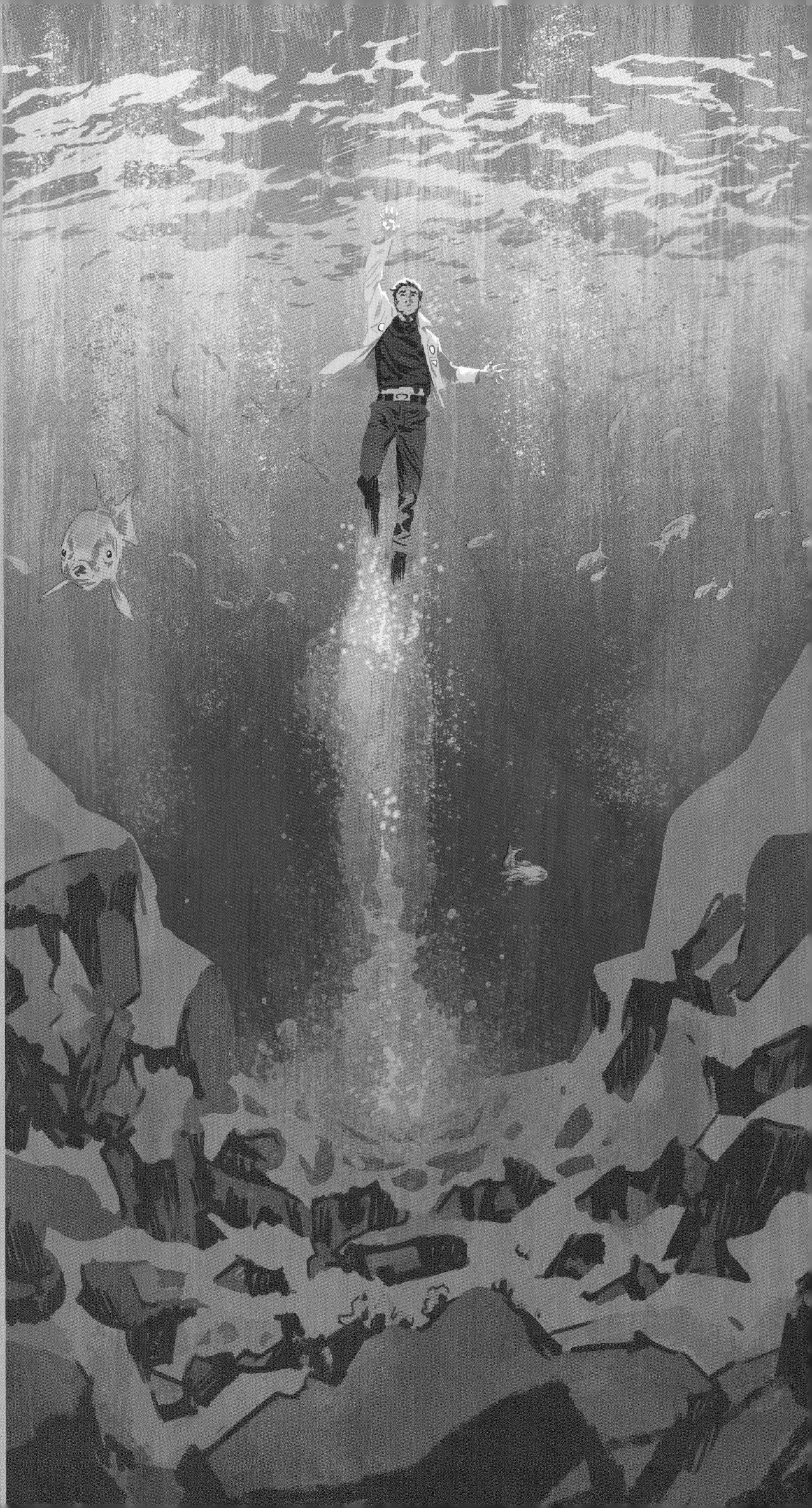

ISSUE 04 COVER ART BY MICHAEL WALSH

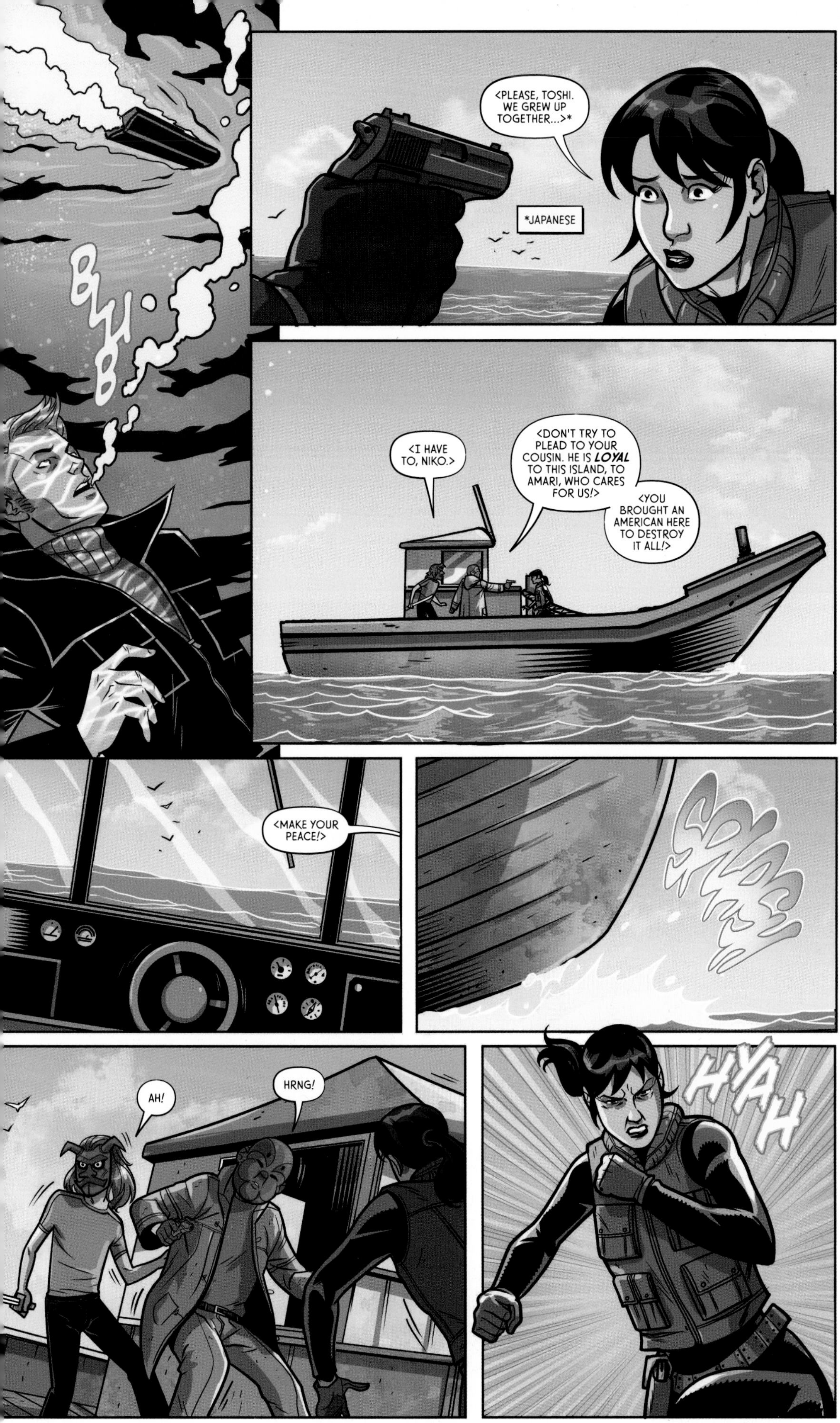

<PLEASE, TOSHI. WE GREW UP TOGETHER...>*
*JAPANESE
BLUB
<I HAVE TO, NIKO.>
<DON'T TRY TO PLEAD TO YOUR COUSIN. HE IS LOYAL TO THIS ISLAND, TO AMARI, WHO CARES FOR US!>
<YOU BROUGHT AN AMERICAN HERE TO DESTROY IT ALL!>
<MAKE YOUR PEACE!>
AH!
HRNG!
HYAH

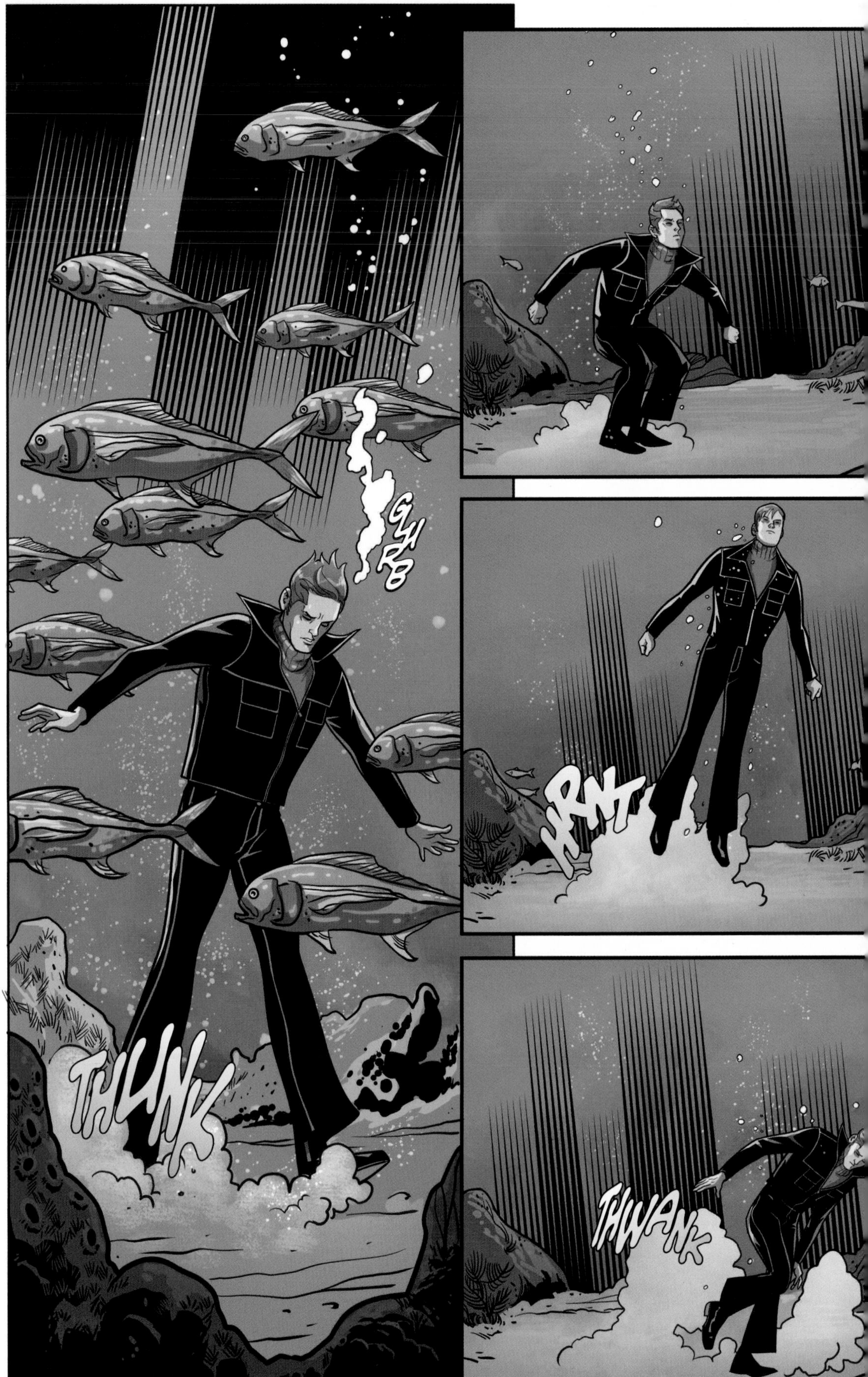
GLURB
THUNK
HRNT
THWANK

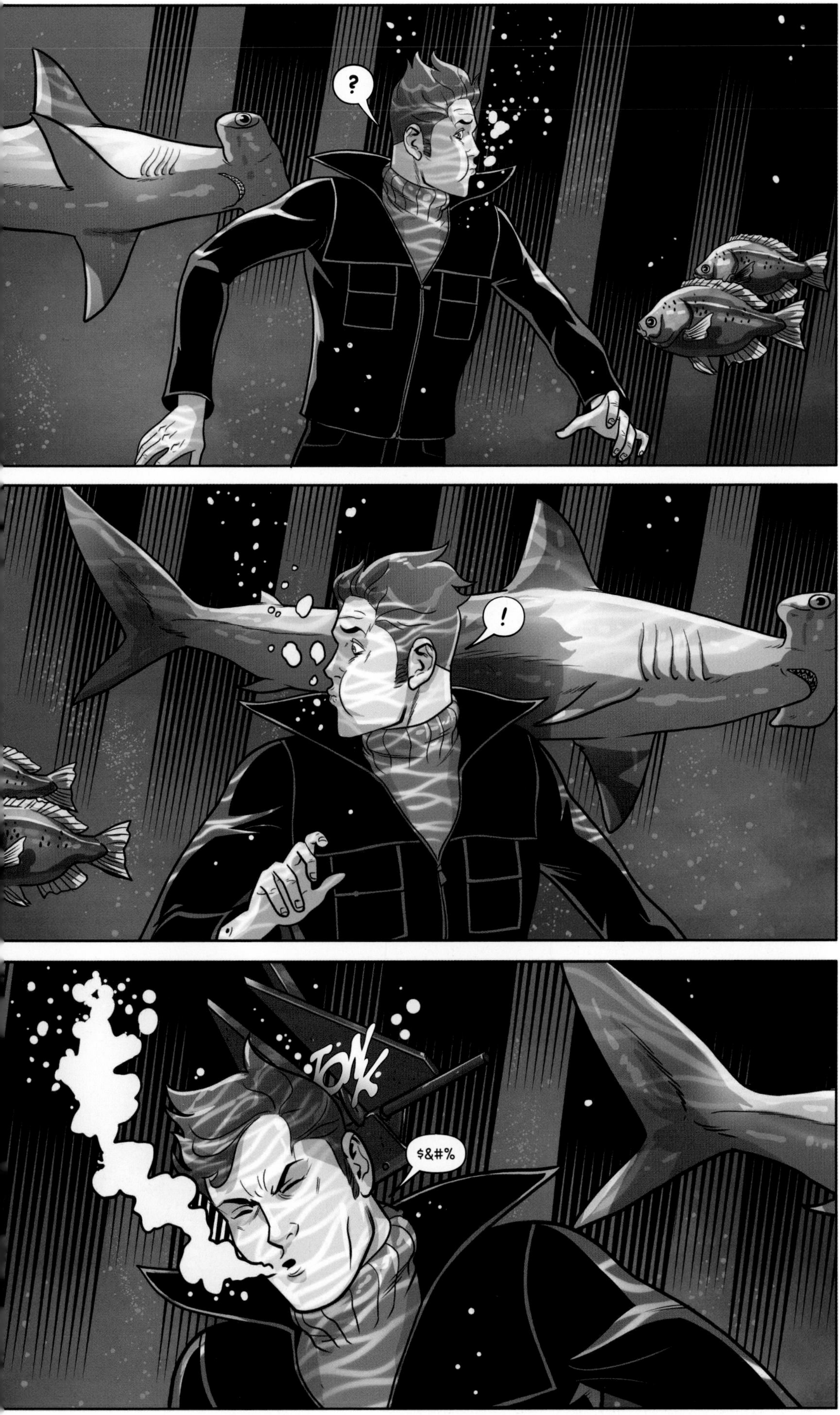
?
!
TONK
$&#%

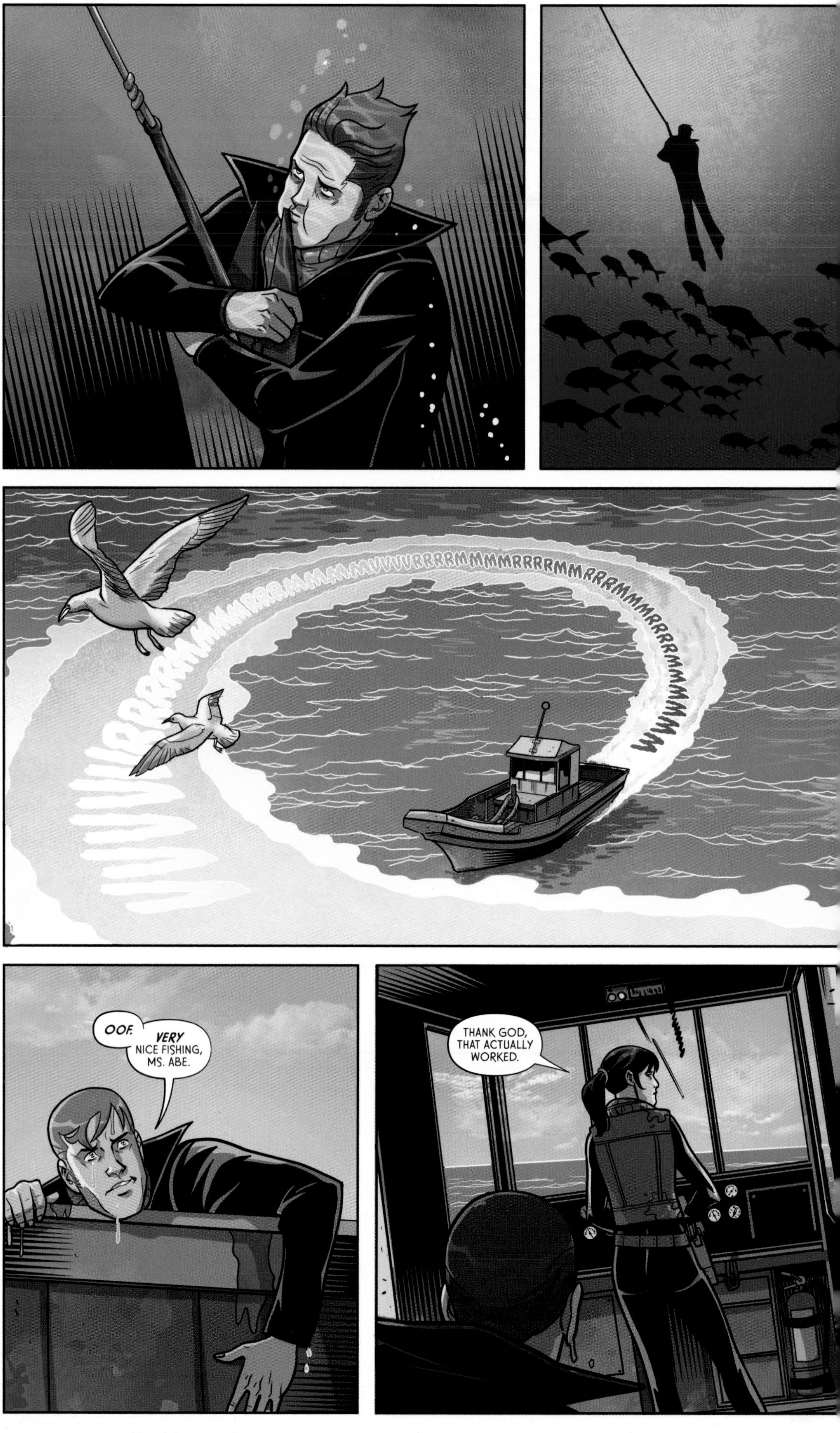
OOF. VERY NICE FISHING, MS. ABE.
THANK GOD, THAT ACTUALLY WORKED.

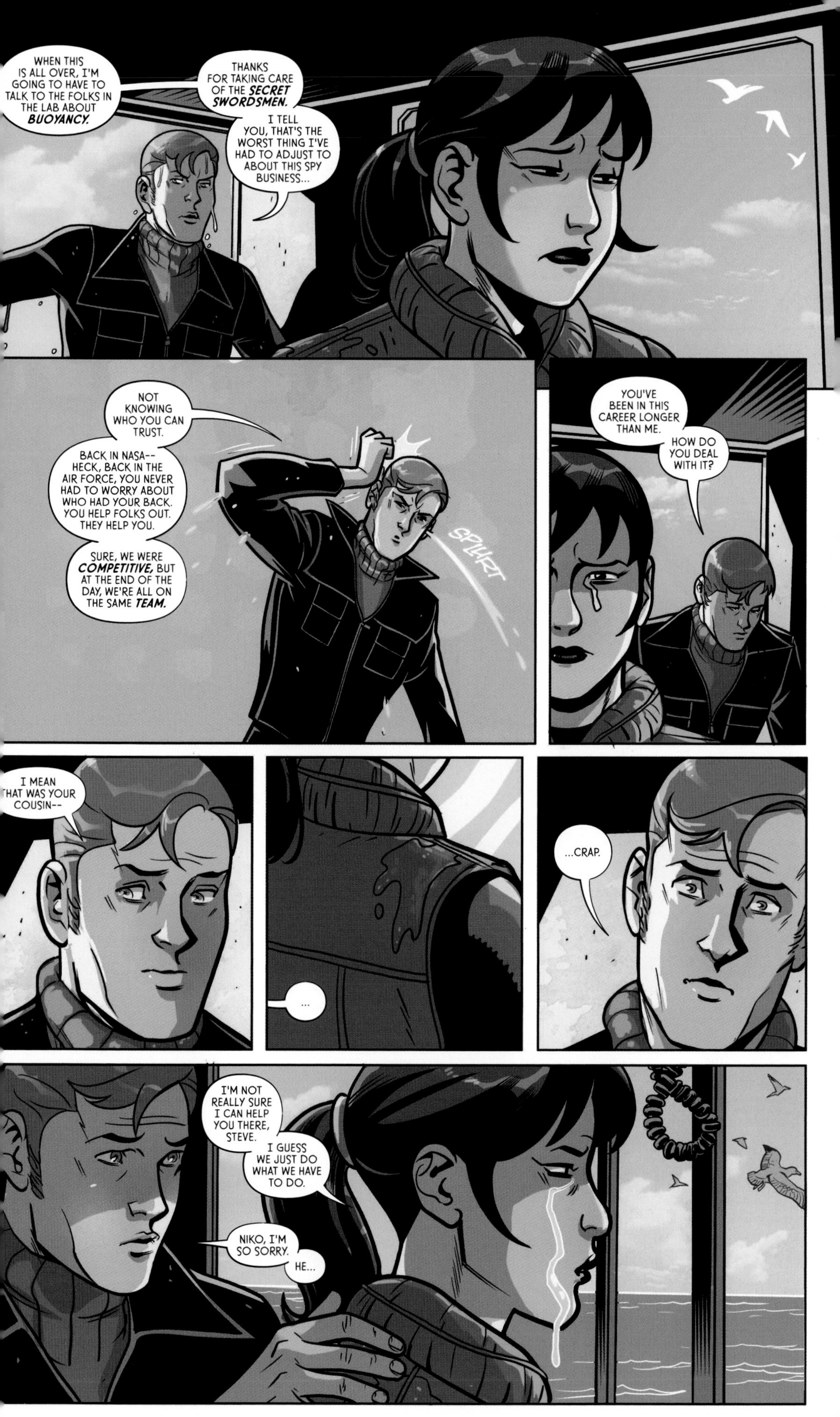
WHEN THIS IS ALL OVER, I'M GOING TO HAVE TO TALK TO THE FOLKS IN THE LAB ABOUT ***BUOYANCY.***
THANKS FOR TAKING CARE OF THE ***SECRET SWORDSMEN.***
I TELL YOU, THAT'S THE WORST THING I'VE HAD TO ADJUST TO ABOUT THIS SPY BUSINESS...
NOT KNOWING WHO YOU CAN TRUST.
BACK IN NASA-- HECK, BACK IN THE AIR FORCE, YOU NEVER HAD TO WORRY ABOUT WHO HAD YOUR BACK. YOU HELP FOLKS OUT. THEY HELP YOU.
SURE, WE WERE ***COMPETITIVE,*** BUT AT THE END OF THE DAY, WE'RE ALL ON THE SAME ***TEAM.***
SPLURT
YOU'VE BEEN IN THIS CAREER LONGER THAN ME.
HOW DO YOU DEAL WITH IT?
I MEAN THAT WAS YOUR COUSIN--
...
...CRAP.
I'M NOT REALLY SURE I CAN HELP YOU THERE, STEVE.
I GUESS WE JUST DO WHAT WE HAVE TO DO.
NIKO, I'M SO SORRY.
HE...

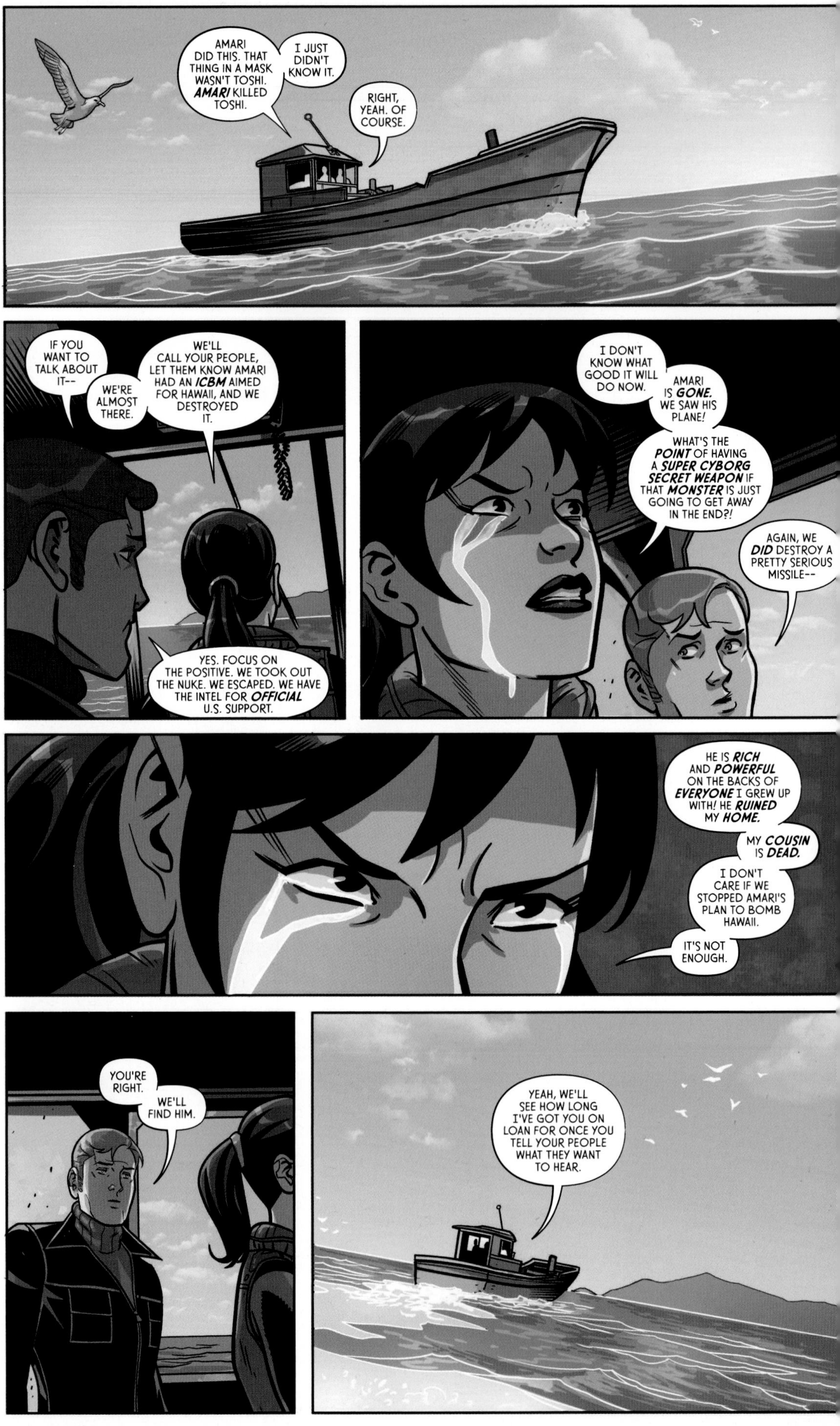
AMARI DID THIS. THAT THING IN A MASK WASN'T TOSHI. AMARI KILLED TOSHI.
I JUST DIDN'T KNOW IT.
RIGHT, YEAH. OF COURSE.
IF YOU WANT TO TALK ABOUT IT--
WE'RE ALMOST THERE.
WE'LL CALL YOUR PEOPLE, LET THEM KNOW AMARI HAD AN ICBM AIMED FOR HAWAII, AND WE DESTROYED IT.
YES. FOCUS ON THE POSITIVE. WE TOOK OUT THE NUKE. WE ESCAPED. WE HAVE THE INTEL FOR OFFICIAL U.S. SUPPORT.
I DON'T KNOW WHAT GOOD IT WILL DO NOW.
AMARI IS GONE. WE SAW HIS PLANE!
WHAT'S THE POINT OF HAVING A SUPER CYBORG SECRET WEAPON IF THAT MONSTER IS JUST GOING TO GET AWAY IN THE END?!
AGAIN, WE DID DESTROY A PRETTY SERIOUS MISSILE--
HE IS RICH AND POWERFUL ON THE BACKS OF EVERYONE I GREW UP WITH! HE RUINED MY HOME.
MY COUSIN IS DEAD.
I DON'T CARE IF WE STOPPED AMARI'S PLAN TO BOMB HAWAII.
IT'S NOT ENOUGH.
YOU'RE RIGHT.
WE'LL FIND HIM.
YEAH, WE'LL SEE HOW LONG I'VE GOT YOU ON LOAN FOR ONCE YOU TELL YOUR PEOPLE WHAT THEY WANT TO HEAR.

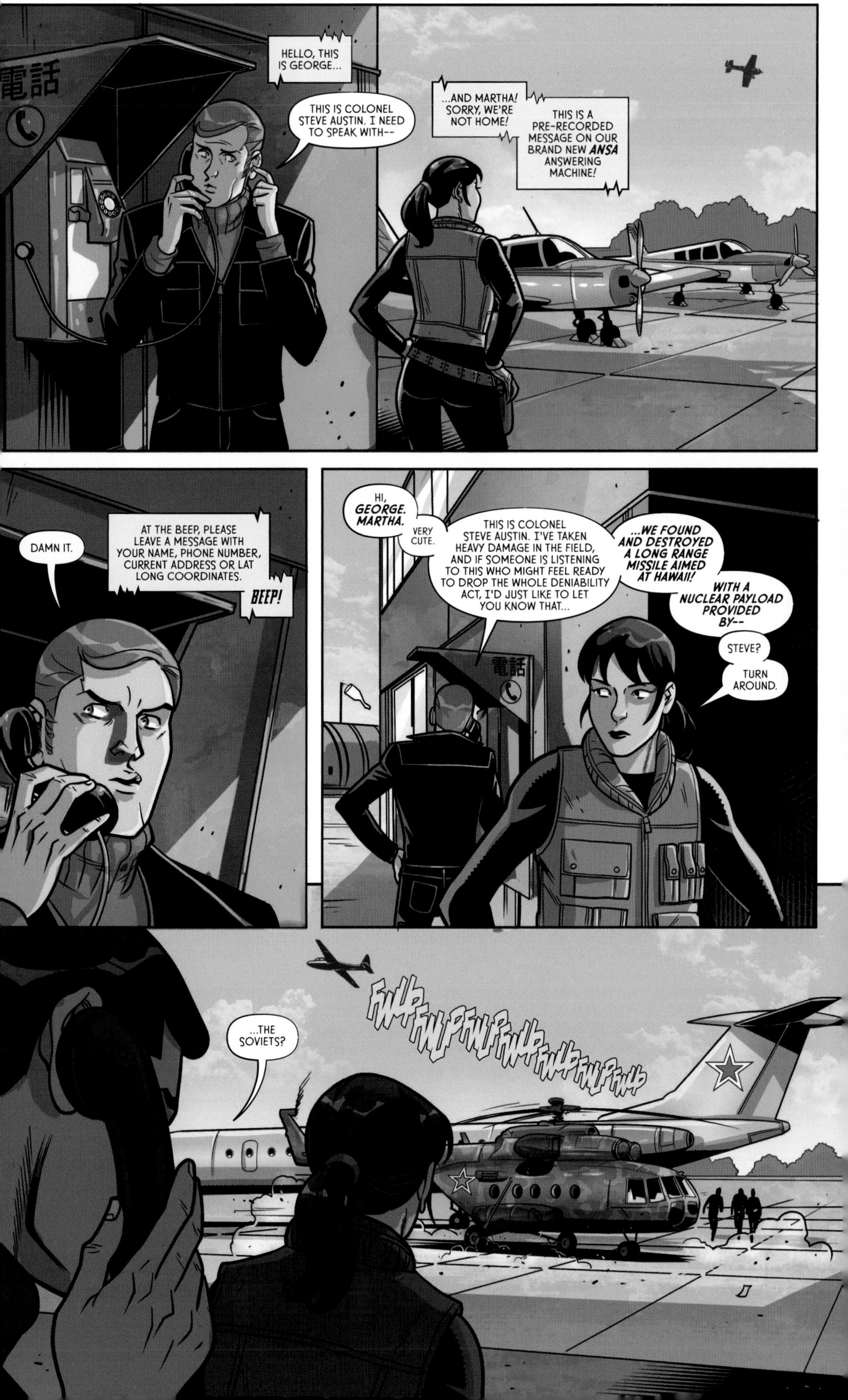

電話
HELLO, THIS IS GEORGE...
THIS IS COLONEL STEVE AUSTIN. I NEED TO SPEAK WITH--
...AND MARTHA! SORRY, WE'RE NOT HOME!
THIS IS A PRE-RECORDED MESSAGE ON OUR BRAND NEW ANSA ANSWERING MACHINE!
DAMN IT.
AT THE BEEP, PLEASE LEAVE A MESSAGE WITH YOUR NAME, PHONE NUMBER, CURRENT ADDRESS OR LAT LONG COORDINATES.
BEEP!
HI, GEORGE. MARTHA.
VERY CUTE.
THIS IS COLONEL STEVE AUSTIN. I'VE TAKEN HEAVY DAMAGE IN THE FIELD, AND IF SOMEONE IS LISTENING TO THIS WHO MIGHT FEEL READY TO DROP THE WHOLE DENIABILITY ACT, I'D JUST LIKE TO LET YOU KNOW THAT...
...WE FOUND AND DESTROYED A LONG RANGE MISSILE AIMED AT HAWAII!
WITH A NUCLEAR PAYLOAD PROVIDED BY--
電話
STEVE?
TURN AROUND.
...THE SOVIETS?

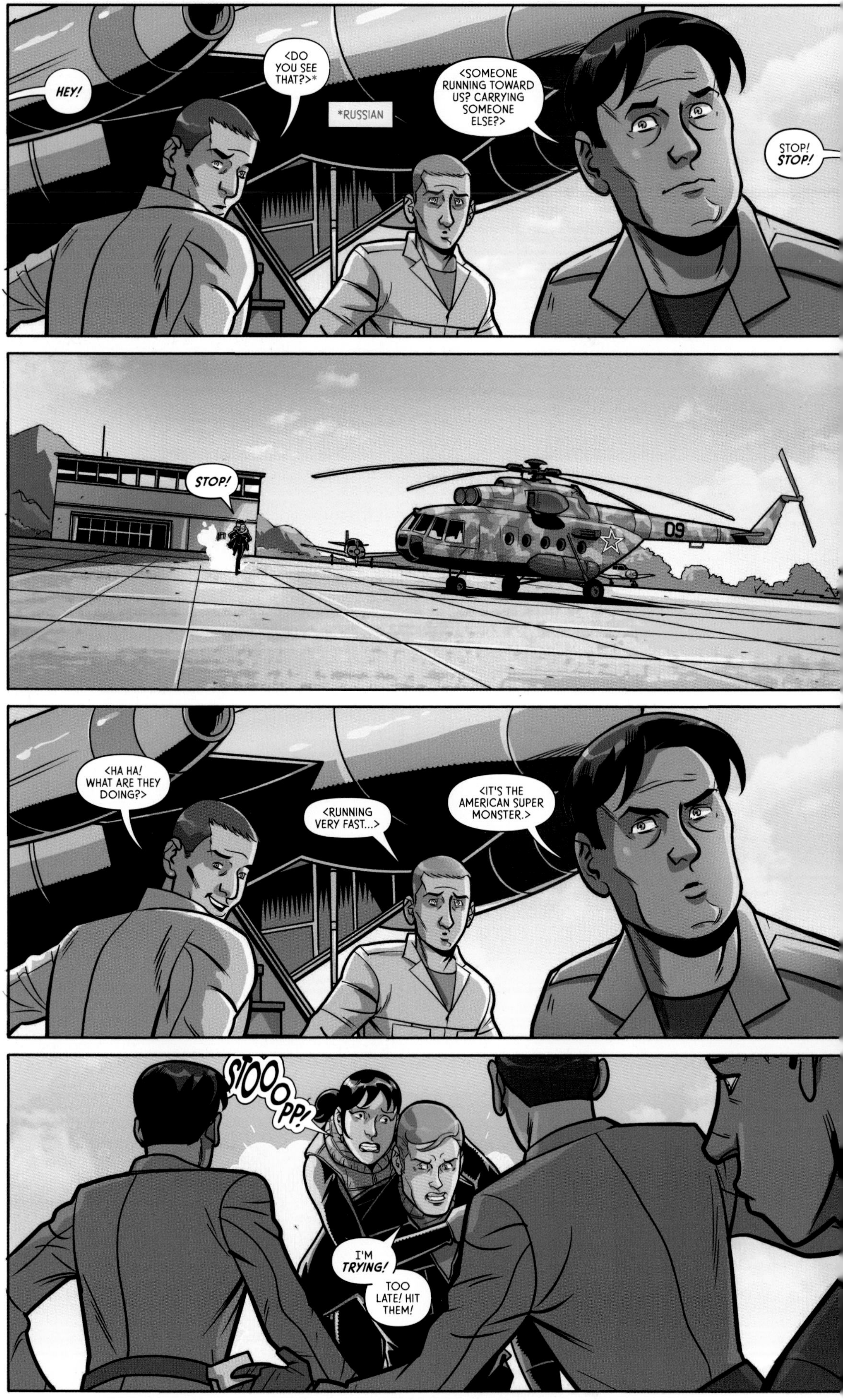
HEY!
<DO YOU SEE THAT?>*
*RUSSIAN
<SOMEONE RUNNING TOWARD US? CARRYING SOMEONE ELSE?>
STOP! STOP!
STOP!
<HA HA! WHAT ARE THEY DOING?>
<RUNNING VERY FAST...>
<IT'S THE AMERICAN SUPER MONSTER.>
STOOOPP!
I'M TRYING!
TOO LATE! HIT THEM!

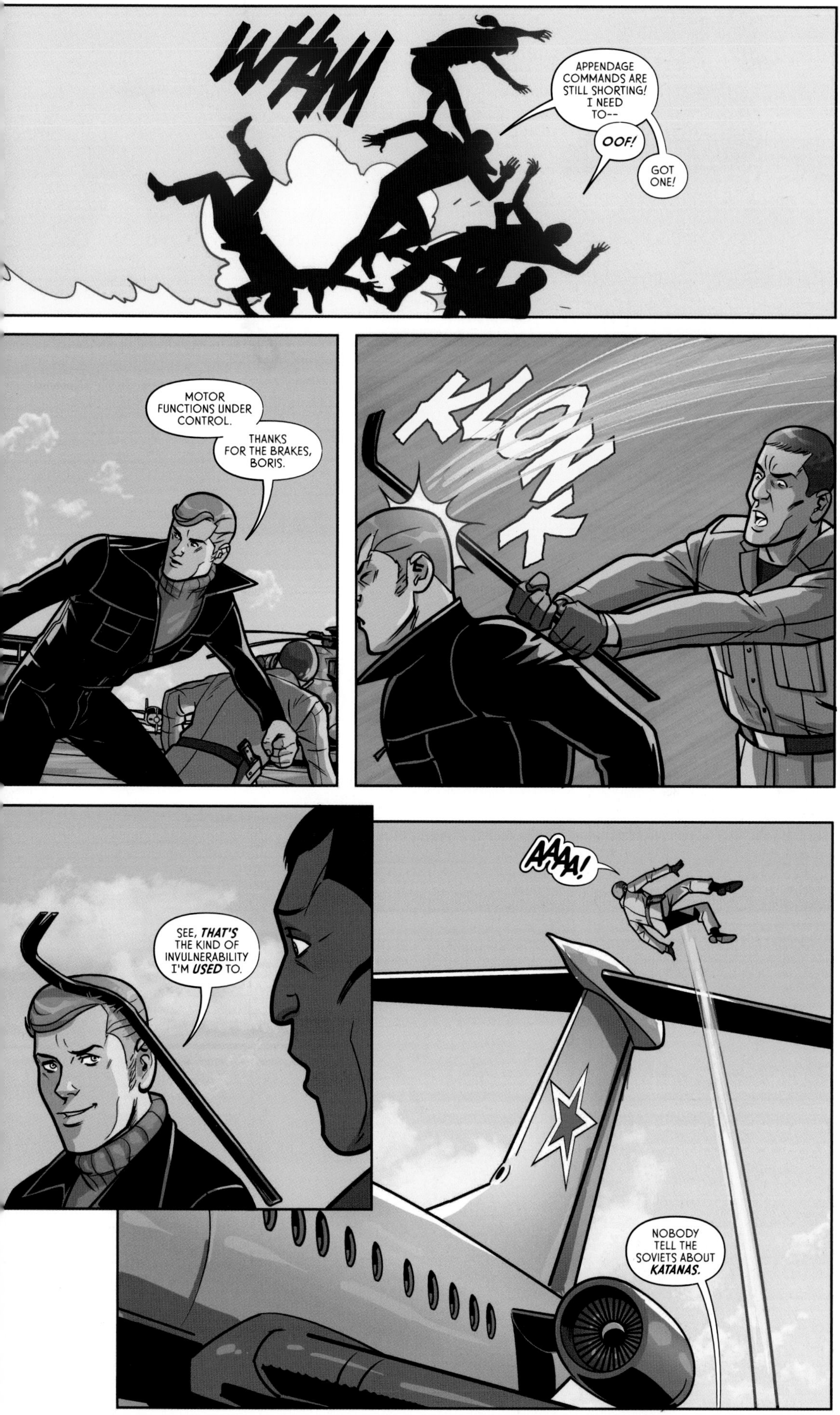
WHAM
APPENDAGE COMMANDS ARE STILL SHORTING! I NEED TO--
OOF!
GOT ONE!
MOTOR FUNCTIONS UNDER CONTROL.
THANKS FOR THE BRAKES, BORIS.
KLONK
SEE, THAT'S THE KIND OF INVULNERABILITY I'M USED TO.
AAAA!
NOBODY TELL THE SOVIETS ABOUT KATANAS.

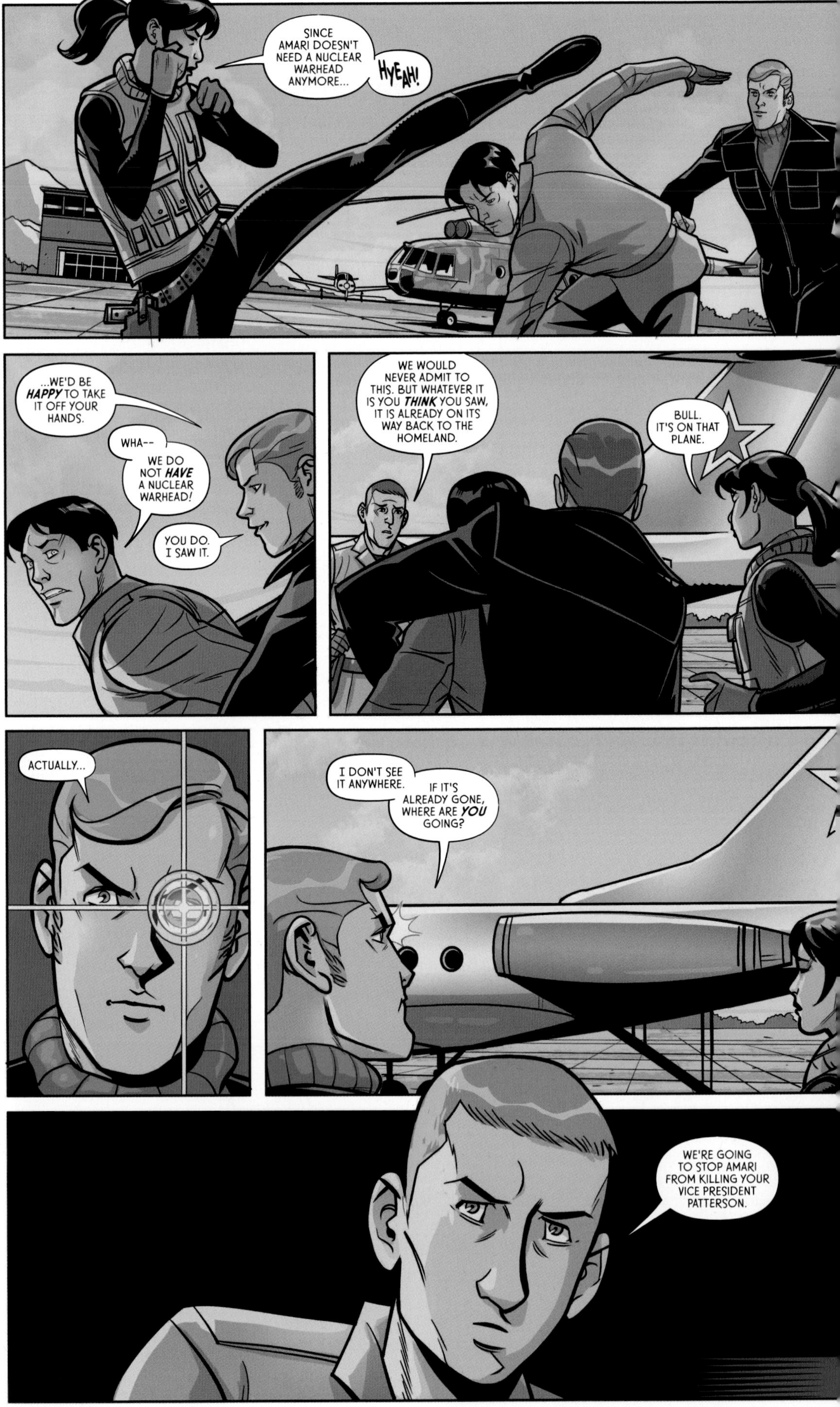

SINCE AMARI DOESN'T NEED A NUCLEAR WARHEAD ANYMORE...
HYEAH!
...WE'D BE HAPPY TO TAKE IT OFF YOUR HANDS.
WHA--
WE DO NOT HAVE A NUCLEAR WARHEAD!
YOU DO. I SAW IT.
WE WOULD NEVER ADMIT TO THIS. BUT WHATEVER IT IS YOU THINK YOU SAW, IT IS ALREADY ON ITS WAY BACK TO THE HOMELAND.
BULL. IT'S ON THAT PLANE.
ACTUALLY...
I DON'T SEE IT ANYWHERE.
IF IT'S ALREADY GONE, WHERE ARE YOU GOING?
WE'RE GOING TO STOP AMARI FROM KILLING YOUR VICE PRESIDENT PATTERSON.

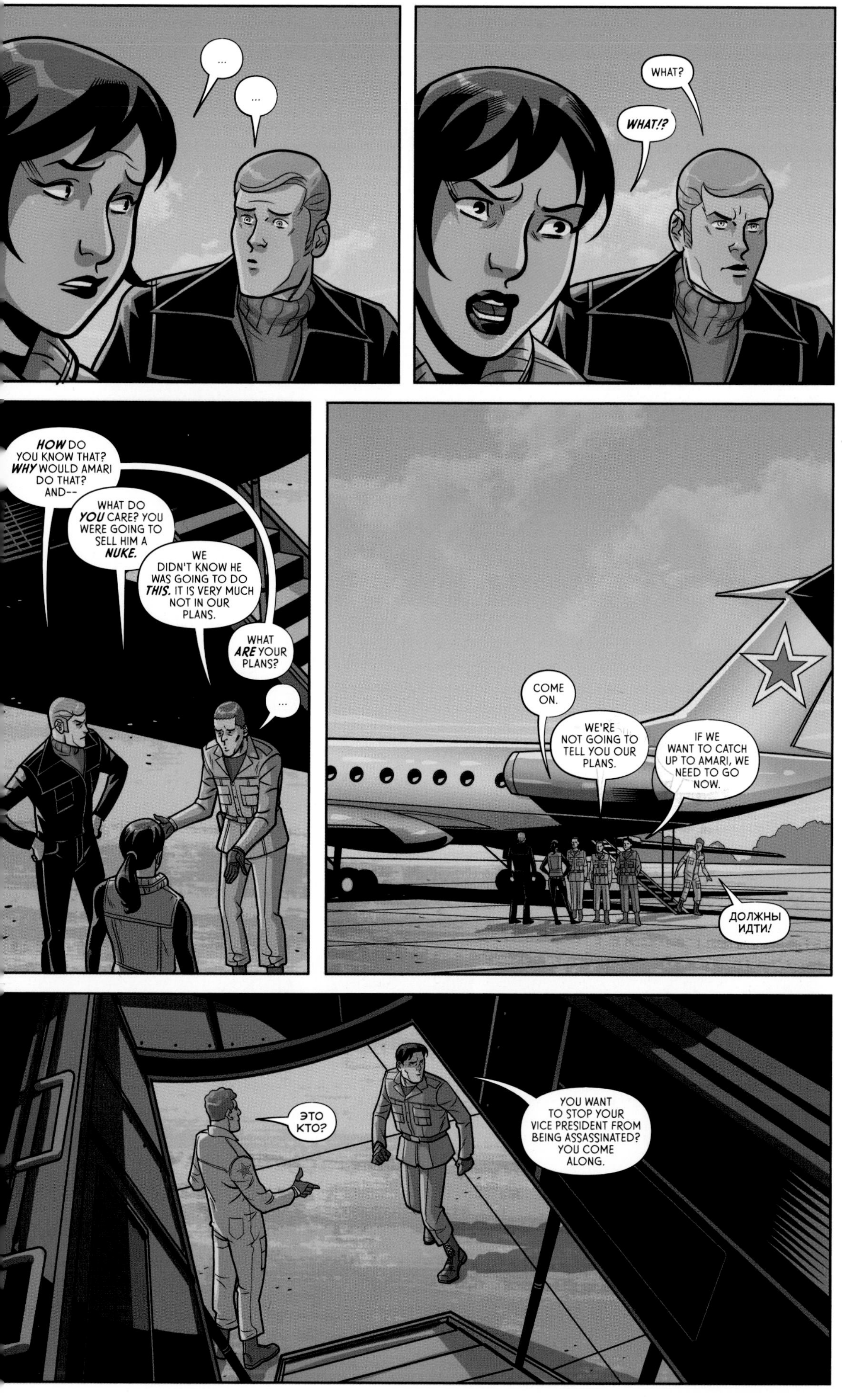
...
...
WHAT?
WHAT!?
HOW DO YOU KNOW THAT? WHY WOULD AMARI DO THAT? AND--
WHAT DO YOU CARE? YOU WERE GOING TO SELL HIM A NUKE.
WE DIDN'T KNOW HE WAS GOING TO DO THIS. IT IS VERY MUCH NOT IN OUR PLANS.
WHAT ARE YOUR PLANS?
...
COME ON.
WE'RE NOT GOING TO TELL YOU OUR PLANS.
IF WE WANT TO CATCH UP TO AMARI, WE NEED TO GO NOW.
ДОЛЖНЫ ИДТИ!
ЭТО КТО?
YOU WANT TO STOP YOUR VICE PRESIDENT FROM BEING ASSASSINATED? YOU COME ALONG.

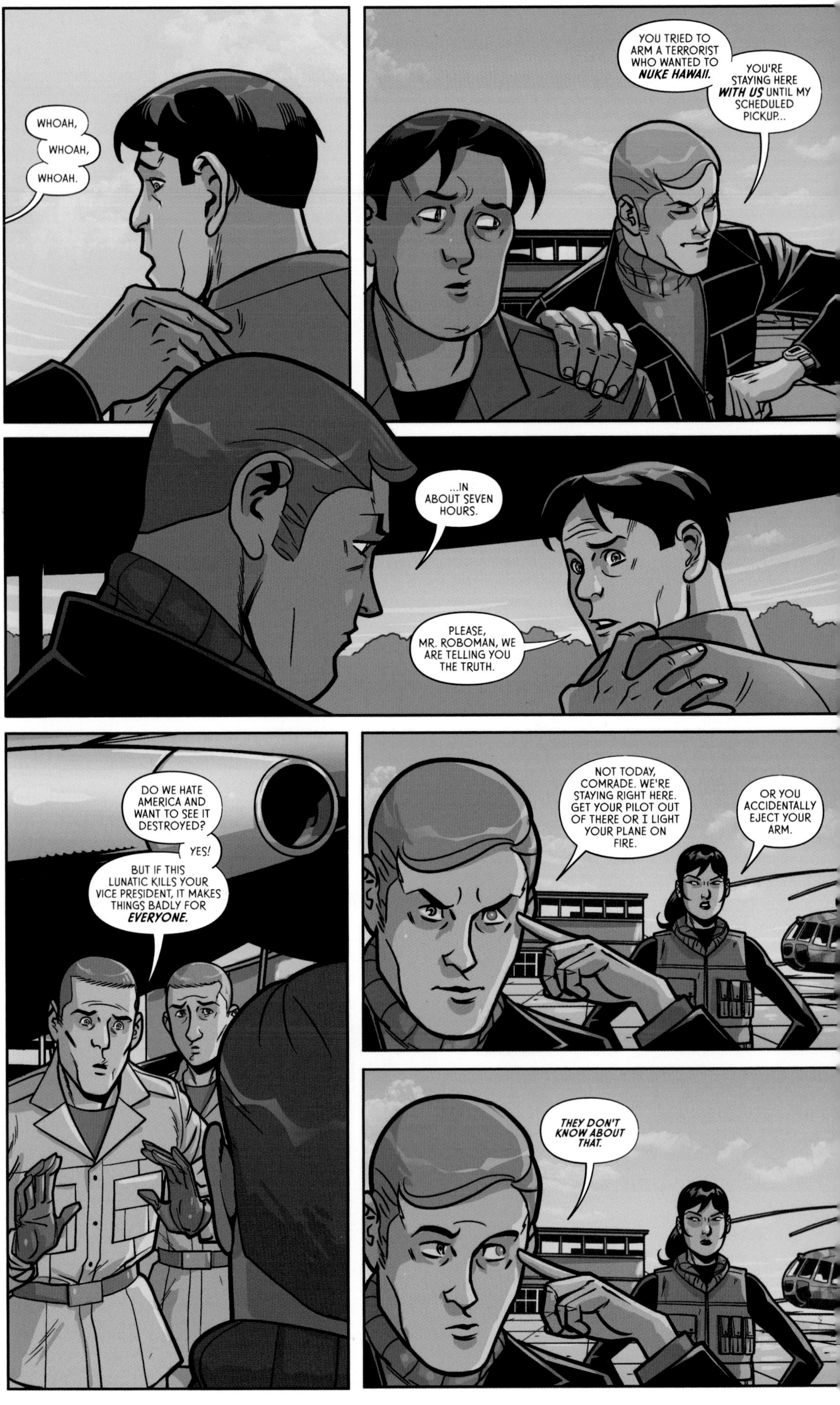
WHOAH,
WHOAH,
WHOAH.
YOU TRIED TO ARM A TERRORIST WHO WANTED TO NUKE HAWAII.
YOU'RE STAYING HERE WITH US UNTIL MY SCHEDULED PICKUP...
...IN ABOUT SEVEN HOURS.
PLEASE, MR. ROBOMAN, WE ARE TELLING YOU THE TRUTH.
DO WE HATE AMERICA AND WANT TO SEE IT DESTROYED?
YES!
BUT IF THIS LUNATIC KILLS YOUR VICE PRESIDENT, IT MAKES THINGS BADLY FOR EVERYONE.
NOT TODAY, COMRADE. WE'RE STAYING RIGHT HERE. GET YOUR PILOT OUT OF THERE OR I LIGHT YOUR PLANE ON FIRE.
OR YOU ACCIDENTALLY EJECT YOUR ARM.
THEY DON'T KNOW ABOUT THAT.

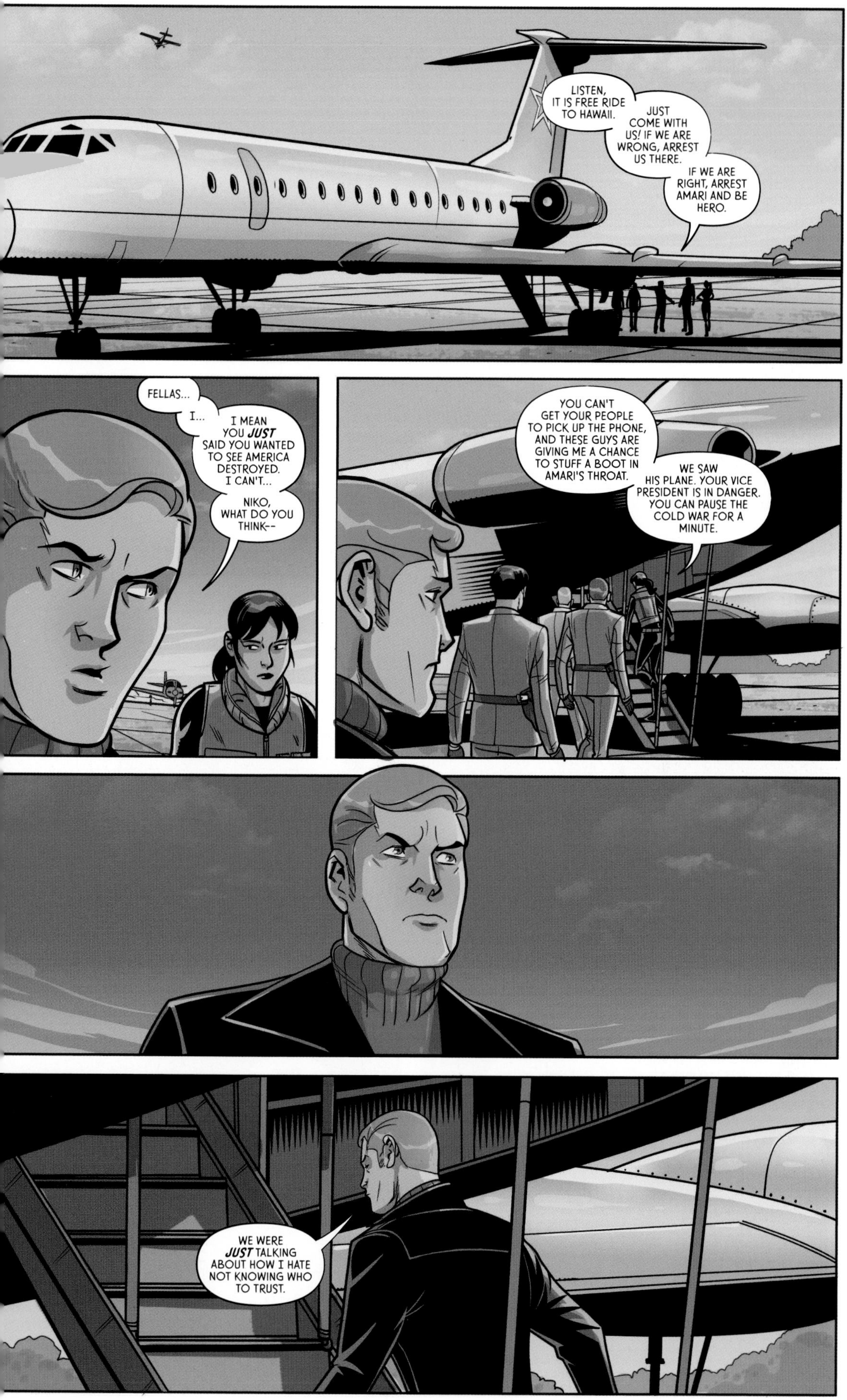
LISTEN, IT IS FREE RIDE TO HAWAII.
JUST COME WITH US! IF WE ARE WRONG, ARREST US THERE.
IF WE ARE RIGHT, ARREST AMARI AND BE HERO.
FELLAS...
I...
I MEAN YOU JUST SAID YOU WANTED TO SEE AMERICA DESTROYED. I CAN'T...
NIKO, WHAT DO YOU THINK--
YOU CAN'T GET YOUR PEOPLE TO PICK UP THE PHONE, AND THESE GUYS ARE GIVING ME A CHANCE TO STUFF A BOOT IN AMARI'S THROAT.
WE SAW HIS PLANE. YOUR VICE PRESIDENT IS IN DANGER. YOU CAN PAUSE THE COLD WAR FOR A MINUTE.
WE WERE JUST TALKING ABOUT HOW I HATE NOT KNOWING WHO TO TRUST.

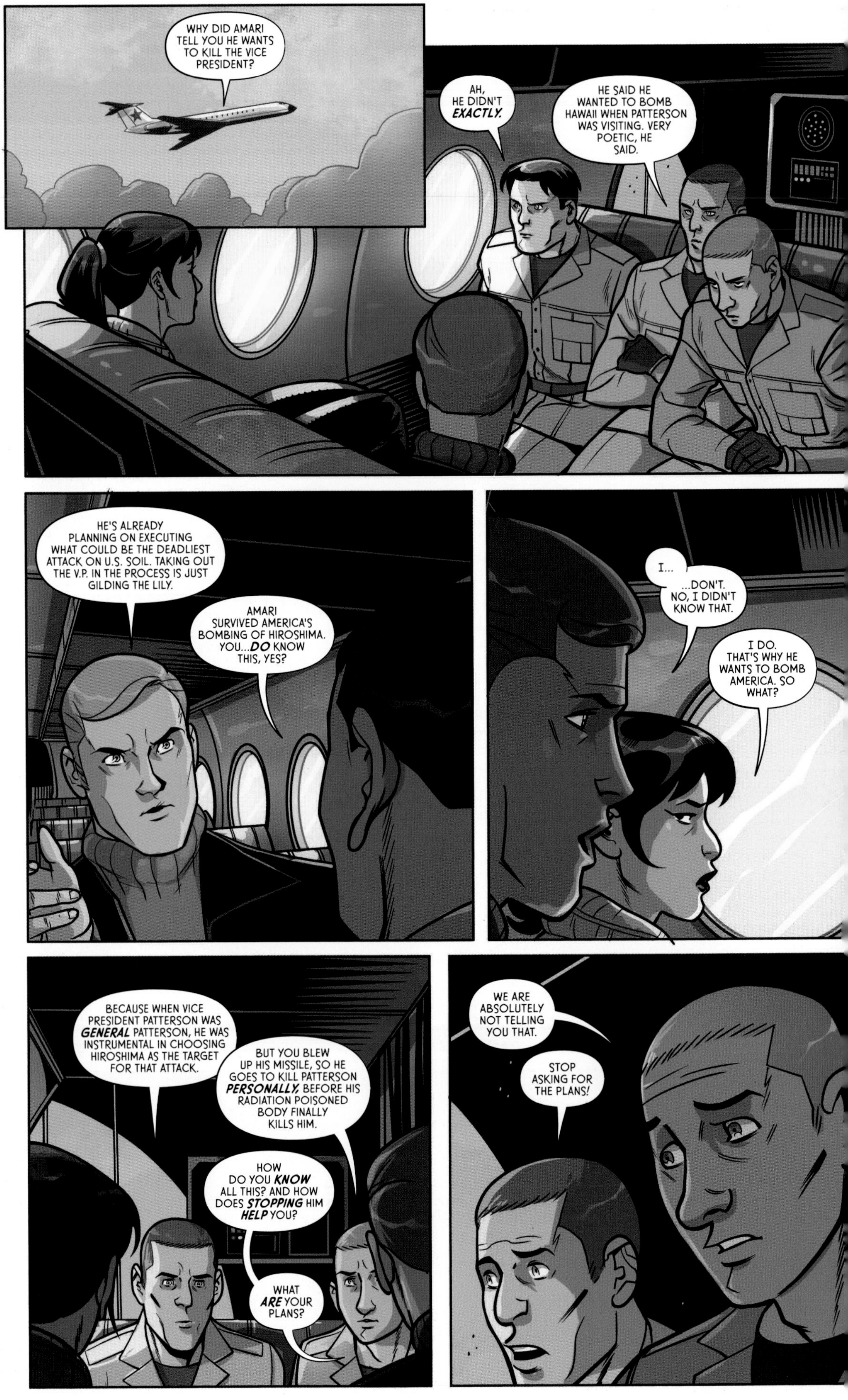
WHY DID AMARI TELL YOU HE WANTS TO KILL THE VICE PRESIDENT?
AH, HE DIDN'T EXACTLY.
HE SAID HE WANTED TO BOMB HAWAII WHEN PATTERSON WAS VISITING. VERY POETIC, HE SAID.
HE'S ALREADY PLANNING ON EXECUTING WHAT COULD BE THE DEADLIEST ATTACK ON U.S. SOIL. TAKING OUT THE V.P. IN THE PROCESS IS JUST GILDING THE LILY.
AMARI SURVIVED AMERICA'S BOMBING OF HIROSHIMA. YOU...DO KNOW THIS, YES?
I...
...DON'T. NO, I DIDN'T KNOW THAT.
I DO. THAT'S WHY HE WANTS TO BOMB AMERICA. SO WHAT?
BECAUSE WHEN VICE PRESIDENT PATTERSON WAS GENERAL PATTERSON, HE WAS INSTRUMENTAL IN CHOOSING HIROSHIMA AS THE TARGET FOR THAT ATTACK.
BUT YOU BLEW UP HIS MISSILE, SO HE GOES TO KILL PATTERSON PERSONALLY, BEFORE HIS RADIATION POISONED BODY FINALLY KILLS HIM.
HOW DO YOU KNOW ALL THIS? AND HOW DOES STOPPING HIM HELP YOU?
WHAT ARE YOUR PLANS?
WE ARE ABSOLUTELY NOT TELLING YOU THAT.
STOP ASKING FOR THE PLANS!

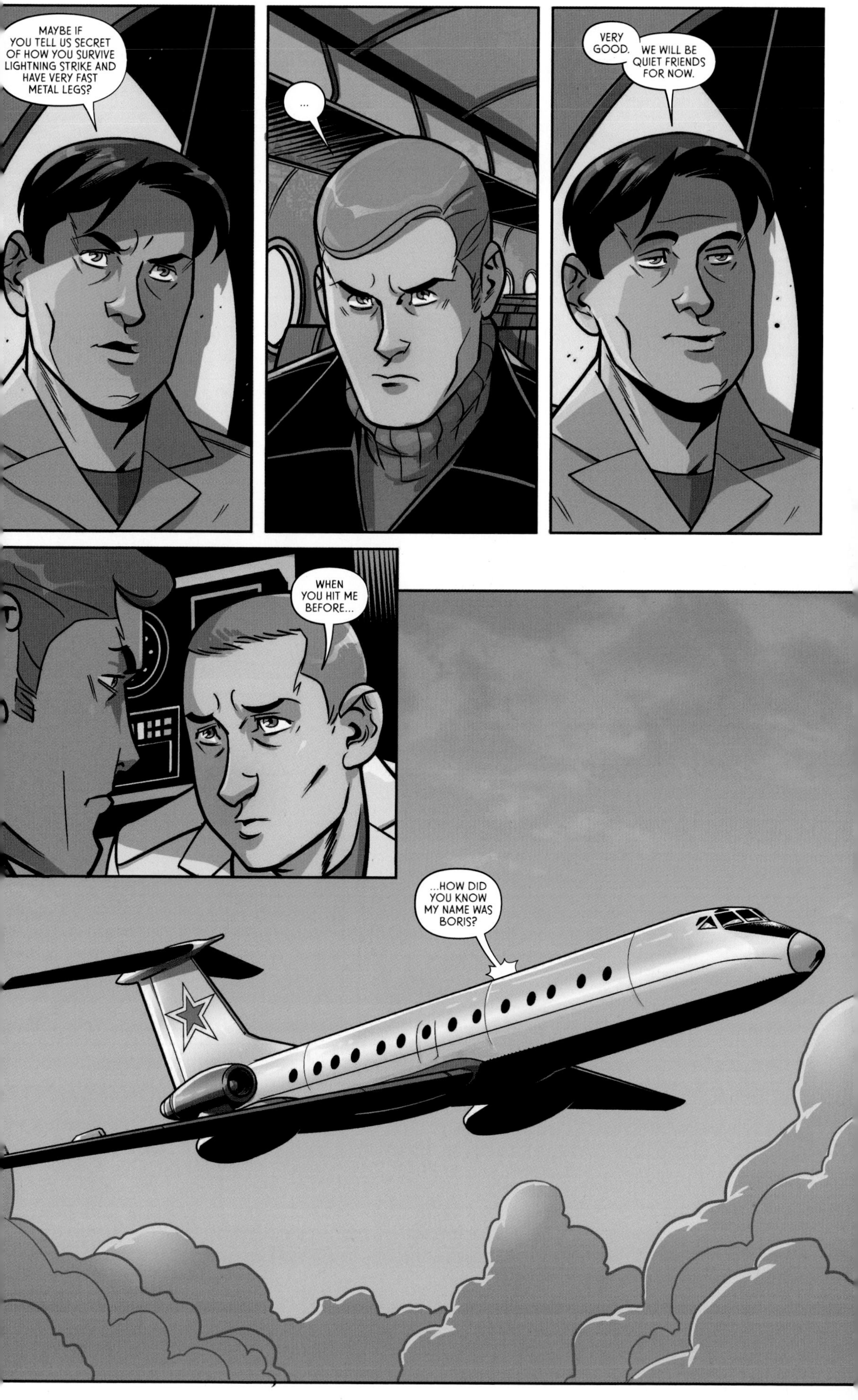
MAYBE IF YOU TELL US SECRET OF HOW YOU SURVIVE LIGHTNING STRIKE AND HAVE VERY FAST METAL LEGS?
...
VERY GOOD.
WE WILL BE QUIET FRIENDS FOR NOW.
WHEN YOU HIT ME BEFORE...
...HOW DID YOU KNOW MY NAME WAS BORIS?

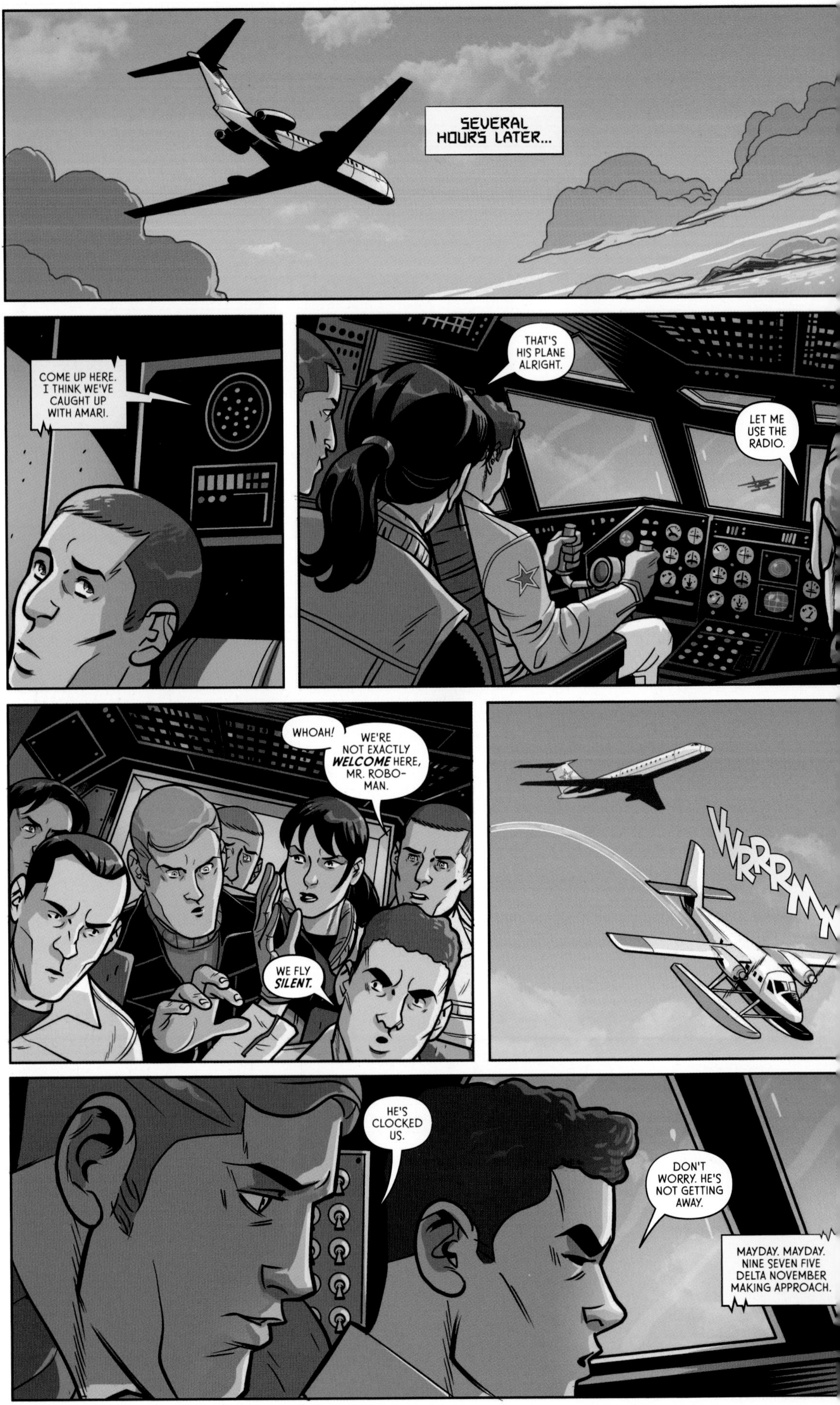
SEVERAL HOURS LATER...
COME UP HERE. I THINK WE'VE CAUGHT UP WITH AMARI.
THAT'S HIS PLANE ALRIGHT.
LET ME USE THE RADIO.
WHOAH!
WE'RE NOT EXACTLY WELCOME HERE, MR. ROBO-MAN.
WE FLY SILENT.
VVRRRMMM
HE'S CLOCKED US.
DON'T WORRY. HE'S NOT GETTING AWAY.
MAYDAY. MAYDAY. NINE SEVEN FIVE DELTA NOVEMBER MAKING APPROACH.

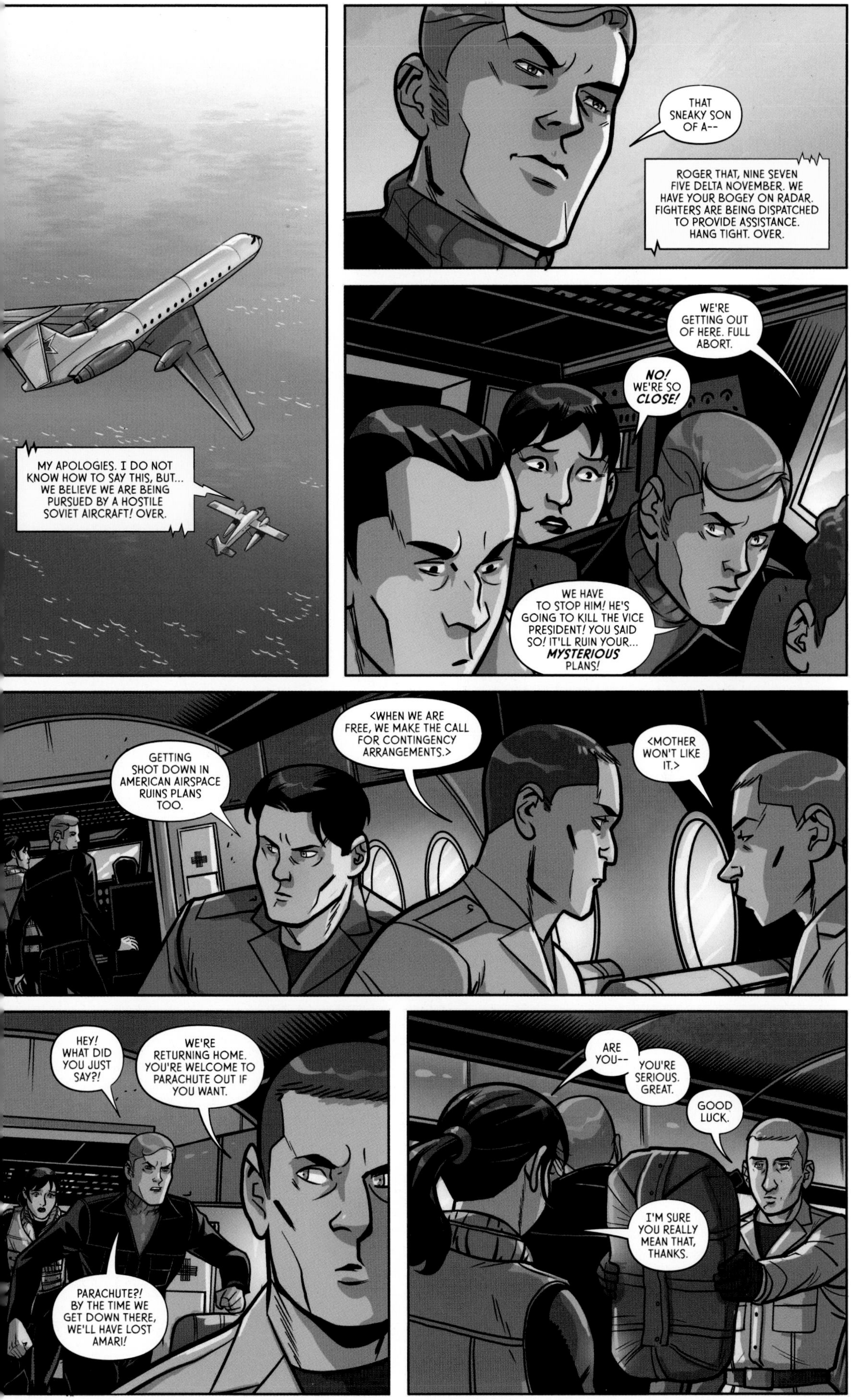
MY APOLOGIES. I DO NOT KNOW HOW TO SAY THIS, BUT... WE BELIEVE WE ARE BEING PURSUED BY A HOSTILE SOVIET AIRCRAFT! OVER.
THAT SNEAKY SON OF A--
ROGER THAT, NINE SEVEN FIVE DELTA NOVEMBER. WE HAVE YOUR BOGEY ON RADAR. FIGHTERS ARE BEING DISPATCHED TO PROVIDE ASSISTANCE. HANG TIGHT. OVER.
WE'RE GETTING OUT OF HERE. FULL ABORT.
NO! WE'RE SO CLOSE!
WE HAVE TO STOP HIM! HE'S GOING TO KILL THE VICE PRESIDENT! YOU SAID SO! IT'LL RUIN YOUR... MYSTERIOUS PLANS!
GETTING SHOT DOWN IN AMERICAN AIRSPACE RUINS PLANS TOO.
<WHEN WE ARE FREE, WE MAKE THE CALL FOR CONTINGENCY ARRANGEMENTS.>
<MOTHER WON'T LIKE IT.>
HEY! WHAT DID YOU JUST SAY?!
WE'RE RETURNING HOME. YOU'RE WELCOME TO PARACHUTE OUT IF YOU WANT.
PARACHUTE?! BY THE TIME WE GET DOWN THERE, WE'LL HAVE LOST AMARI!
ARE YOU--
YOU'RE SERIOUS. GREAT.
GOOD LUCK.
I'M SURE YOU REALLY MEAN THAT, THANKS.

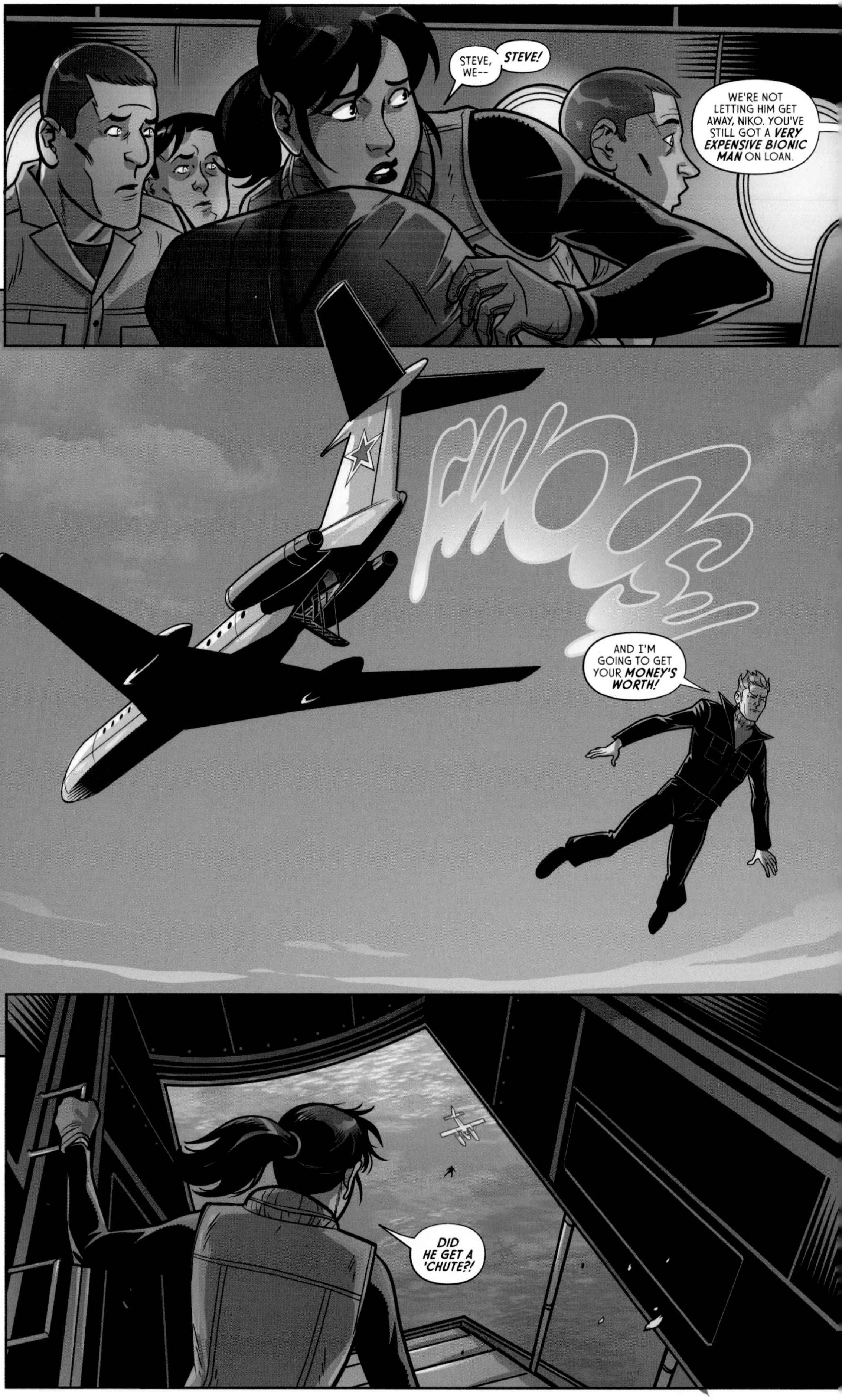
STEVE, WE--
STEVE!
WE'RE NOT LETTING HIM GET AWAY, NIKO. YOU'VE STILL GOT A VERY EXPENSIVE BIONIC MAN ON LOAN.
FWOOSH!
AND I'M GOING TO GET YOUR MONEY'S WORTH!
DID HE GET A 'CHUTE?!

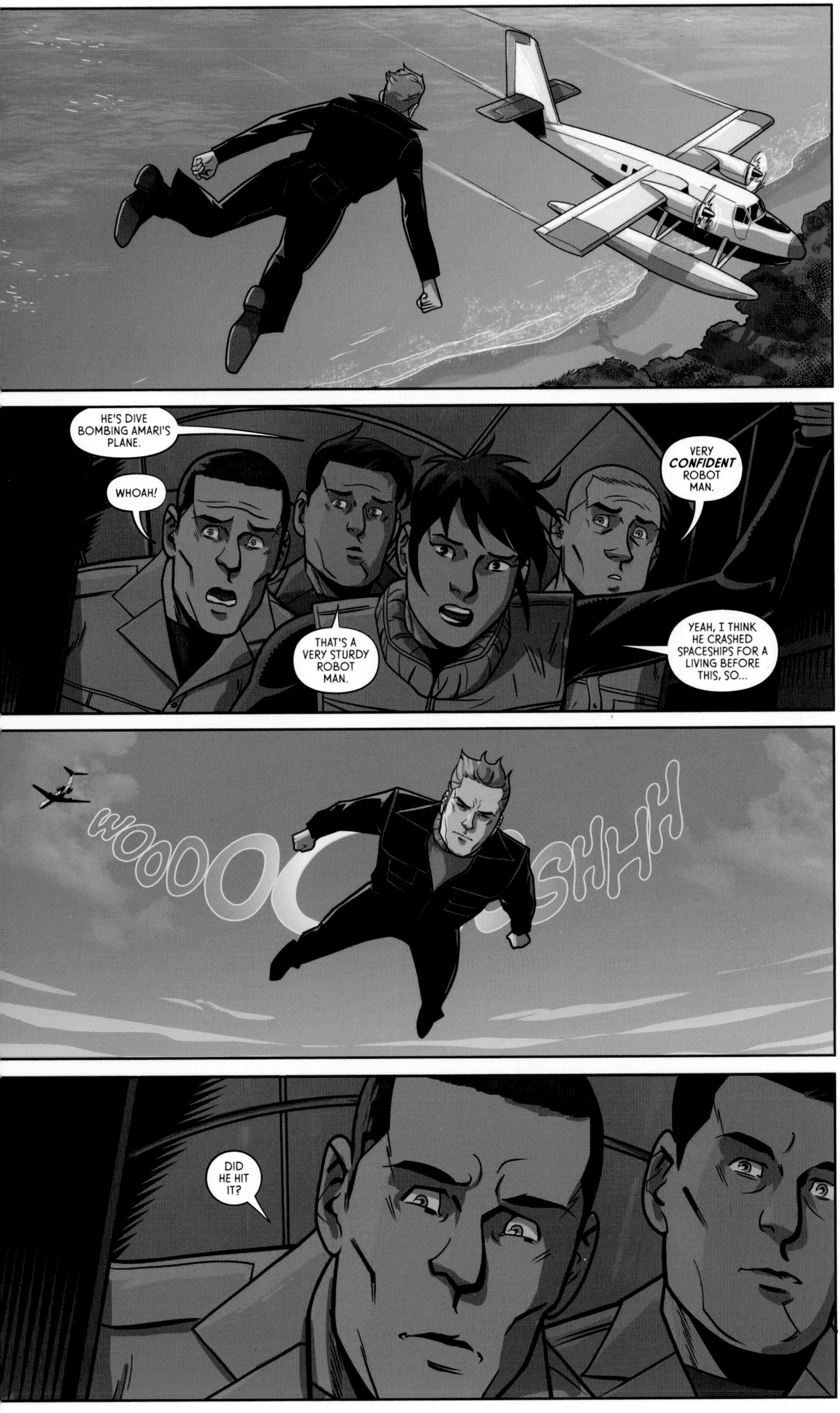
HE'S DIVE BOMBING AMARI'S PLANE.
WHOAH!
VERY CONFIDENT ROBOT MAN.
THAT'S A VERY STURDY ROBOT MAN.
YEAH, I THINK HE CRASHED SPACESHIPS FOR A LIVING BEFORE THIS, SO...
WOOOOOOSHHH
DID HE HIT IT?

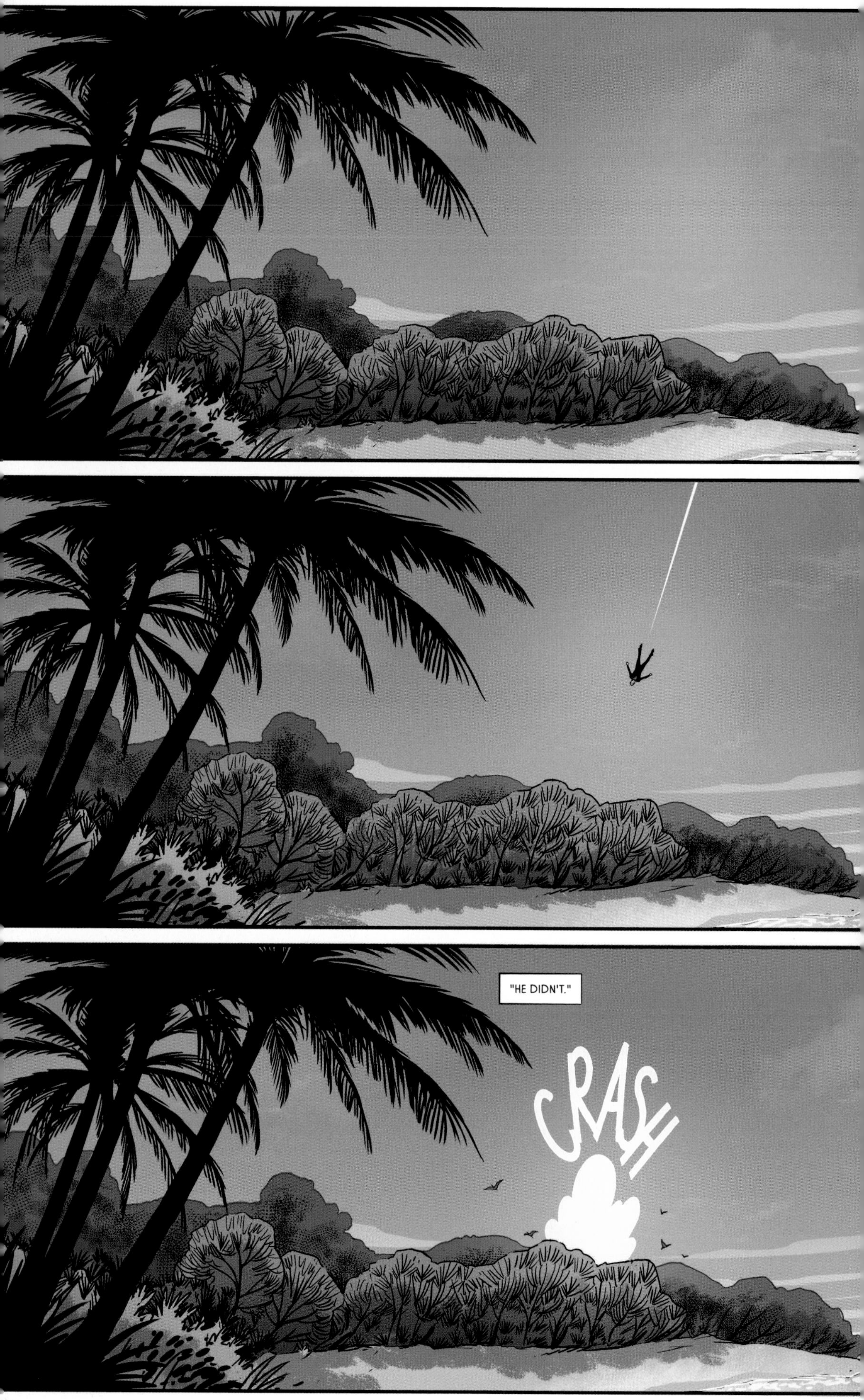
"HE DIDN'T."
CRASH

TEVE AUSTIN. ASTRONAUT. A MAN BARELY ALIVE AFTER A HORRIBLE ACCIDENT. REBUILT AS THE WORLD'S FIRST BIONIC MAN. BETTER THAN HE WAS BEFORE.

BETTER, STRONGER, FASTER.

THE

0,003,238

DOLLAR MAN

[...EXCEPT HE RECENTLY JUMPED OUT OF A PLANE WITHOUT A PARACHUTE, IN ORDER TO SAVE THE VICE-PRESIDENT FROM BEING ASSASSINATED, AND LAMMED INTO THE GROUND. HARD. BUT WE WOULDN'T DEFINE THAT AS "BAD."]

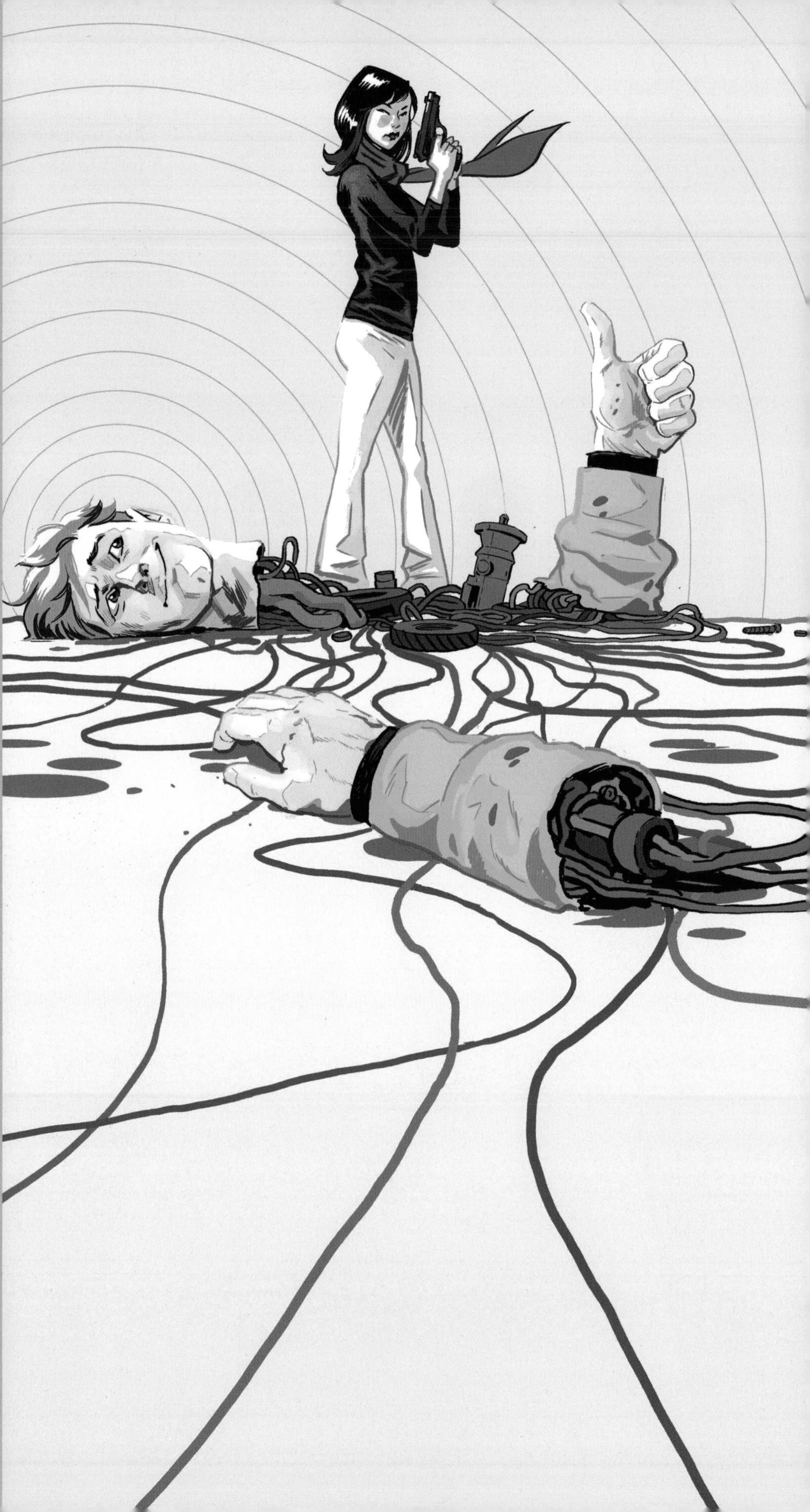

ISSUE 05 COVER ART BY MICHAEL WALSH

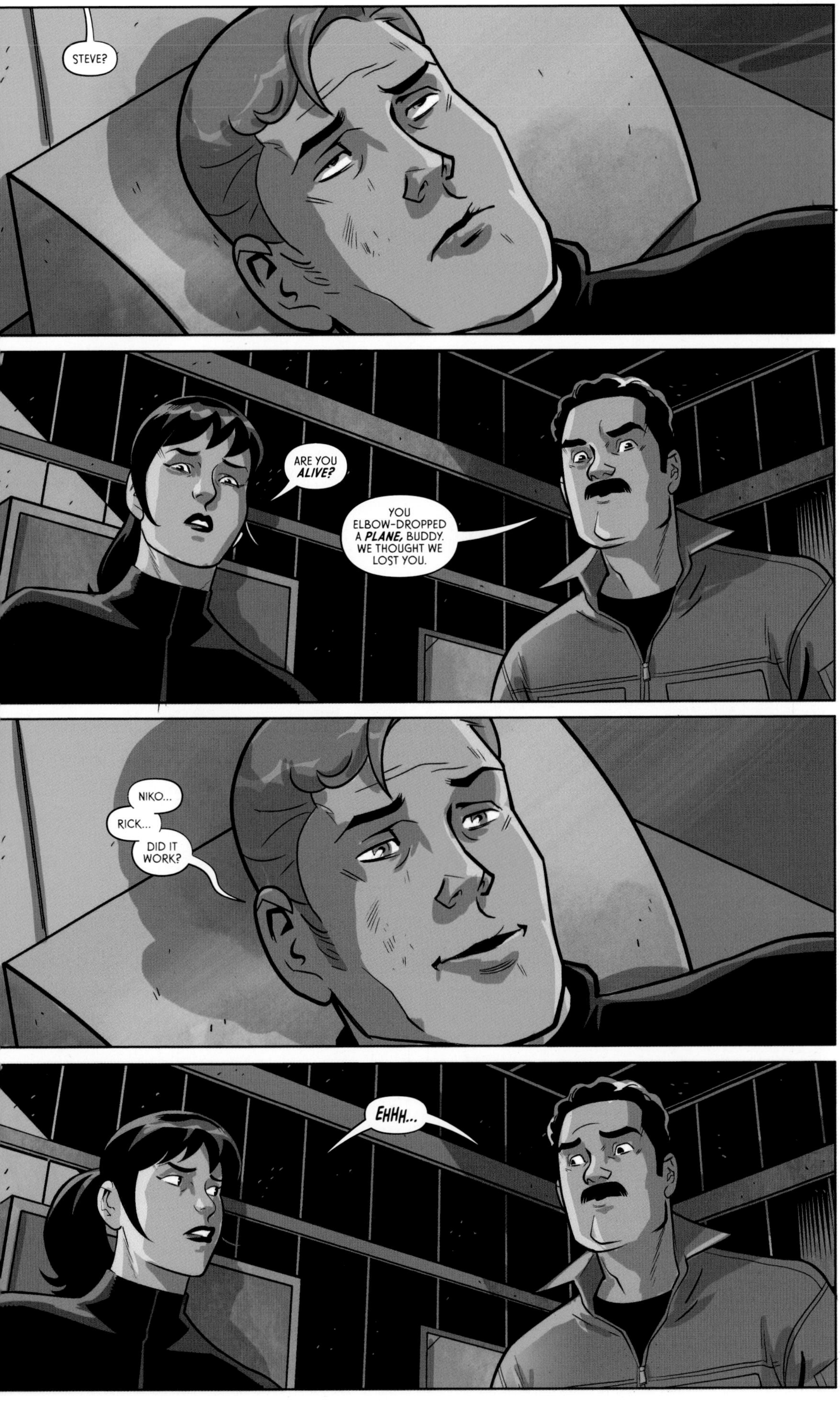
STEVE?
ARE YOU *ALIVE?*
YOU ELBOW-DROPPED A ***PLANE,*** BUDDY. WE THOUGHT WE LOST YOU.
NIKO...
RICK...
DID IT WORK?
EHHH...

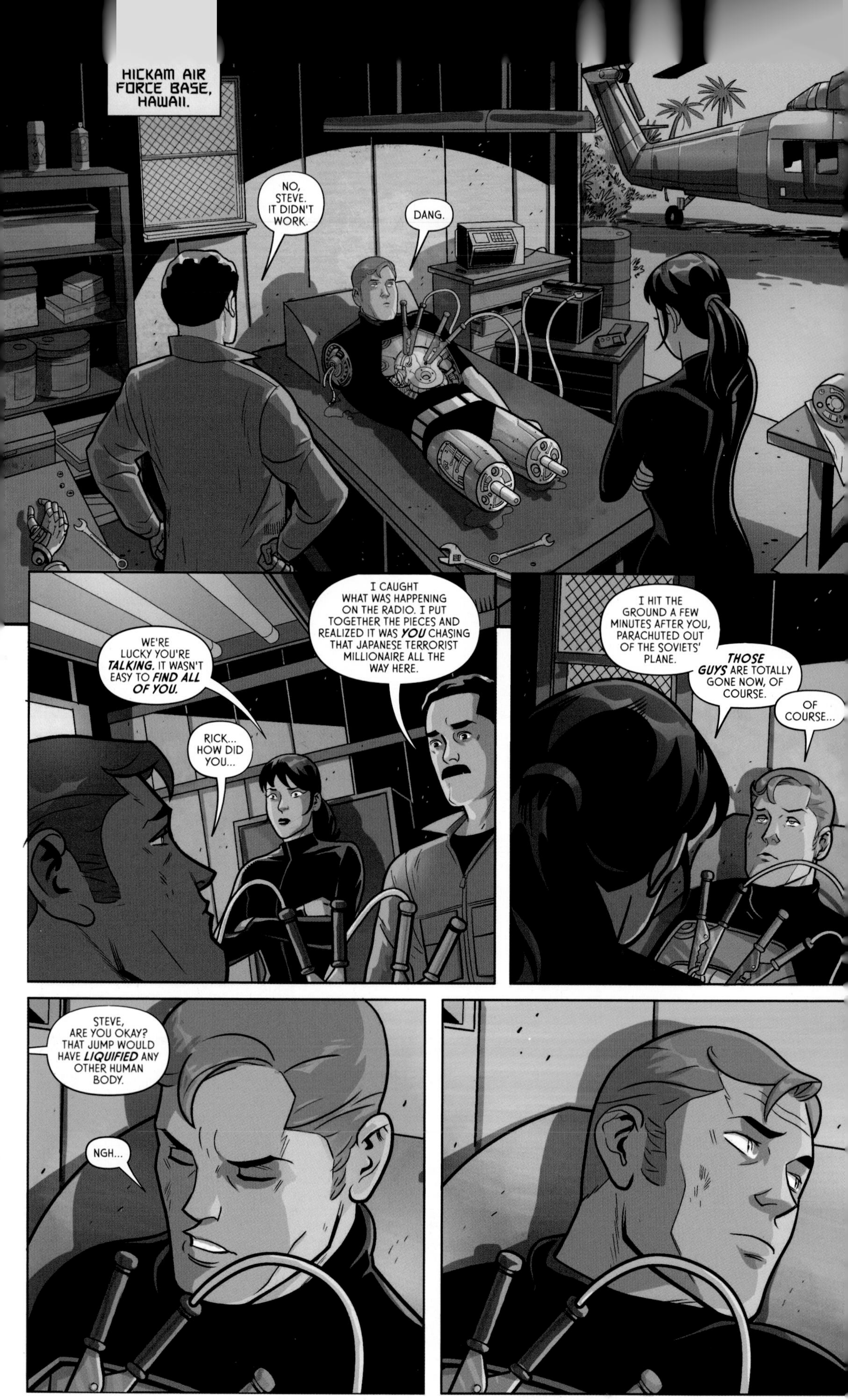
HICKAM AIR FORCE BASE, HAWAII.
NO, STEVE. IT DIDN'T WORK.
DANG.
WE'RE LUCKY YOU'RE **TALKING.** IT WASN'T EASY TO **FIND ALL OF YOU.**
RICK... HOW DID YOU...
I CAUGHT WHAT WAS HAPPENING ON THE RADIO. I PUT TOGETHER THE PIECES AND REALIZED IT WAS **YOU** CHASING THAT JAPANESE TERRORIST MILLIONAIRE ALL THE WAY HERE.
I HIT THE GROUND A FEW MINUTES AFTER YOU, PARACHUTED OUT OF THE SOVIETS' PLANE.
THOSE GUYS ARE TOTALLY GONE NOW, OF COURSE.
OF COURSE...
STEVE, ARE YOU OKAY? THAT JUMP WOULD HAVE **LIQUIFIED** ANY OTHER HUMAN BODY.
NGH...

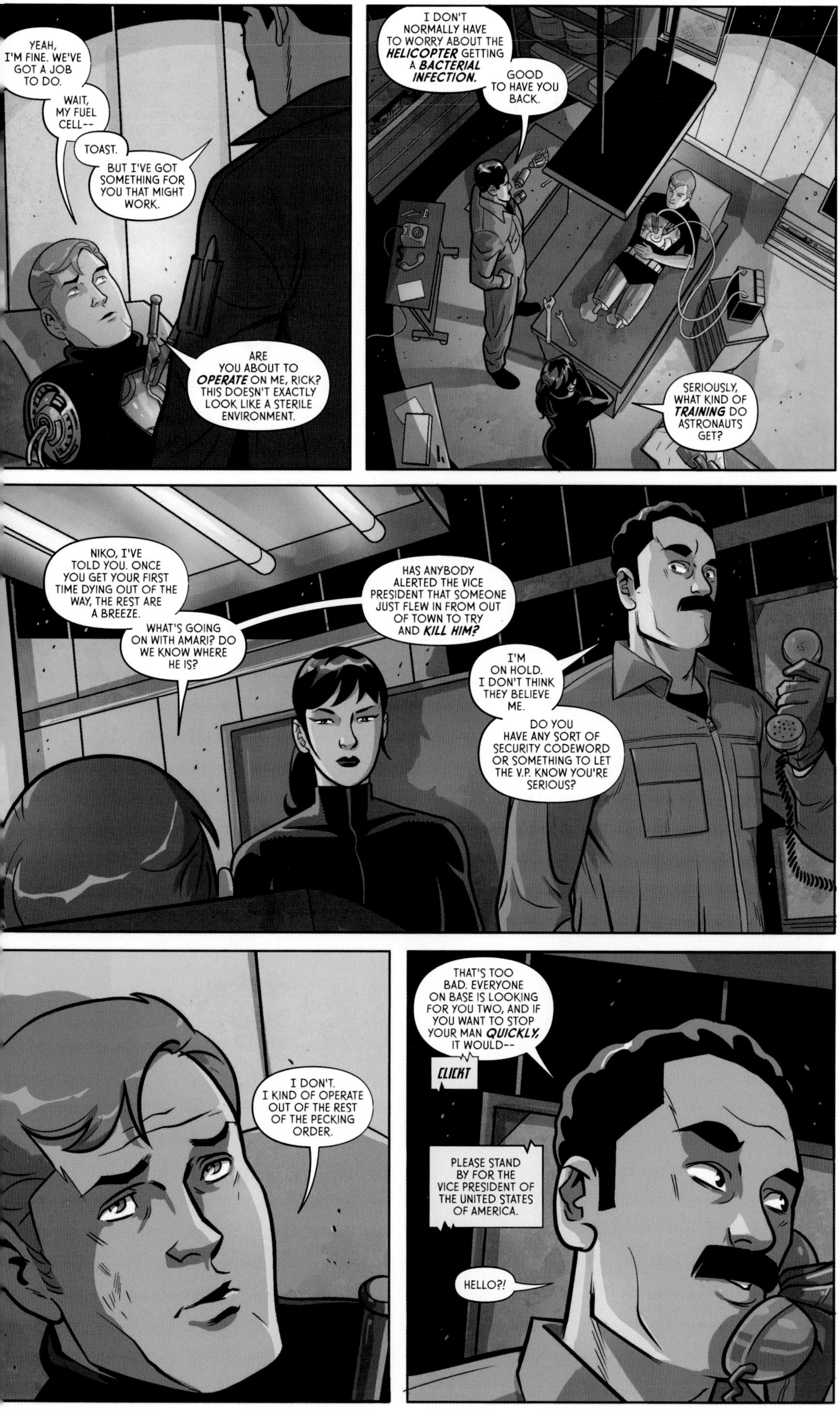
YEAH, I'M FINE. WE'VE GOT A JOB TO DO.
WAIT, MY FUEL CELL--
TOAST.
BUT I'VE GOT SOMETHING FOR YOU THAT MIGHT WORK.
ARE YOU ABOUT TO OPERATE ON ME, RICK? THIS DOESN'T EXACTLY LOOK LIKE A STERILE ENVIRONMENT.
I DON'T NORMALLY HAVE TO WORRY ABOUT THE HELICOPTER GETTING A BACTERIAL INFECTION.
GOOD TO HAVE YOU BACK.
SERIOUSLY, WHAT KIND OF TRAINING DO ASTRONAUTS GET?
NIKO, I'VE TOLD YOU. ONCE YOU GET YOUR FIRST TIME DYING OUT OF THE WAY, THE REST ARE A BREEZE.
WHAT'S GOING ON WITH AMARI? DO WE KNOW WHERE HE IS?
HAS ANYBODY ALERTED THE VICE PRESIDENT THAT SOMEONE JUST FLEW IN FROM OUT OF TOWN TO TRY AND KILL HIM?
I'M ON HOLD. I DON'T THINK THEY BELIEVE ME.
DO YOU HAVE ANY SORT OF SECURITY CODEWORD OR SOMETHING TO LET THE V.P. KNOW YOU'RE SERIOUS?
I DON'T. I KIND OF OPERATE OUT OF THE REST OF THE PECKING ORDER.
THAT'S TOO BAD. EVERYONE ON BASE IS LOOKING FOR YOU TWO, AND IF YOU WANT TO STOP YOUR MAN QUICKLY, IT WOULD--
CLICKT
PLEASE STAND BY FOR THE VICE PRESIDENT OF THE UNITED STATES OF AMERICA.
HELLO?!

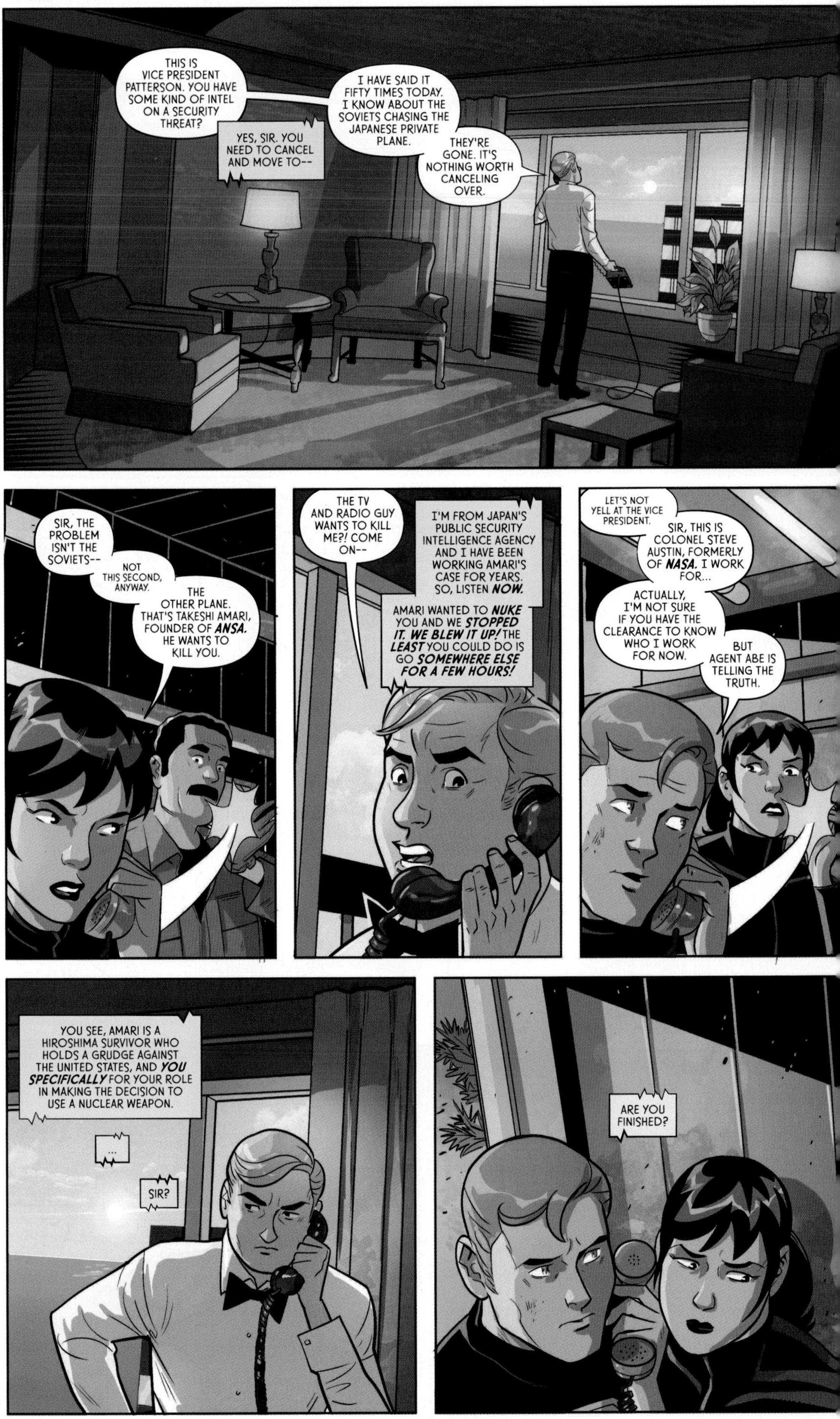

THIS IS VICE PRESIDENT PATTERSON. YOU HAVE SOME KIND OF INTEL ON A SECURITY THREAT?
YES, SIR. YOU NEED TO CANCEL AND MOVE TO--
I HAVE SAID IT FIFTY TIMES TODAY. I KNOW ABOUT THE SOVIETS CHASING THE JAPANESE PRIVATE PLANE.
THEY'RE GONE. IT'S NOTHING WORTH CANCELING OVER.
SIR, THE PROBLEM ISN'T THE SOVIETS--
NOT THIS SECOND, ANYWAY.
THE OTHER PLANE. THAT'S TAKESHI AMARI, FOUNDER OF ANSA. HE WANTS TO KILL YOU.
THE TV AND RADIO GUY WANTS TO KILL ME?! COME ON--
I'M FROM JAPAN'S PUBLIC SECURITY INTELLIGENCE AGENCY AND I HAVE BEEN WORKING AMARI'S CASE FOR YEARS. SO, LISTEN NOW.
AMARI WANTED TO NUKE YOU AND WE STOPPED IT. WE BLEW IT UP! THE LEAST YOU COULD DO IS GO SOMEWHERE ELSE FOR A FEW HOURS!
LET'S NOT YELL AT THE VICE PRESIDENT.
SIR, THIS IS COLONEL STEVE AUSTIN, FORMERLY OF NASA. I WORK FOR...
ACTUALLY, I'M NOT SURE IF YOU HAVE THE CLEARANCE TO KNOW WHO I WORK FOR NOW.
BUT AGENT ABE IS TELLING THE TRUTH.
YOU SEE, AMARI IS A HIROSHIMA SURVIVOR WHO HOLDS A GRUDGE AGAINST THE UNITED STATES, AND YOU SPECIFICALLY FOR YOUR ROLE IN MAKING THE DECISION TO USE A NUCLEAR WEAPON.
...
SIR?
ARE YOU FINISHED?

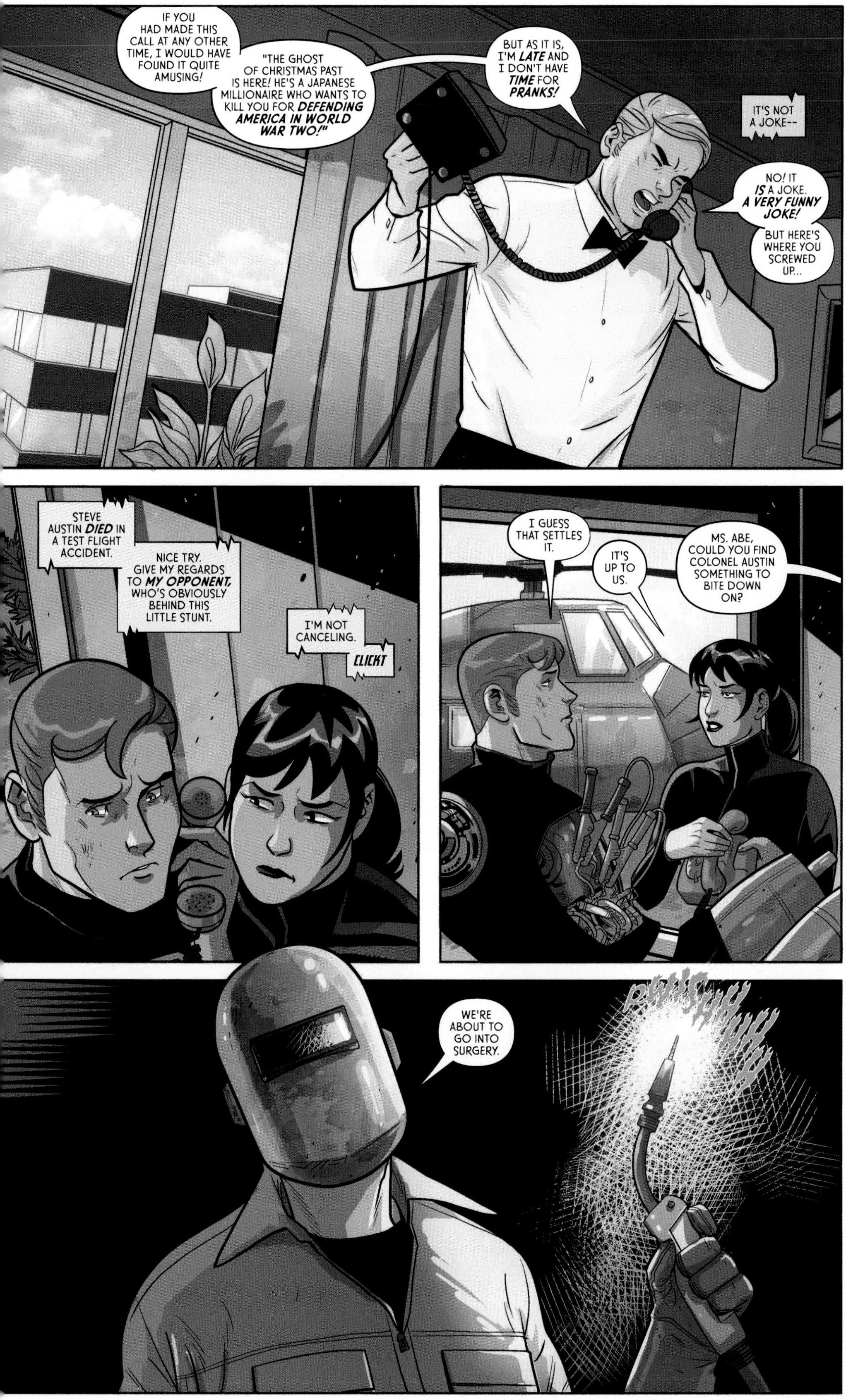
IF YOU HAD MADE THIS CALL AT ANY OTHER TIME, I WOULD HAVE FOUND IT QUITE AMUSING!
"THE GHOST OF CHRISTMAS PAST IS HERE! HE'S A JAPANESE MILLIONAIRE WHO WANTS TO KILL YOU FOR DEFENDING AMERICA IN WORLD WAR TWO!"
BUT AS IT IS, I'M LATE AND I DON'T HAVE TIME FOR PRANKS!
IT'S NOT A JOKE--
NO! IT IS A JOKE. A VERY FUNNY JOKE!
BUT HERE'S WHERE YOU SCREWED UP...
STEVE AUSTIN DIED IN A TEST FLIGHT ACCIDENT.
NICE TRY. GIVE MY REGARDS TO MY OPPONENT, WHO'S OBVIOUSLY BEHIND THIS LITTLE STUNT.
I'M NOT CANCELING.
CLICKT
I GUESS THAT SETTLES IT.
IT'S UP TO US.
MS. ABE, COULD YOU FIND COLONEL AUSTIN SOMETHING TO BITE DOWN ON?
WE'RE ABOUT TO GO INTO SURGERY.

IS PATTERSON EVEN *HERE*?

I SAW SECRET SERVICE RUNNING AROUND JUST A FEW MINUTES AGO. DO YOU THINK THEY LOST HIM?

HA HA HA!

PATTERSON '76

AMERICA CAN,
AMERICA MUS

WHAT IS THAT NOISE?

wwwwrrrrrMMMMmmmVRMm

VRRMMM

VRMMM

mmm

RRRMMMmmm

I'M NOT SURE IF IT WAS BEST TO BRING ME ALONG HERE.

IN THE PAST TWENTY-FOUR HOURS YOU'VE FOUGHT OFF WAVES OF DEMON-FACED SWORDSMEN, BLEW UP AN INTERCONTINENTAL ROCKET, WON A FIGHT WITH A COMBAT HELICOPTER, AND SURVIVED A 30,000 FOOT DIVE OUT OF A PLANE.

THESE DRIPS MAKE YOU NERVOUS?

I'M JUST NOT EXACTLY HELPFUL LIKE THIS.

HOLD ON.

GETTING A GOOD LOOK?! THIS MAN NEARLY *DIED* FOR THIS COUNTRY. HAVE SOME RESPECT!

S-SO SORRY!

YOU ARE BEING *VERY* HELPFUL.

YOU JUST GOT MY GUN PAST SECURITY!

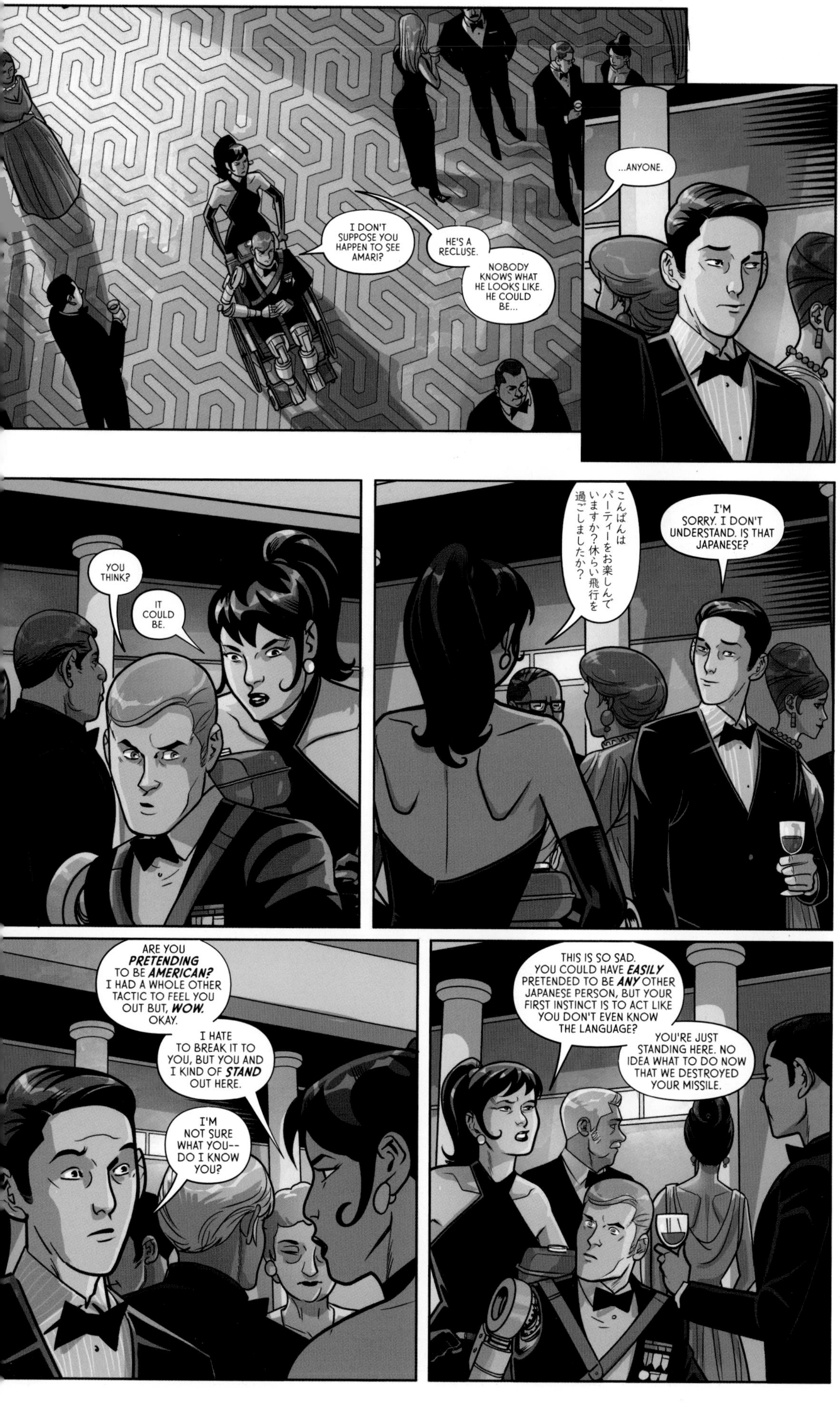
I DON'T SUPPOSE YOU HAPPEN TO SEE AMARI?
HE'S A RECLUSE.
NOBODY KNOWS WHAT HE LOOKS LIKE. HE COULD BE...
...ANYONE.
YOU THINK?
IT COULD BE.
こんばんはパーティーをお楽しんでいますか？休らい飛行を過ごしましたか？
I'M SORRY. I DON'T UNDERSTAND. IS THAT JAPANESE?
ARE YOU ***PRETENDING*** TO BE ***AMERICAN?*** I HAD A WHOLE OTHER TACTIC TO FEEL YOU OUT BUT, ***WOW.*** OKAY.
I HATE TO BREAK IT TO YOU, BUT YOU AND I KIND OF ***STAND*** OUT HERE.
I'M NOT SURE WHAT YOU-- DO I KNOW YOU?
THIS IS SO SAD. YOU COULD HAVE ***EASILY*** PRETENDED TO BE ***ANY*** OTHER JAPANESE PERSON, BUT YOUR FIRST INSTINCT IS TO ACT LIKE YOU DON'T EVEN KNOW THE LANGUAGE?
YOU'RE JUST STANDING HERE. NO IDEA WHAT TO DO NOW THAT WE DESTROYED YOUR MISSILE.

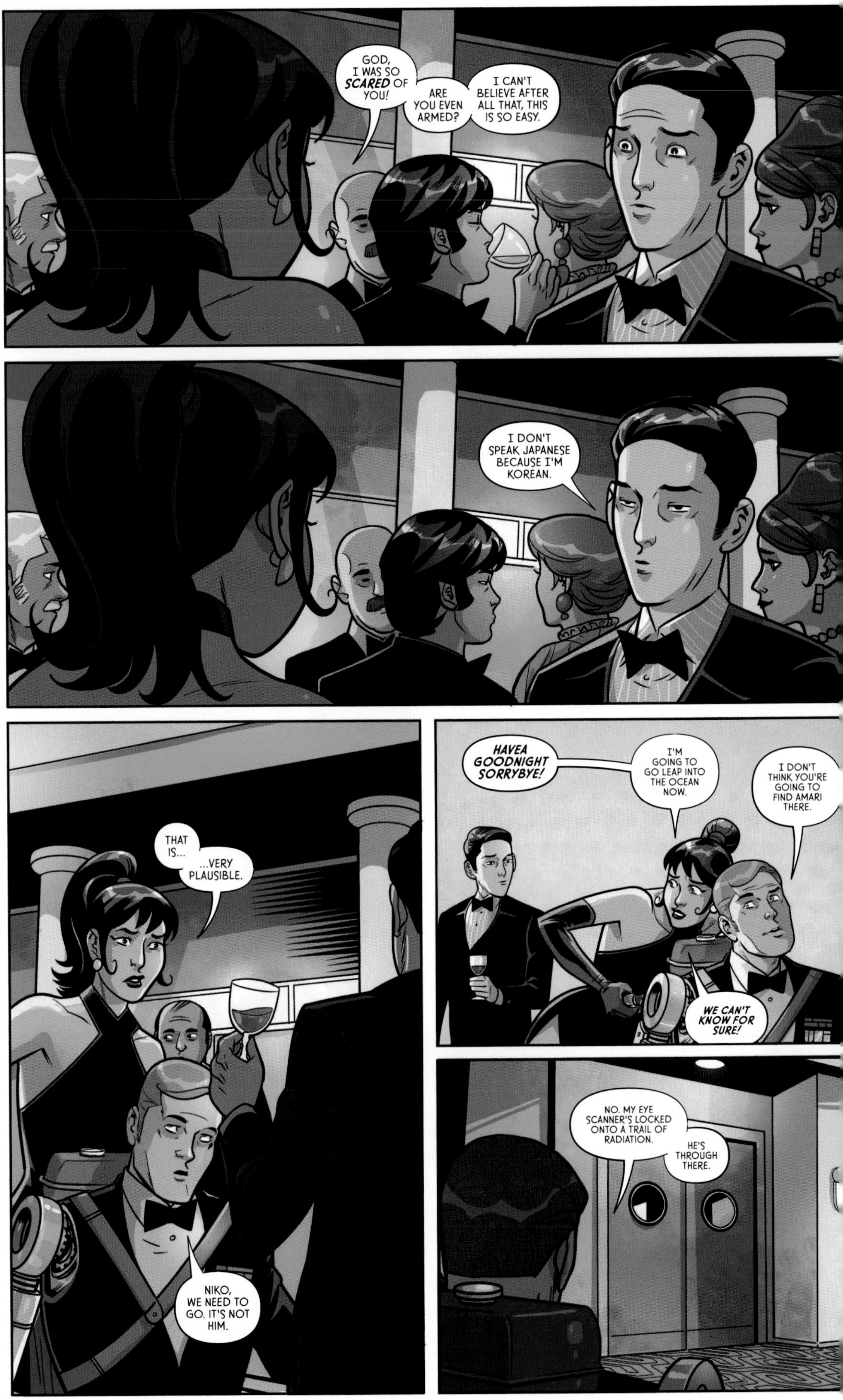
GOD, I WAS SO SCARED OF YOU!
ARE YOU EVEN ARMED?
I CAN'T BELIEVE AFTER ALL THAT, THIS IS SO EASY.
I DON'T SPEAK JAPANESE BECAUSE I'M KOREAN.
THAT IS...
...VERY PLAUSIBLE.
NIKO, WE NEED TO GO. IT'S NOT HIM.
HAVEA GOODNIGHT SORRYBYE!
I'M GOING TO GO LEAP INTO THE OCEAN NOW.
I DON'T THINK YOU'RE GOING TO FIND AMARI THERE.
WE CAN'T KNOW FOR SURE!
NO. MY EYE SCANNER'S LOCKED ONTO A TRAIL OF RADIATION.
HE'S THROUGH THERE.

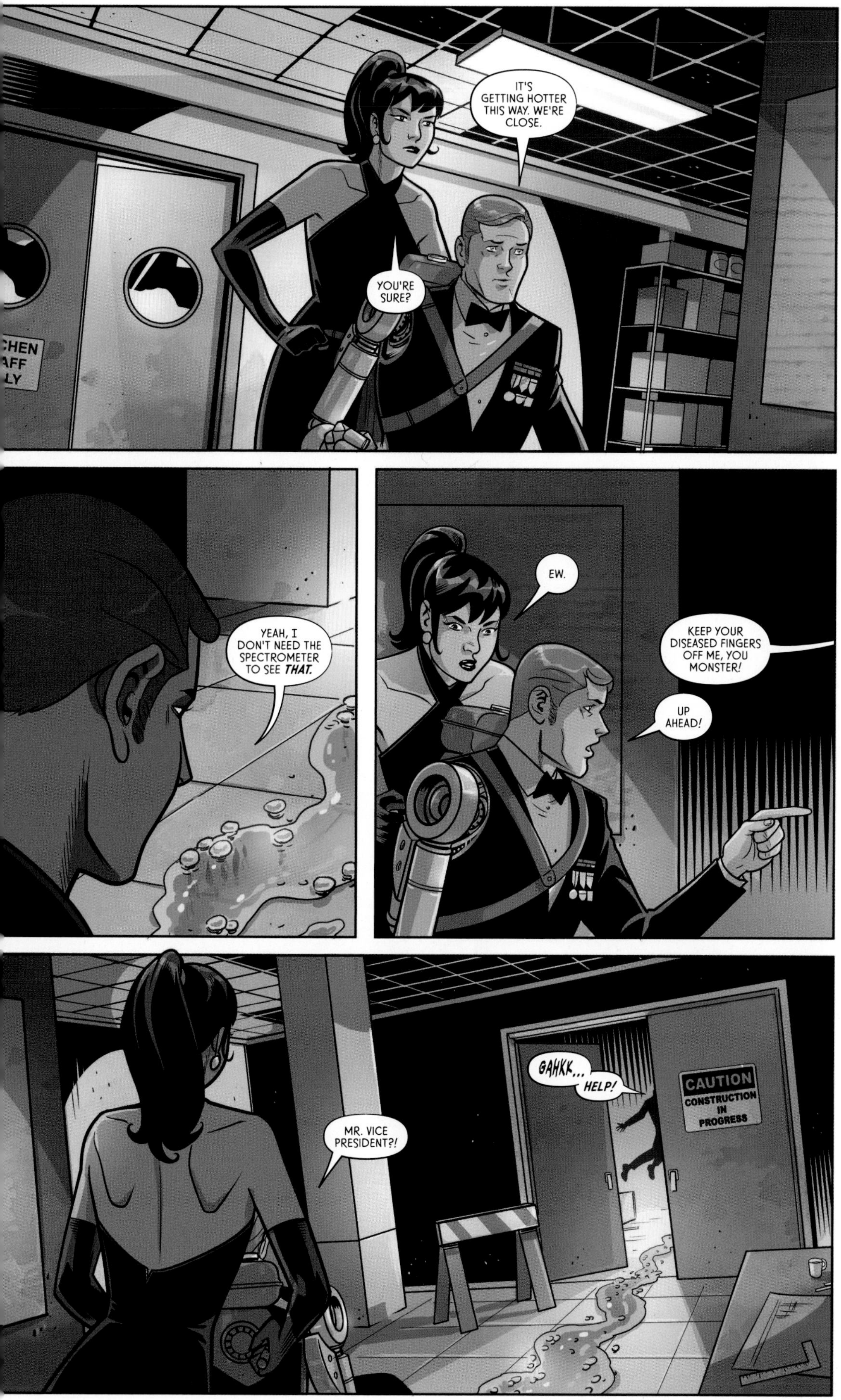
CHEN
AFF
LY
IT'S GETTING HOTTER THIS WAY. WE'RE CLOSE.
YOU'RE SURE?
YEAH, I DON'T NEED THE SPECTROMETER TO SEE *THAT.*
EW.
KEEP YOUR DISEASED FINGERS OFF ME, YOU MONSTER!
UP AHEAD!
MR. VICE PRESIDENT?!
GAHKK... HELP!
CAUTION
CONSTRUCTION IN PROGRESS

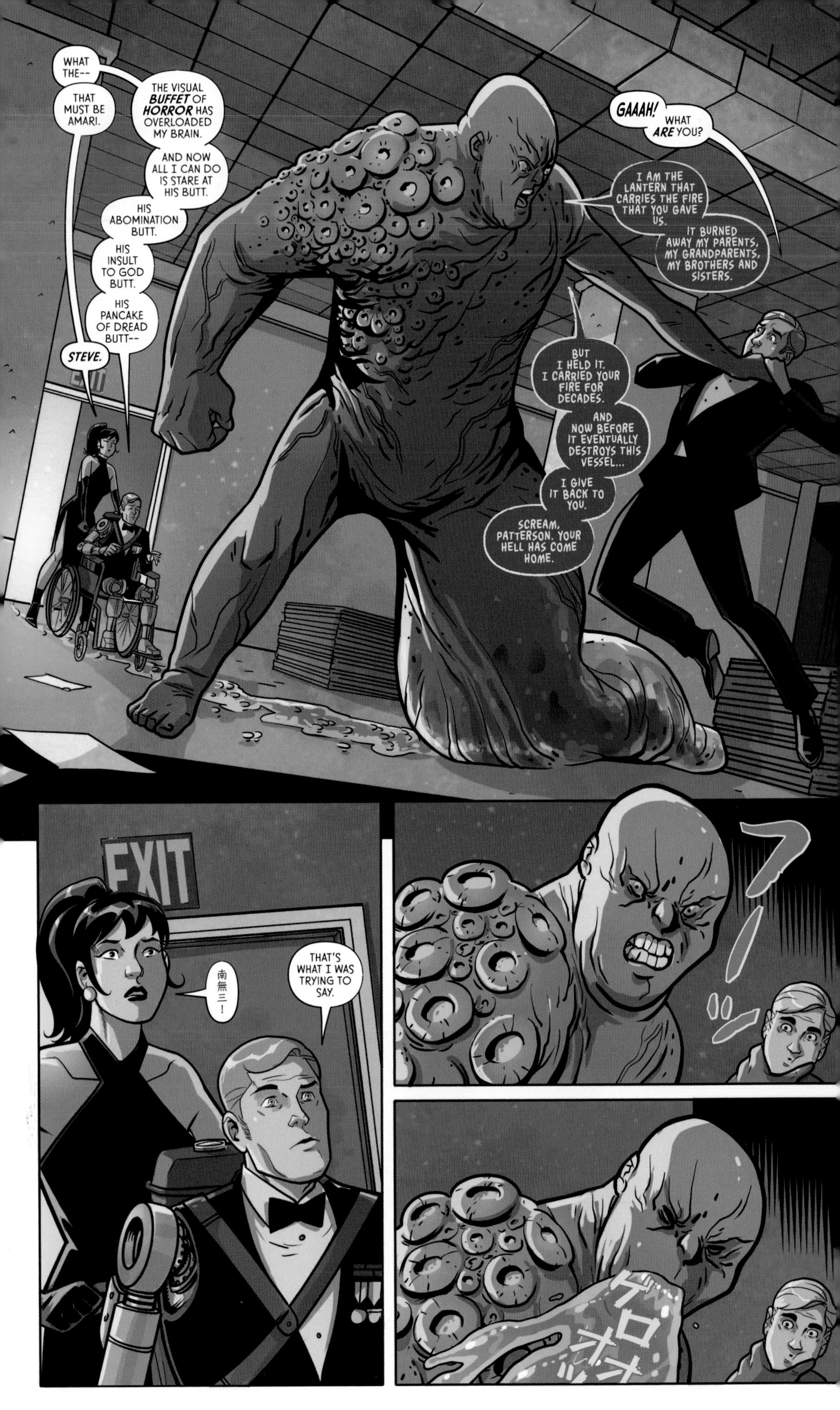
WHAT THE--
THAT MUST BE AMARI.
THE VISUAL BUFFET OF HORROR HAS OVERLOADED MY BRAIN.
AND NOW ALL I CAN DO IS STARE AT HIS BUTT.
HIS ABOMINATION BUTT.
HIS INSULT TO GOD BUTT.
HIS PANCAKE OF DREAD BUTT--
STEVE.
GAAAH! WHAT ARE YOU?
I AM THE LANTERN THAT CARRIES THE FIRE THAT YOU GAVE US.
IT BURNED AWAY MY PARENTS, MY GRANDPARENTS, MY BROTHERS AND SISTERS.
BUT I HELD IT. I CARRIED YOUR FIRE FOR DECADES.
AND NOW BEFORE IT EVENTUALLY DESTROYS THIS VESSEL...
I GIVE IT BACK TO YOU.
SCREAM, PATTERSON. YOUR HELL HAS COME HOME.
EXIT
南無三!
THAT'S WHAT I WAS TRYING TO SAY.

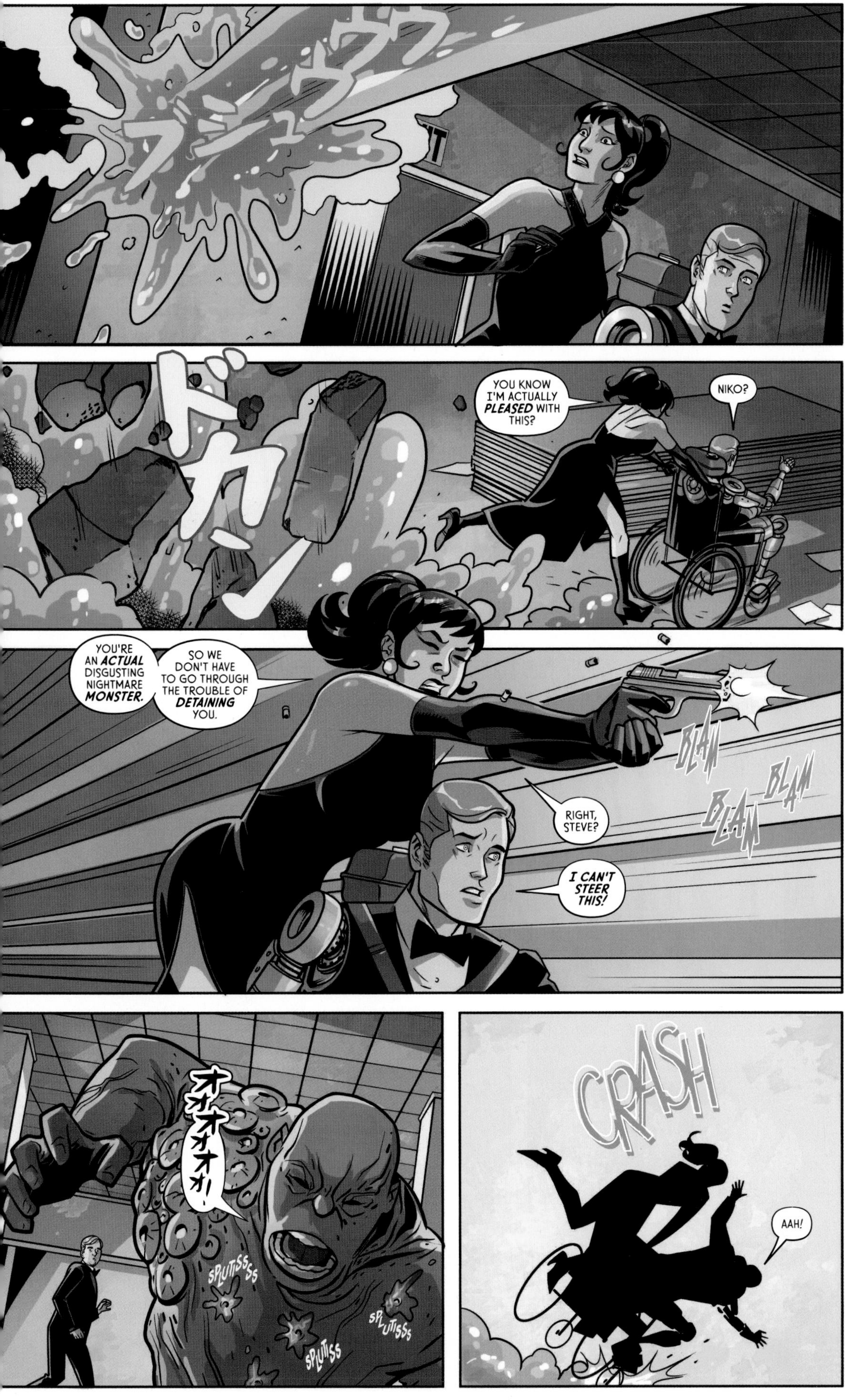

ドカン
YOU KNOW I'M ACTUALLY ***PLEASED*** WITH THIS?
NIKO?
YOU'RE AN ***ACTUAL*** DISGUSTING NIGHTMARE ***MONSTER.***
SO WE DON'T HAVE TO GO THROUGH THE TROUBLE OF ***DETAINING*** YOU.
BLAM
BLAM
BLAM
RIGHT, STEVE?
I CAN'T STEER THIS!
オオオオオオ!
SPLUTISSSS
SPLUTISS
SPLUTISSSS
CRASH
AAH!

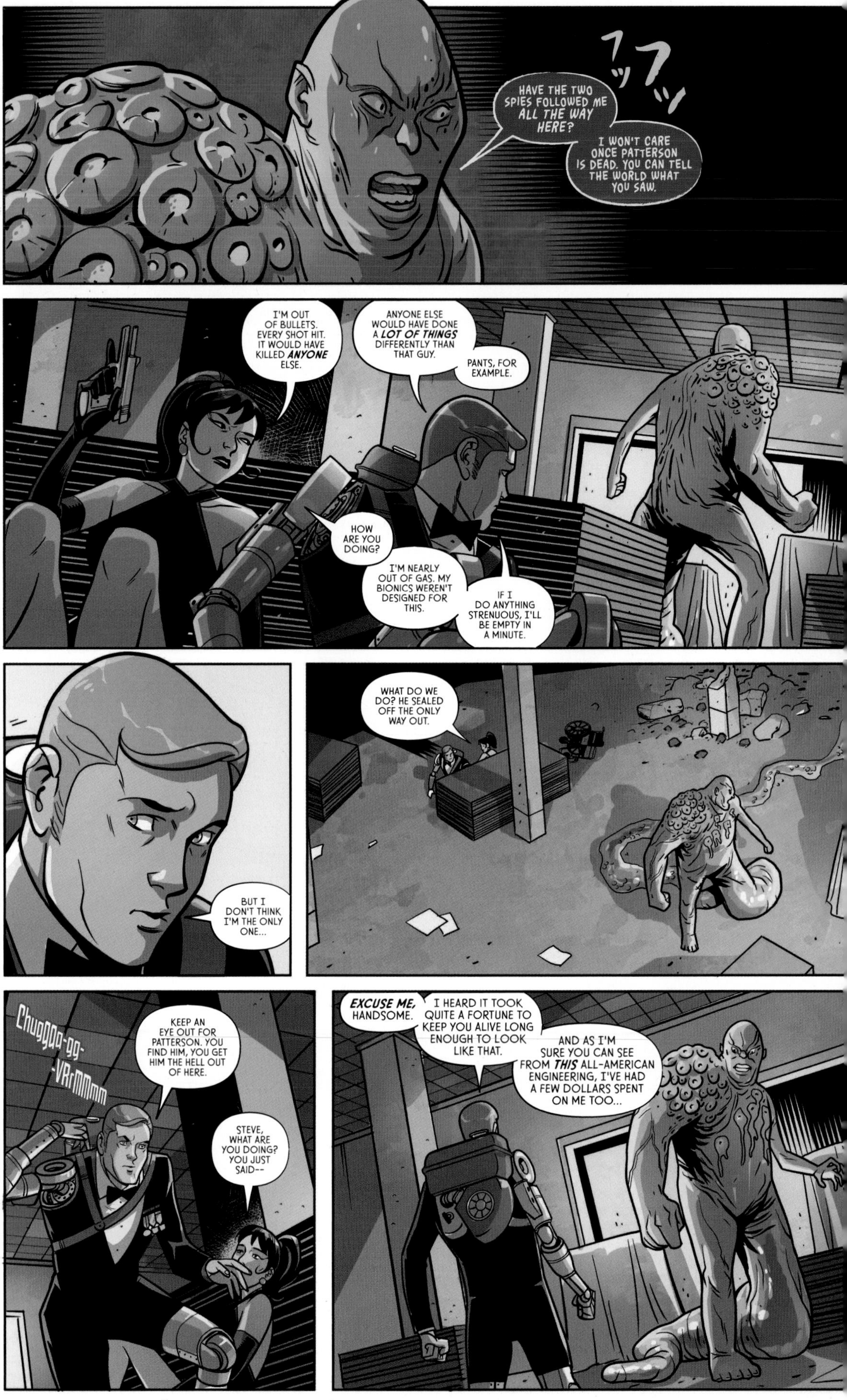

フッフッ
HAVE THE TWO SPIES FOLLOWED ME ALL THE WAY HERE?
I WON'T CARE ONCE PATTERSON IS DEAD. YOU CAN TELL THE WORLD WHAT YOU SAW.
I'M OUT OF BULLETS. EVERY SHOT HIT. IT WOULD HAVE KILLED ANYONE ELSE.
ANYONE ELSE WOULD HAVE DONE A LOT OF THINGS DIFFERENTLY THAN THAT GUY.
PANTS, FOR EXAMPLE.
HOW ARE YOU DOING?
I'M NEARLY OUT OF GAS. MY BIONICS WEREN'T DESIGNED FOR THIS.
IF I DO ANYTHING STRENUOUS, I'LL BE EMPTY IN A MINUTE.
WHAT DO WE DO? HE SEALED OFF THE ONLY WAY OUT.
BUT I DON'T THINK I'M THE ONLY ONE...
Chuggga-gg-
-VRrMMmm
KEEP AN EYE OUT FOR PATTERSON. YOU FIND HIM, YOU GET HIM THE HELL OUT OF HERE.
STEVE, WHAT ARE YOU DOING? YOU JUST SAID--
EXCUSE ME, HANDSOME.
I HEARD IT TOOK QUITE A FORTUNE TO KEEP YOU ALIVE LONG ENOUGH TO LOOK LIKE THAT.
AND AS I'M SURE YOU CAN SEE FROM THIS ALL-AMERICAN ENGINEERING, I'VE HAD A FEW DOLLARS SPENT ON ME TOO...

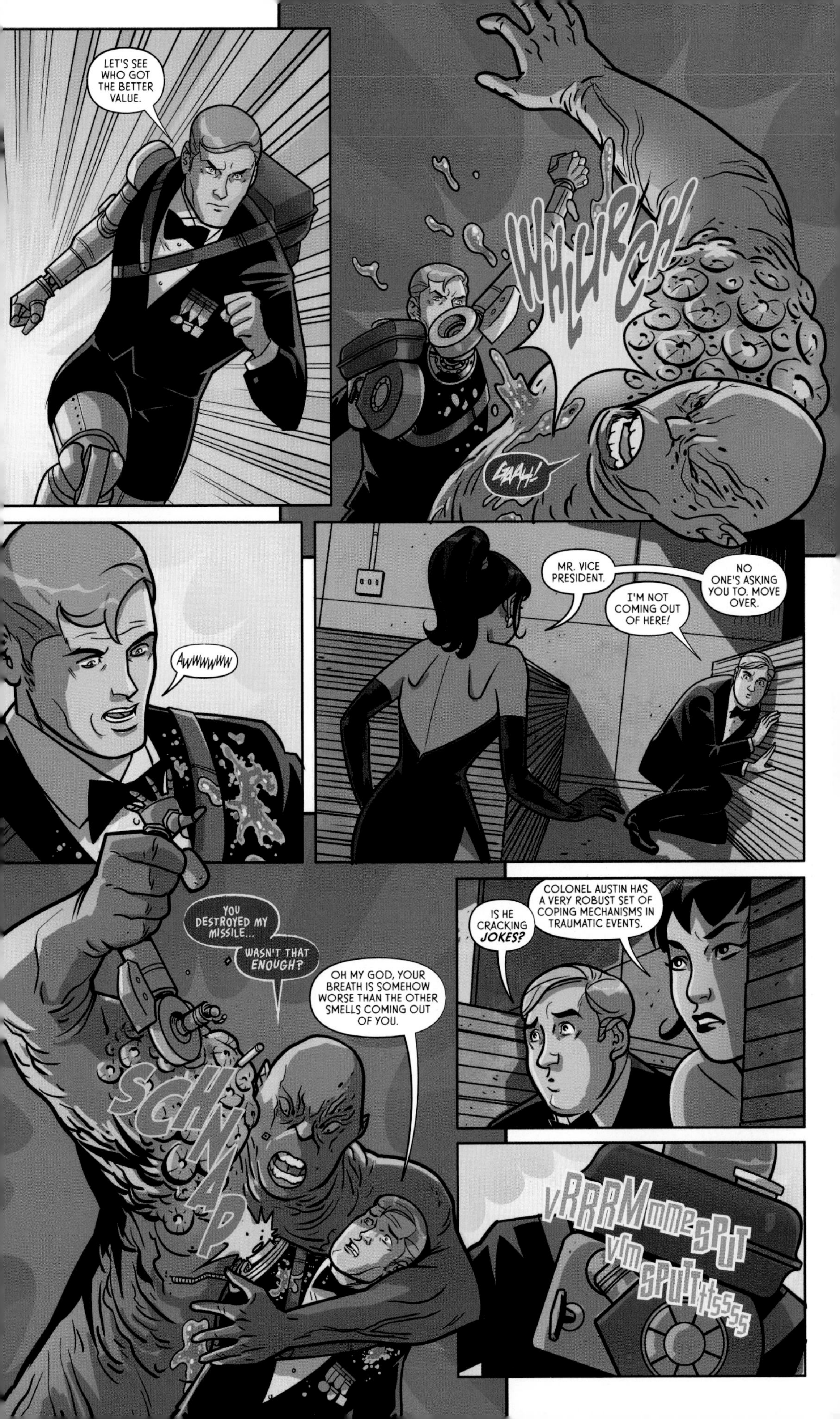
LET'S SEE WHO GOT THE BETTER VALUE.
WHLLRCH
GAAH!
AWWWWWW
MR. VICE PRESIDENT.
I'M NOT COMING OUT OF HERE!
NO ONE'S ASKING YOU TO. MOVE OVER.
YOU DESTROYED MY MISSILE...
WASN'T THAT ENOUGH?
OH MY GOD, YOUR BREATH IS SOMEHOW WORSE THAN THE OTHER SMELLS COMING OUT OF YOU.
SCHNAP
IS HE CRACKING *JOKES?*
COLONEL AUSTIN HAS A VERY ROBUST SET OF COPING MECHANISMS IN TRAUMATIC EVENTS.
vRRRMmmeSPUT vm SPUTttssss

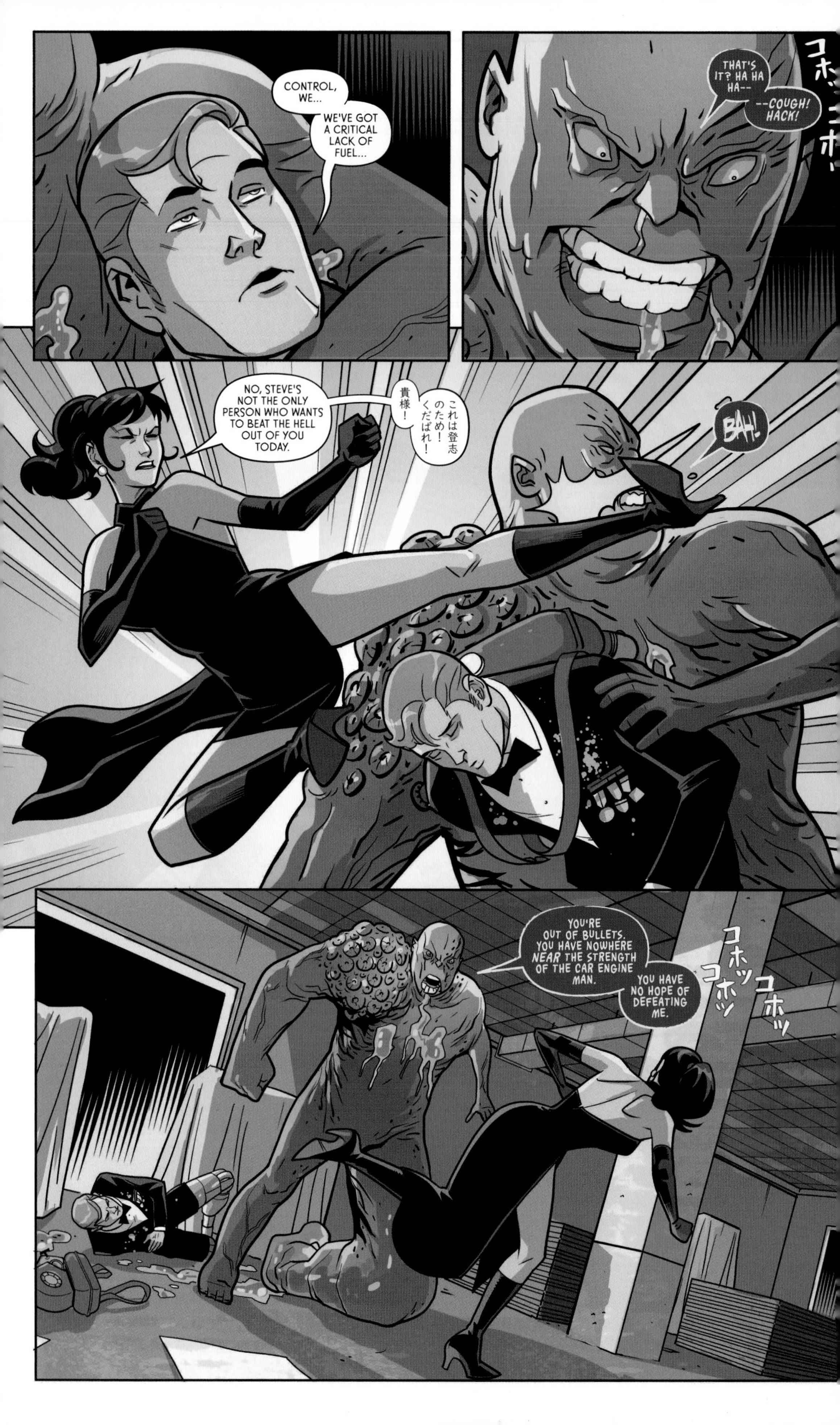
CONTROL, WE...
WE'VE GOT A CRITICAL LACK OF FUEL...
THAT'S IT? HA HA HA--
--COUGH! HACK!
コホッコホッ
NO, STEVE'S NOT THE ONLY PERSON WHO WANTS TO BEAT THE HELL OUT OF YOU TODAY.
これは登志のため！くだばれ！貴様！
BAH!
YOU'RE OUT OF BULLETS. YOU HAVE NOWHERE NEAR THE STRENGTH OF THE CAR ENGINE MAN.
YOU HAVE NO HOPE OF DEFEATING ME.
コホッコホッコホッ

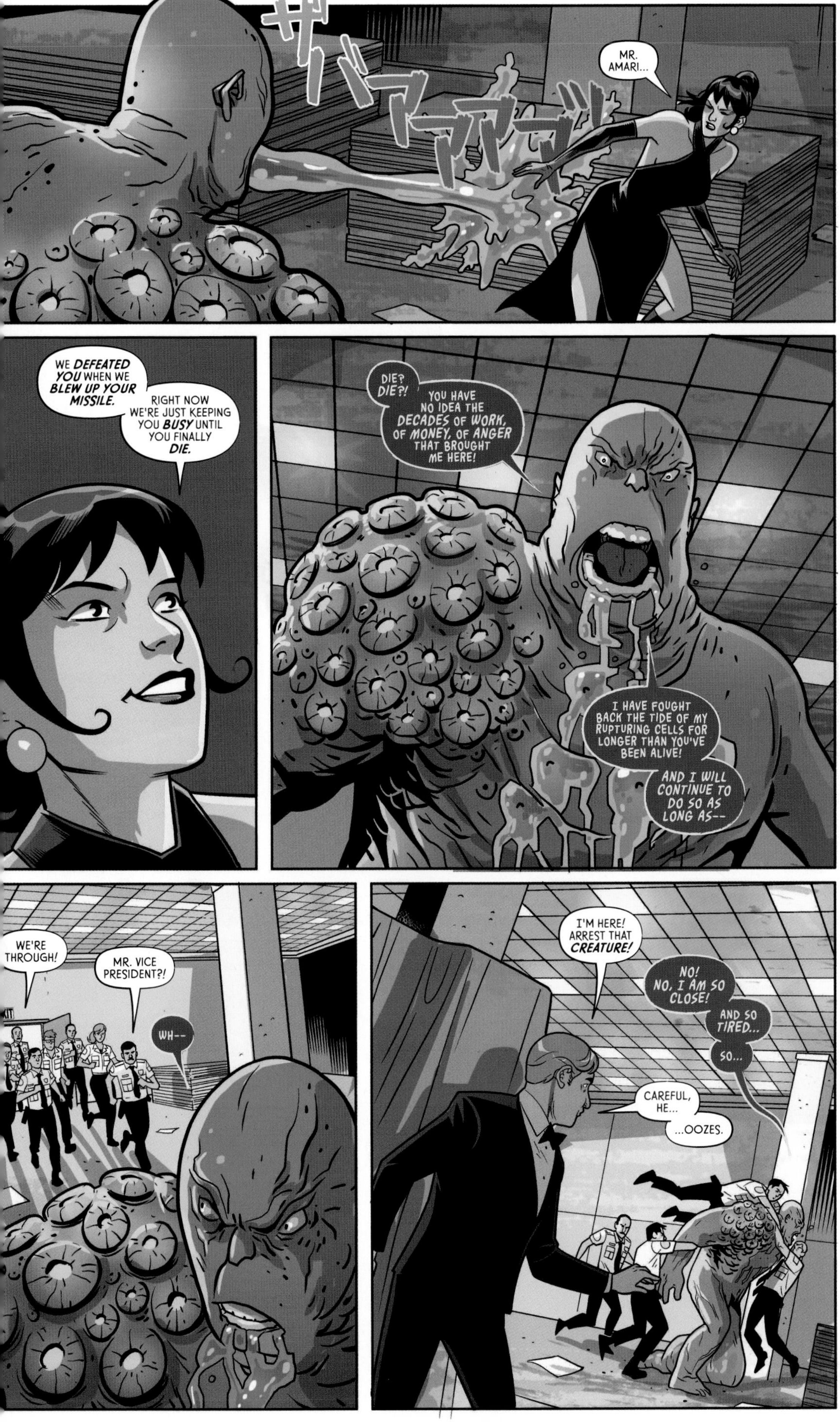
MR. AMARI...
WE DEFEATED YOU WHEN WE BLEW UP YOUR MISSILE.
RIGHT NOW WE'RE JUST KEEPING YOU BUSY UNTIL YOU FINALLY DIE.
DIE? DIE?!
YOU HAVE NO IDEA THE DECADES OF WORK, OF MONEY, OF ANGER THAT BROUGHT ME HERE!
I HAVE FOUGHT BACK THE TIDE OF MY RUPTURING CELLS FOR LONGER THAN YOU'VE BEEN ALIVE!
AND I WILL CONTINUE TO DO SO AS LONG AS--
WE'RE THROUGH!
MR. VICE PRESIDENT?!
WH--
I'M HERE! ARREST THAT CREATURE!
NO! NO, I AM SO CLOSE!
AND SO TIRED...
SO...
CAREFUL, HE...
...OOZES.

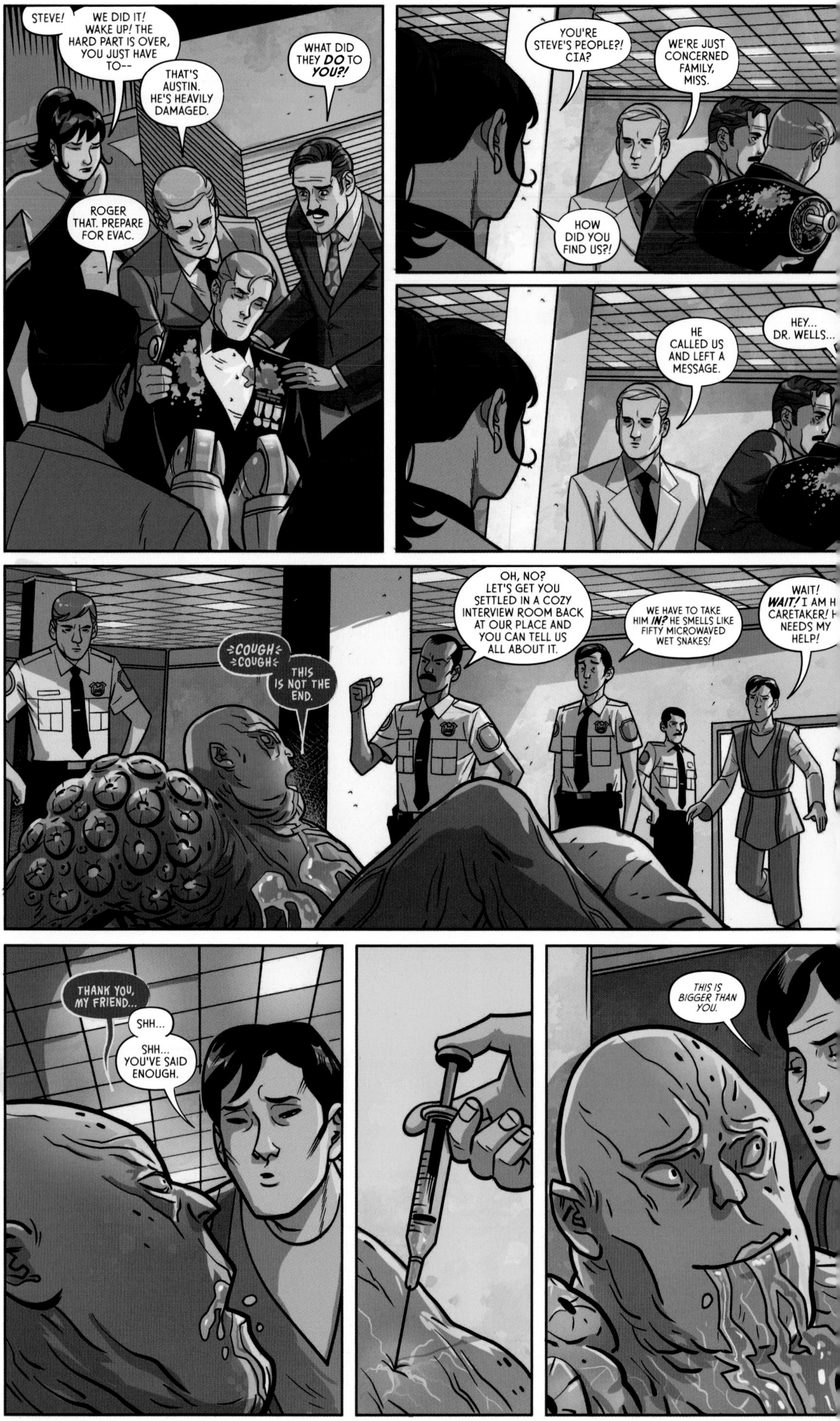

STEVE!
WE DID IT! WAKE UP! THE HARD PART IS OVER, YOU JUST HAVE TO--
THAT'S AUSTIN. HE'S HEAVILY DAMAGED.
WHAT DID THEY **DO** TO ***YOU?!***
ROGER THAT. PREPARE FOR EVAC.
YOU'RE STEVE'S PEOPLE?! CIA?
WE'RE JUST CONCERNED FAMILY, MISS.
HOW DID YOU FIND US?!
HE CALLED US AND LEFT A MESSAGE.
HEY... DR. WELLS...
COUGH COUGH
THIS IS NOT THE END.
OH, NO? LET'S GET YOU SETTLED IN A COZY INTERVIEW ROOM BACK AT OUR PLACE AND YOU CAN TELL US ALL ABOUT IT.
WE HAVE TO TAKE HIM ***IN?*** HE SMELLS LIKE FIFTY MICROWAVED WET SNAKES!
WAIT! ***WAIT!*** I AM H CARETAKER! H NEEDS MY HELP!
THANK YOU, MY FRIEND...
SHH...
SHH... YOU'VE SAID ENOUGH.
THIS IS BIGGER THAN YOU.

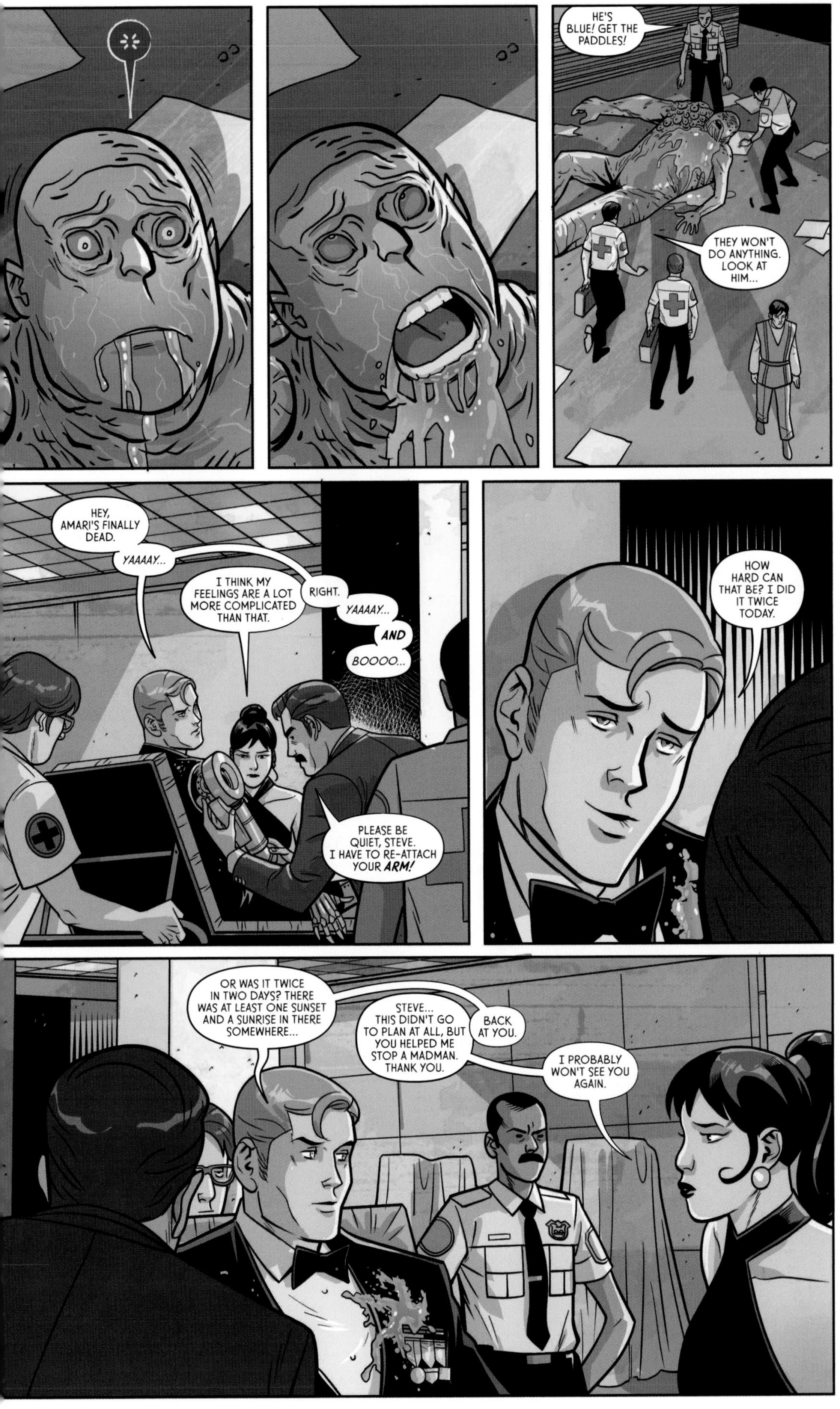
HE'S BLUE! GET THE PADDLES!
THEY WON'T DO ANYTHING. LOOK AT HIM...
HEY, AMARI'S FINALLY DEAD.
YAAAAY...
I THINK MY FEELINGS ARE A LOT MORE COMPLICATED THAN THAT.
RIGHT.
YAAAAY...
AND
BOOOO...
PLEASE BE QUIET, STEVE. I HAVE TO RE-ATTACH YOUR ARM!
HOW HARD CAN THAT BE? I DID IT TWICE TODAY.
OR WAS IT TWICE IN TWO DAYS? THERE WAS AT LEAST ONE SUNSET AND A SUNRISE IN THERE SOMEWHERE...
STEVE... THIS DIDN'T GO TO PLAN AT ALL, BUT YOU HELPED ME STOP A MADMAN. THANK YOU.
BACK AT YOU.
I PROBABLY WON'T SEE YOU AGAIN.

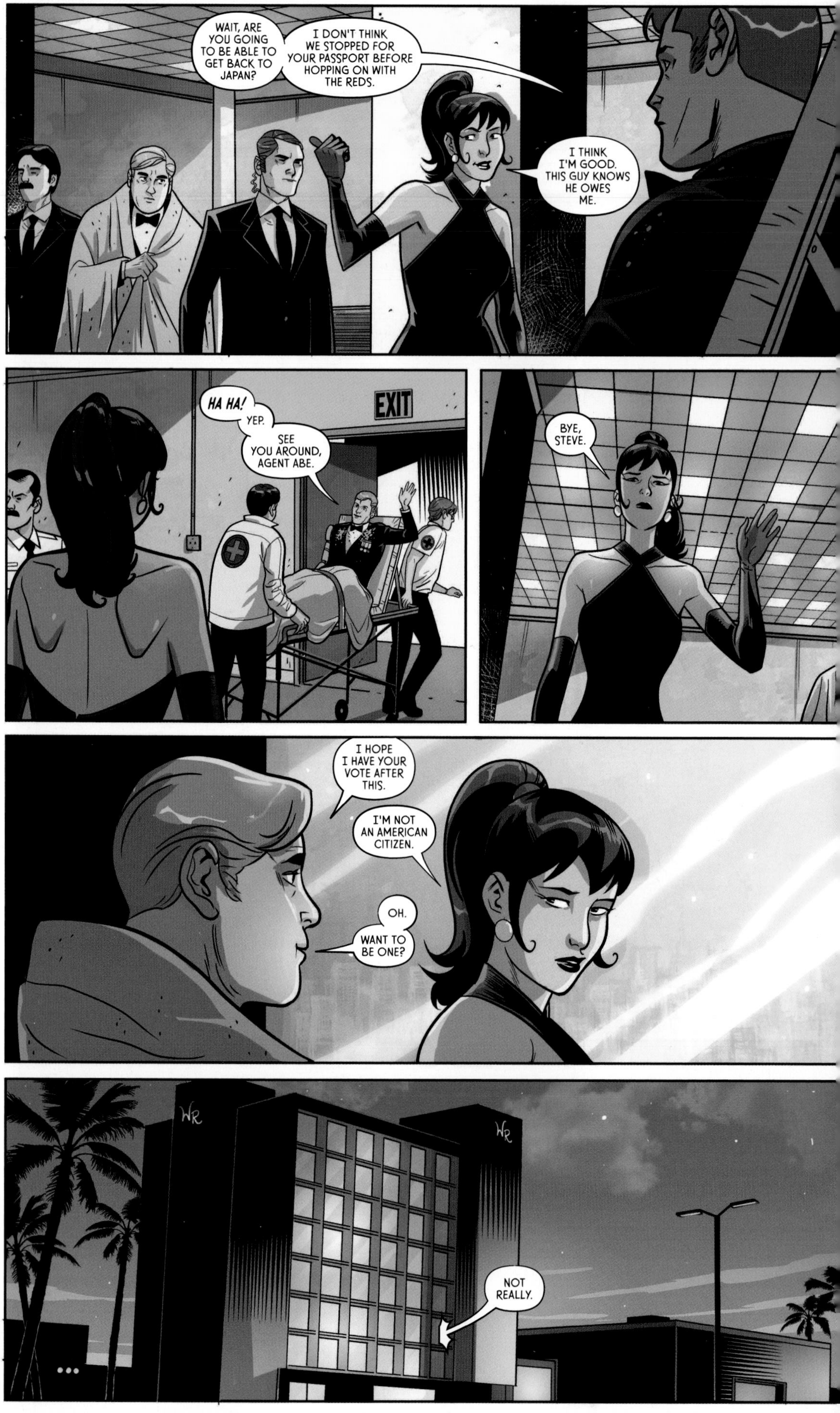
WAIT, ARE YOU GOING TO BE ABLE TO GET BACK TO JAPAN?
I DON'T THINK WE STOPPED FOR YOUR PASSPORT BEFORE HOPPING ON WITH THE REDS.
I THINK I'M GOOD. THIS GUY KNOWS HE OWES ME.
HA HA!
YEP.
SEE YOU AROUND, AGENT ABE.
EXIT
BYE, STEVE.
I HOPE I HAVE YOUR VOTE AFTER THIS.
I'M NOT AN AMERICAN CITIZEN.
OH.
WANT TO BE ONE?
NOT REALLY.
...

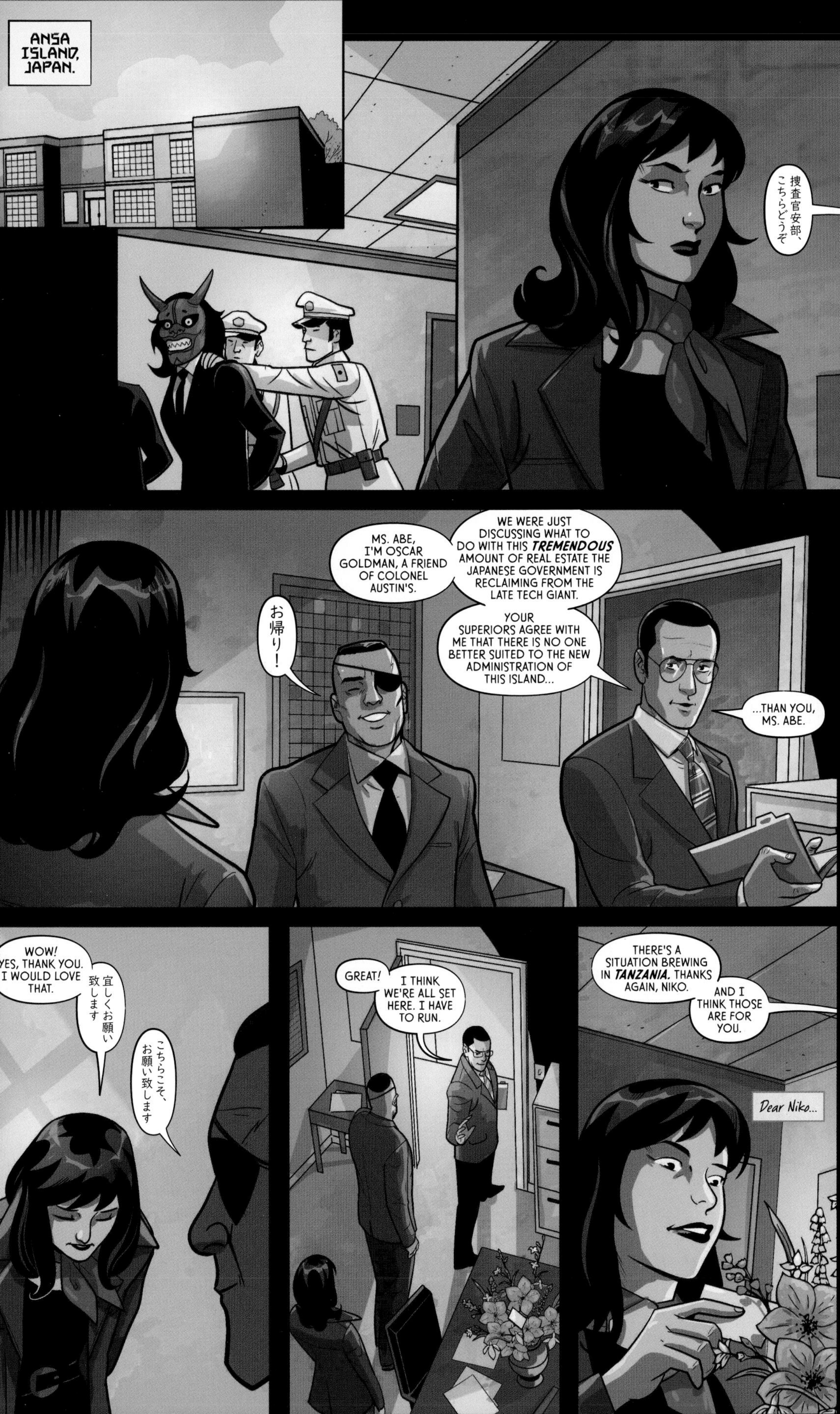
ANSA ISLAND, JAPAN.
捜査官安部、こちらどうぞ
MS. ABE, I'M OSCAR GOLDMAN, A FRIEND OF COLONEL AUSTIN'S.
WE WERE JUST DISCUSSING WHAT TO DO WITH THIS *TREMENDOUS* AMOUNT OF REAL ESTATE THE JAPANESE GOVERNMENT IS RECLAIMING FROM THE LATE TECH GIANT.
お帰り！
YOUR SUPERIORS AGREE WITH ME THAT THERE IS NO ONE BETTER SUITED TO THE NEW ADMINISTRATION OF THIS ISLAND...
...THAN YOU, MS. ABE.
WOW! YES, THANK YOU. I WOULD LOVE THAT.
宜しくお願い致します
こちらこそ、お願い致します
GREAT!
I THINK WE'RE ALL SET HERE. I HAVE TO RUN.
THERE'S A SITUATION BREWING IN *TANZANIA.* THANKS AGAIN, NIKO.
AND I THINK THOSE ARE FOR YOU.
Dear Niko...

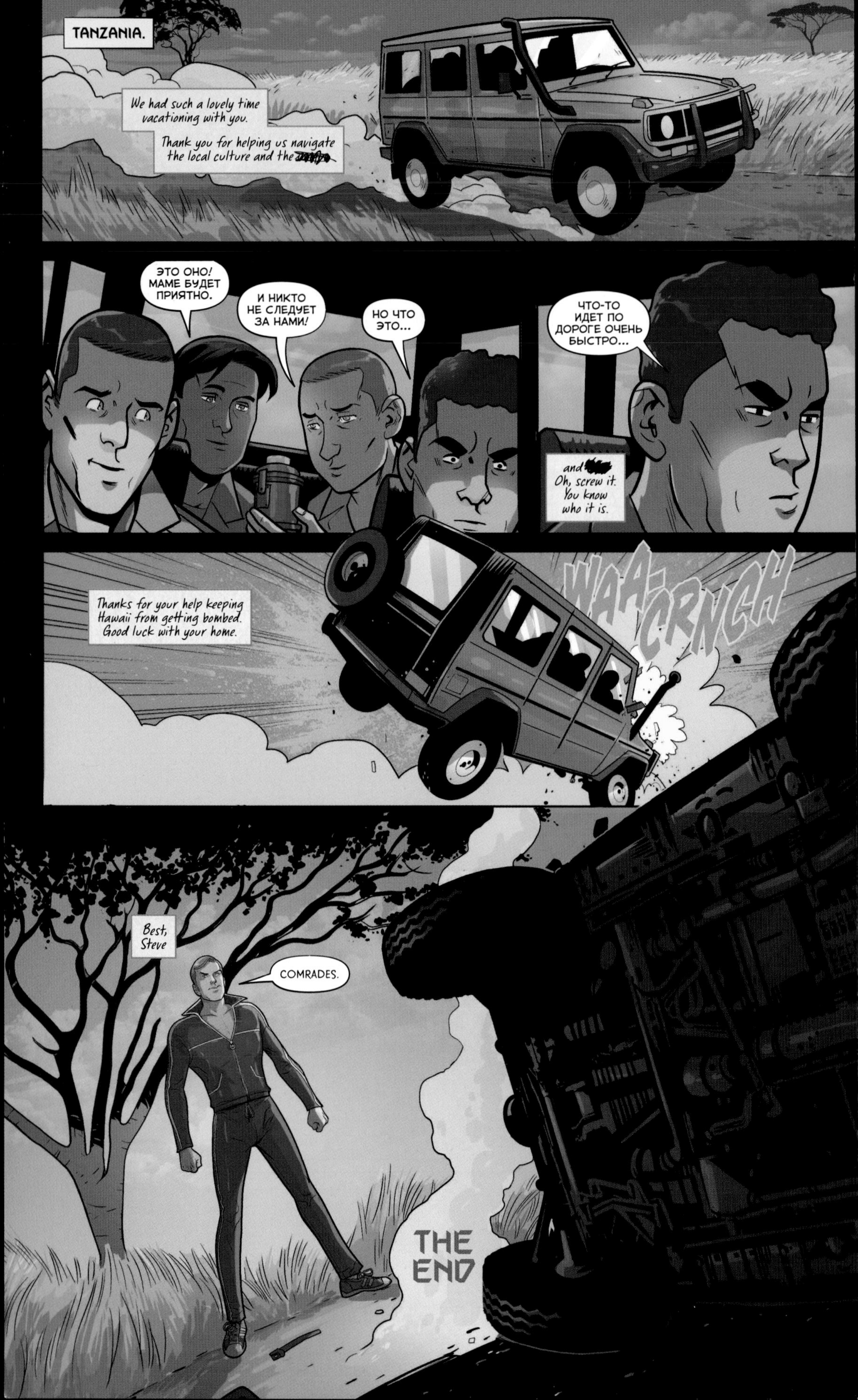
TANZANIA.
We had such a lovely time vacationing with you.
Thank you for helping us navigate the local culture and the [redacted]
ЭТО ОНО! МАМЕ БУДЕТ ПРИЯТНО.
И НИКТО НЕ СЛЕДУЕТ ЗА НАМИ!
НО ЧТО ЭТО...
ЧТО-ТО ИДЕТ ПО ДОРОГЕ ОЧЕНЬ БЫСТРО...
and [redacted] Oh, screw it. You know who it is.
Thanks for your help keeping Hawaii from getting bombed. Good luck with your home.
WAA-CRNCH
Best, Steve
COMRADES.
THE END

COVER GALLERY

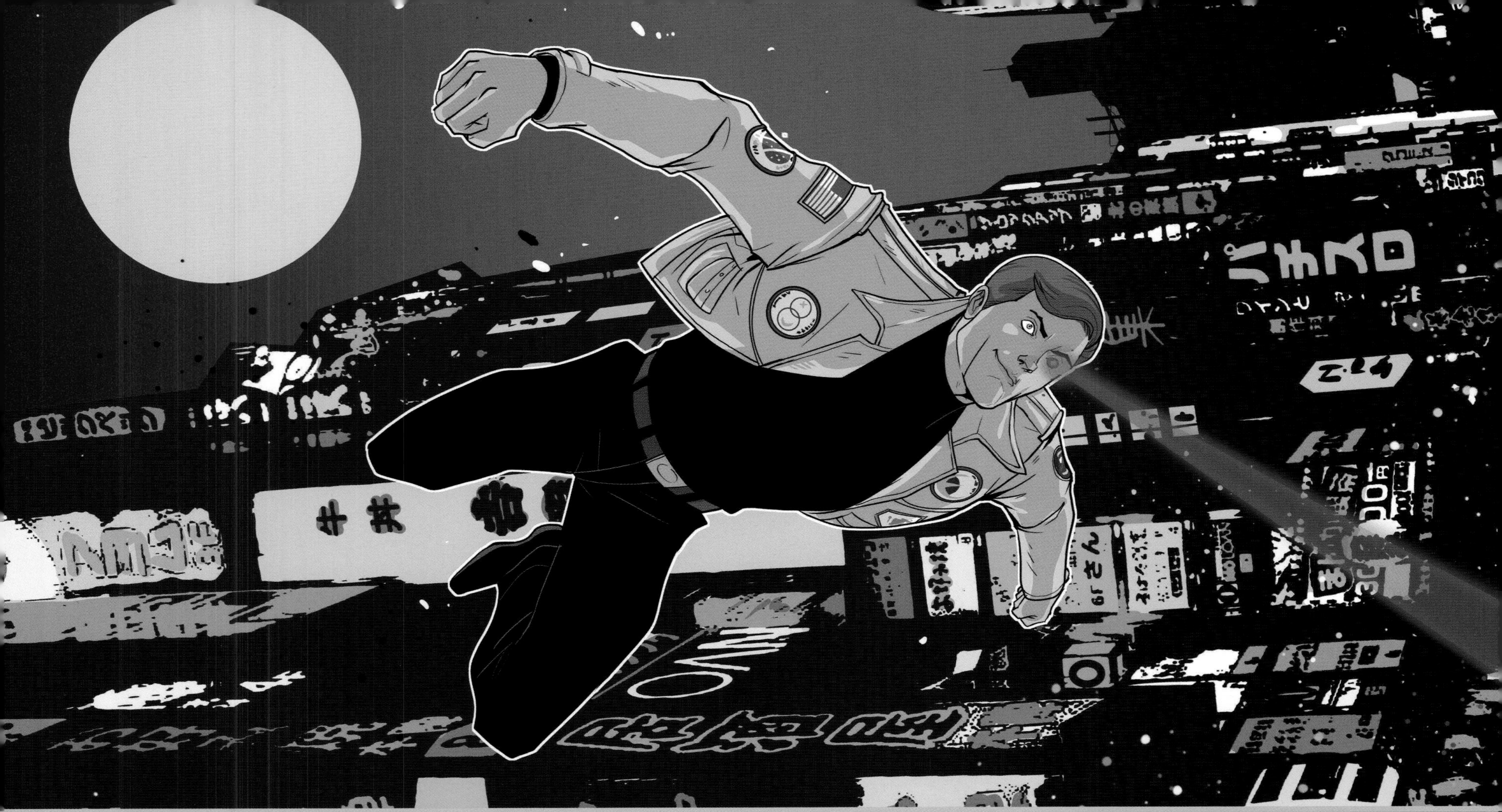

ISSUE 01 VARIANT COVER ART BY DENIS MEDRI

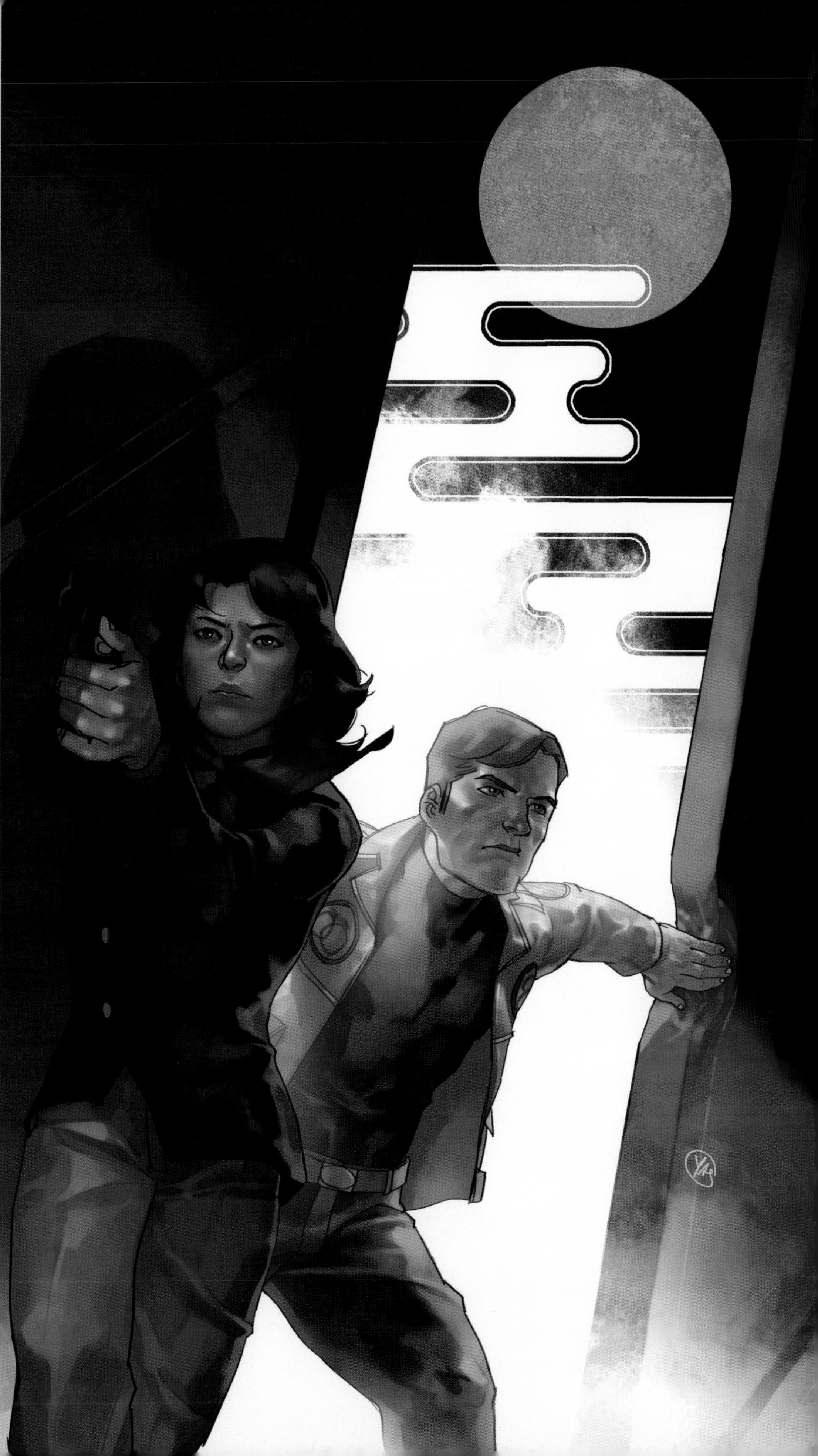

ISSUE 01 VARIANT COVER ART BY YASMINE PUTRI

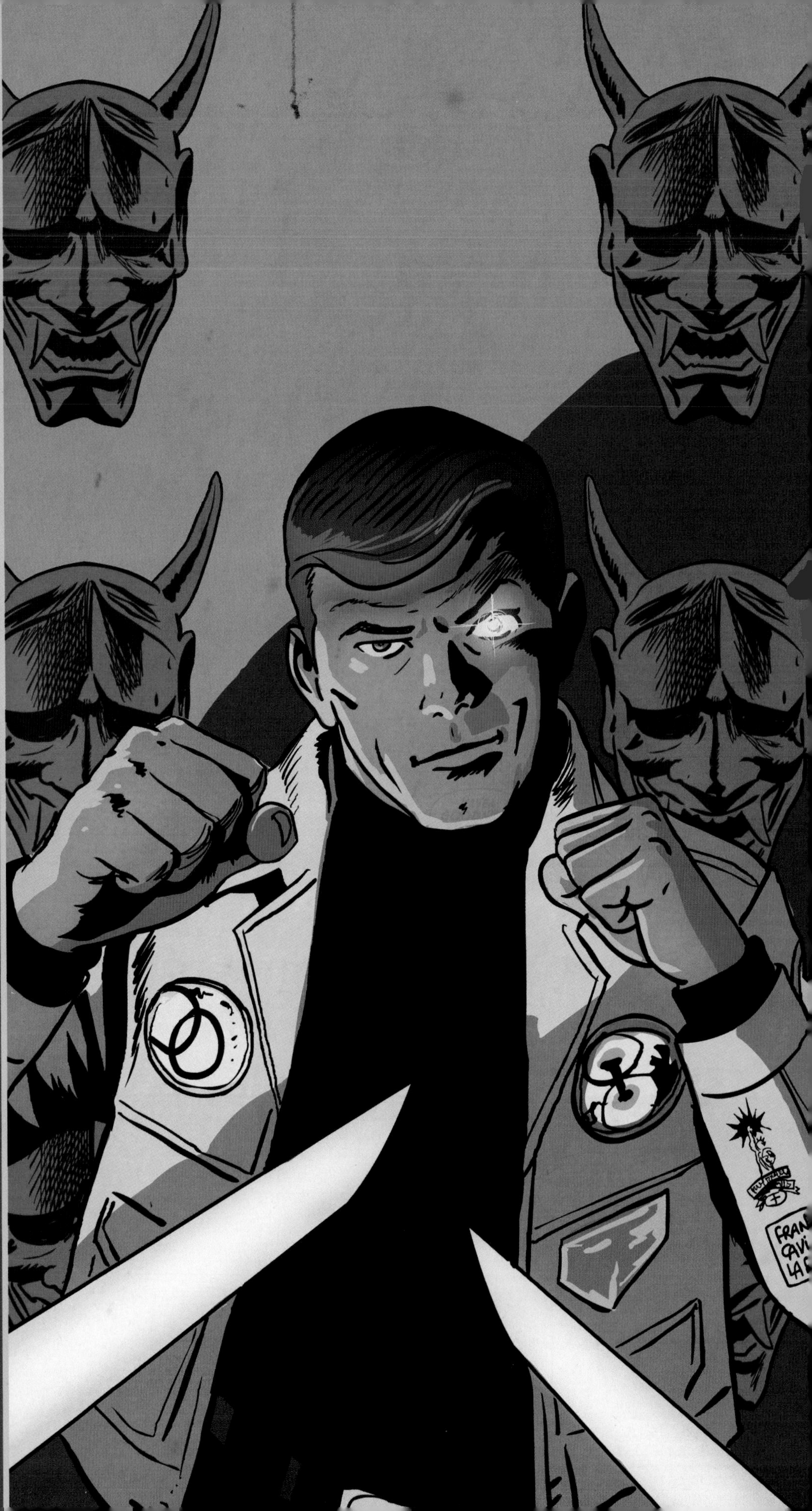

ISSUE 01 VARIANT COVER ART BY FRANCESCO FRANCAVILLA

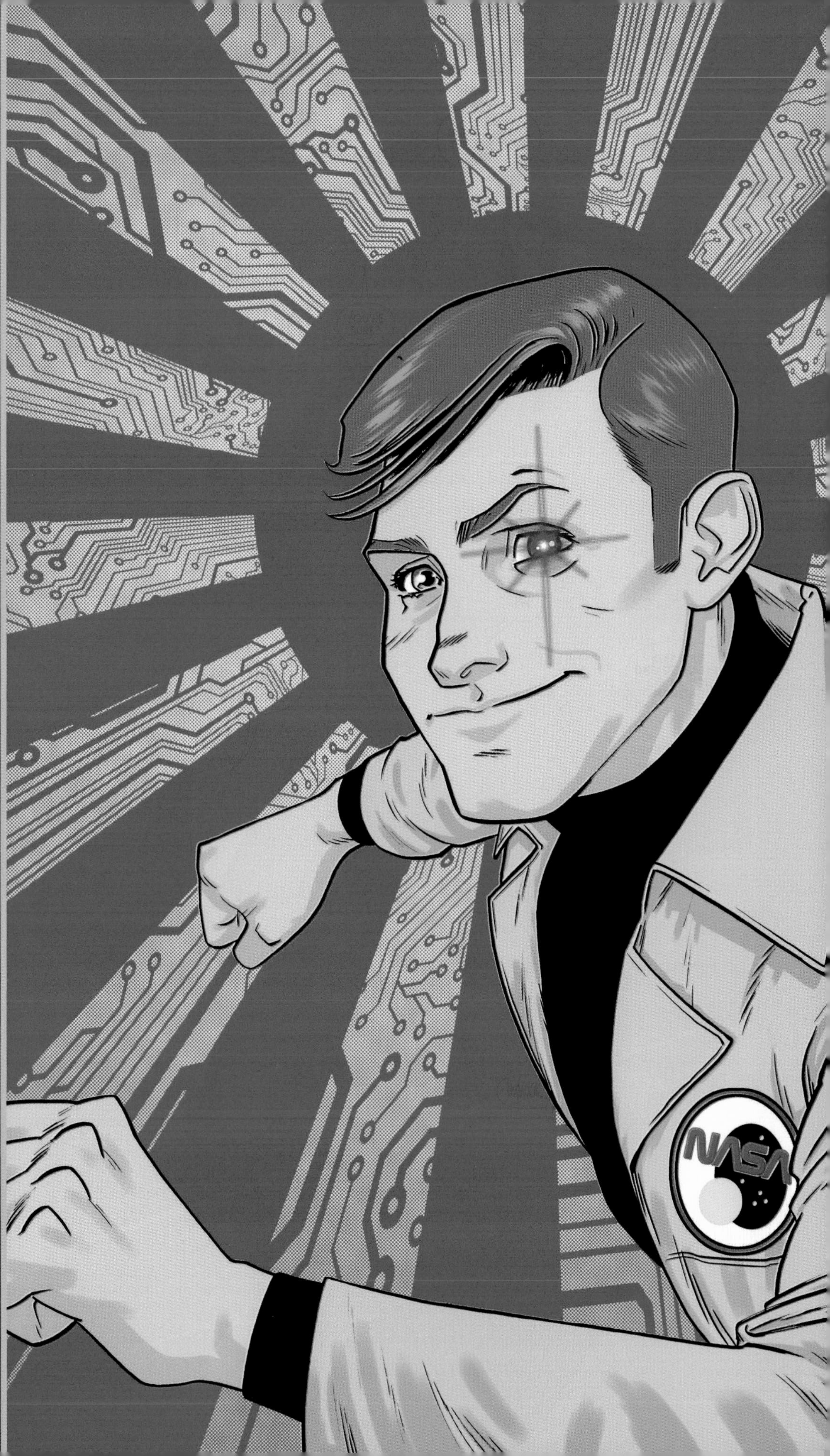

ISSUE 08 VARIANT COVER ART BY ADAM GORHAM

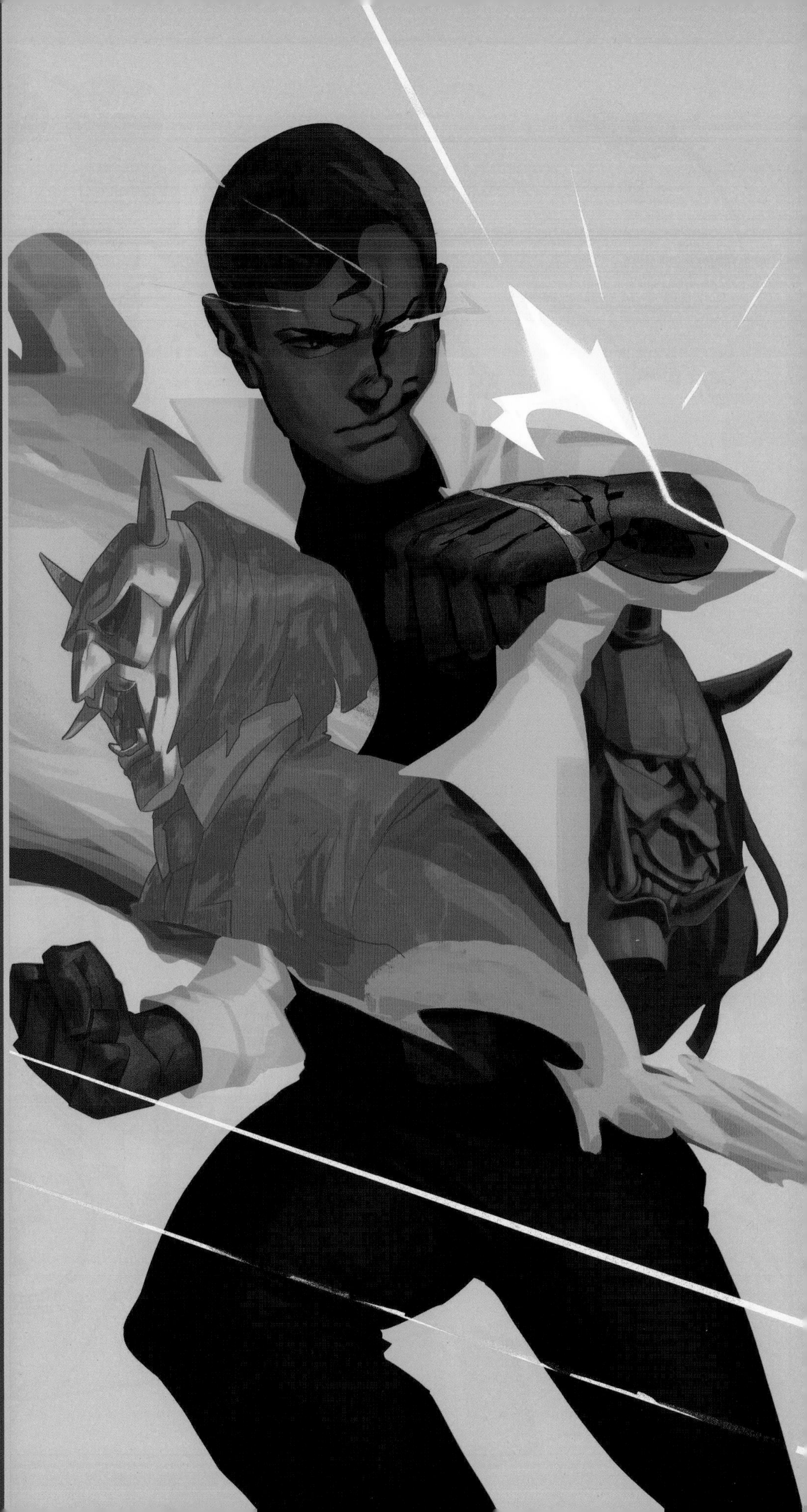

ISSUE 02 VARIANT COVER ART BY FELIPE MAGAÑA

ISSUE 03 VARIANT COVER ART BY ERIC GAPSTUR, COLORS BY CHRIS O'HALLORAN

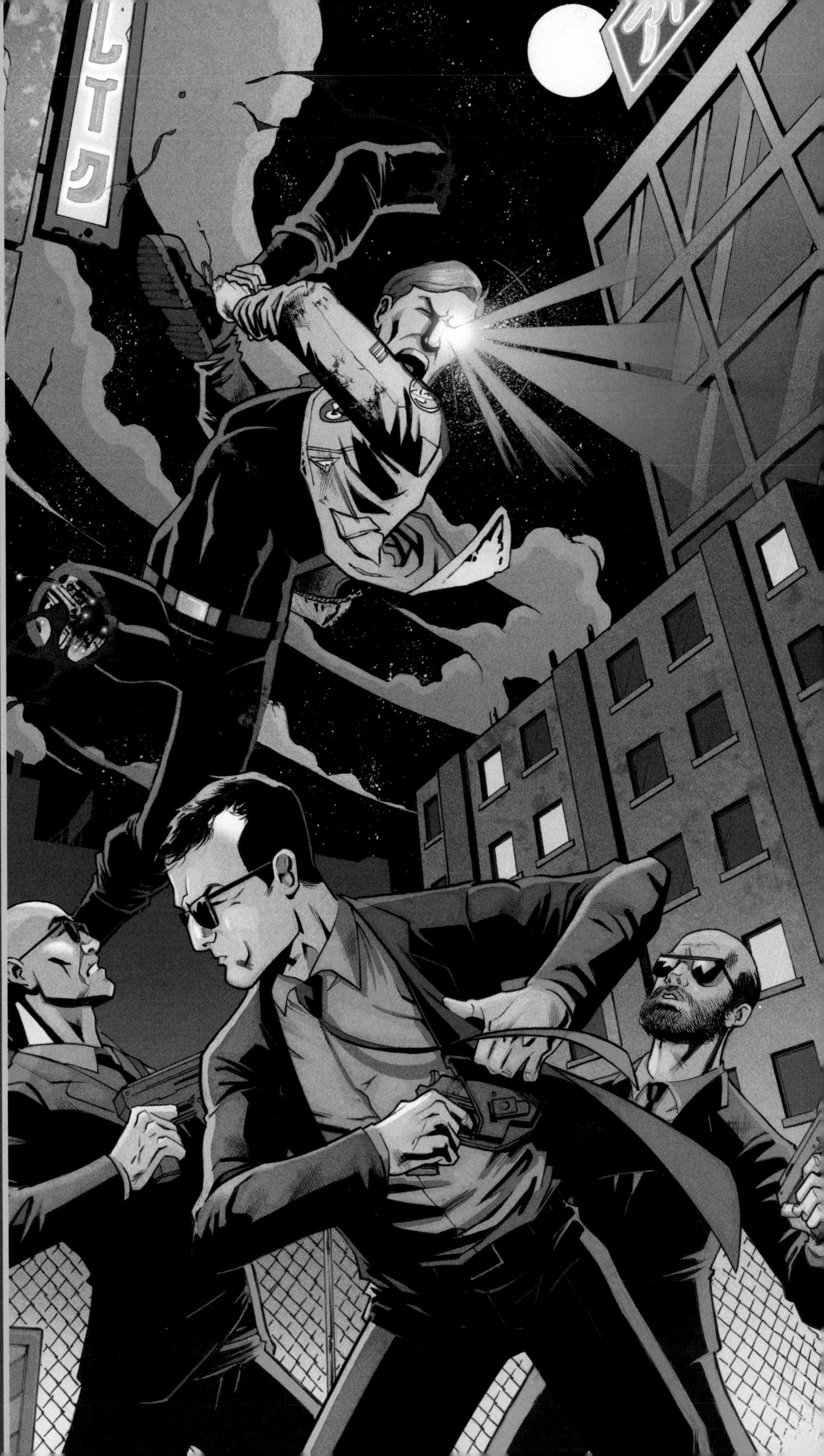

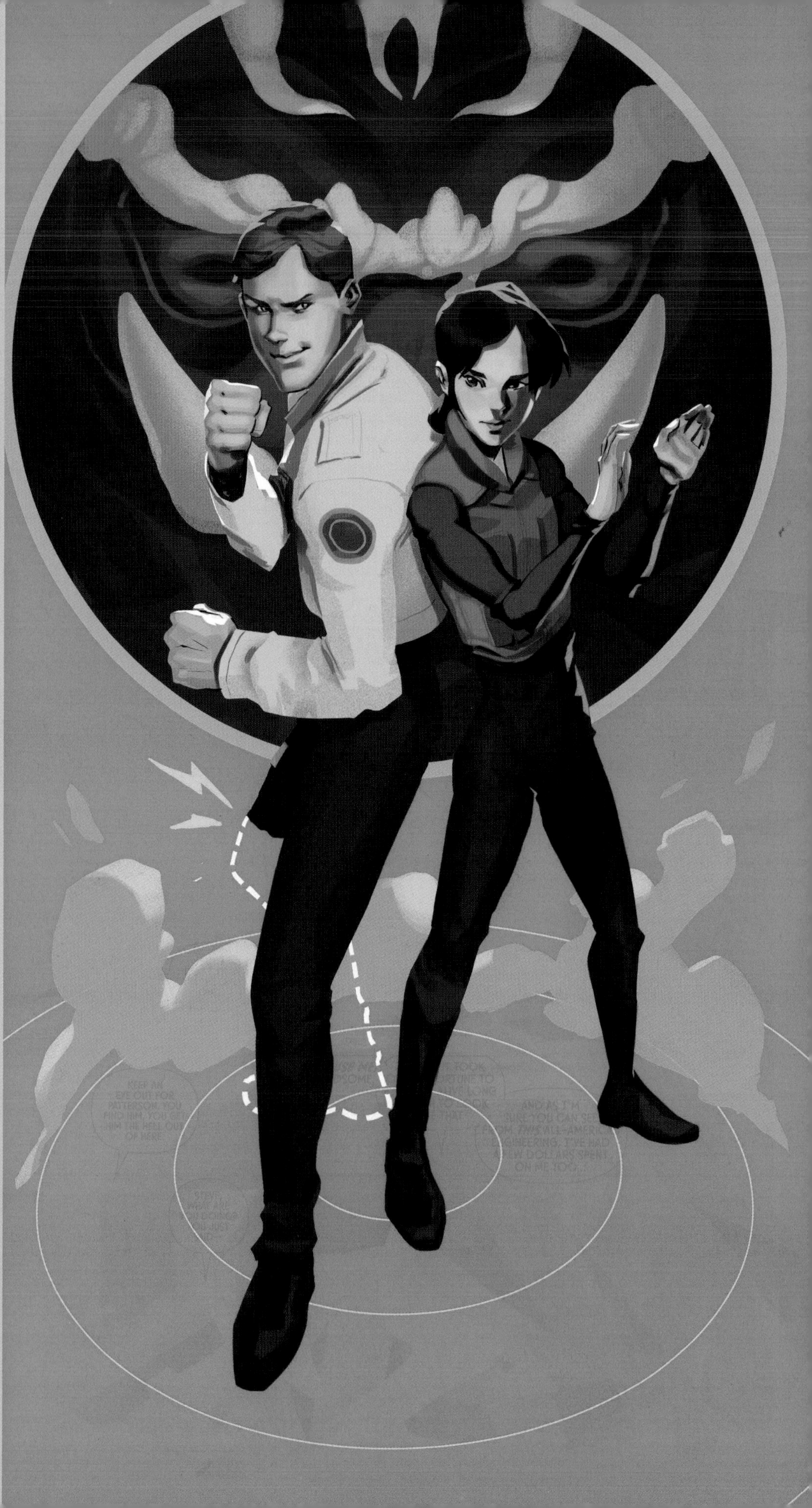

ISSUE 03 VARIANT COVER ART BY FELIPE MAGAÑA

ISSUE 01 VARIANT COVER ART BY SEBASTIAN PIRIZ

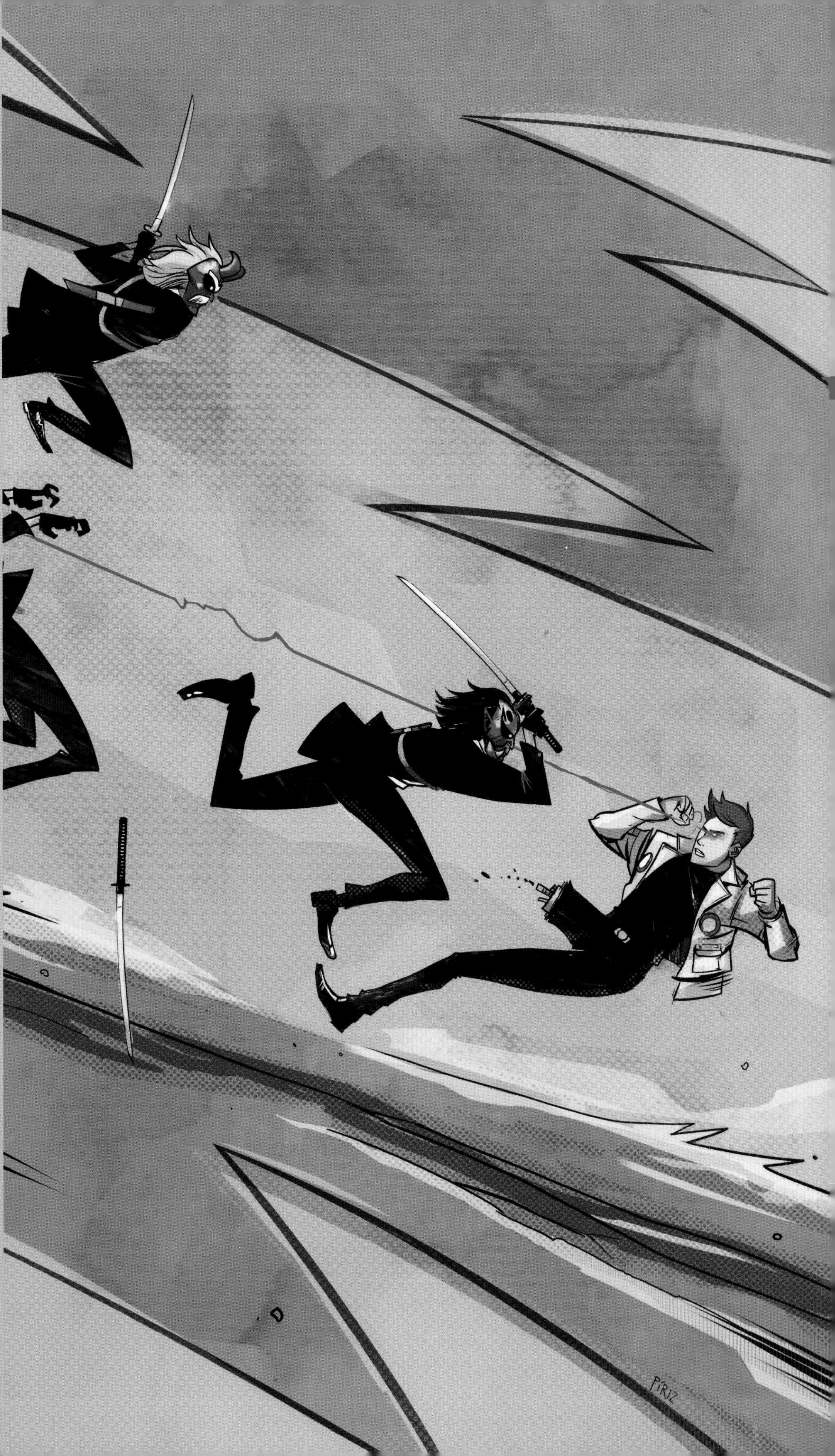
PÍRIZ

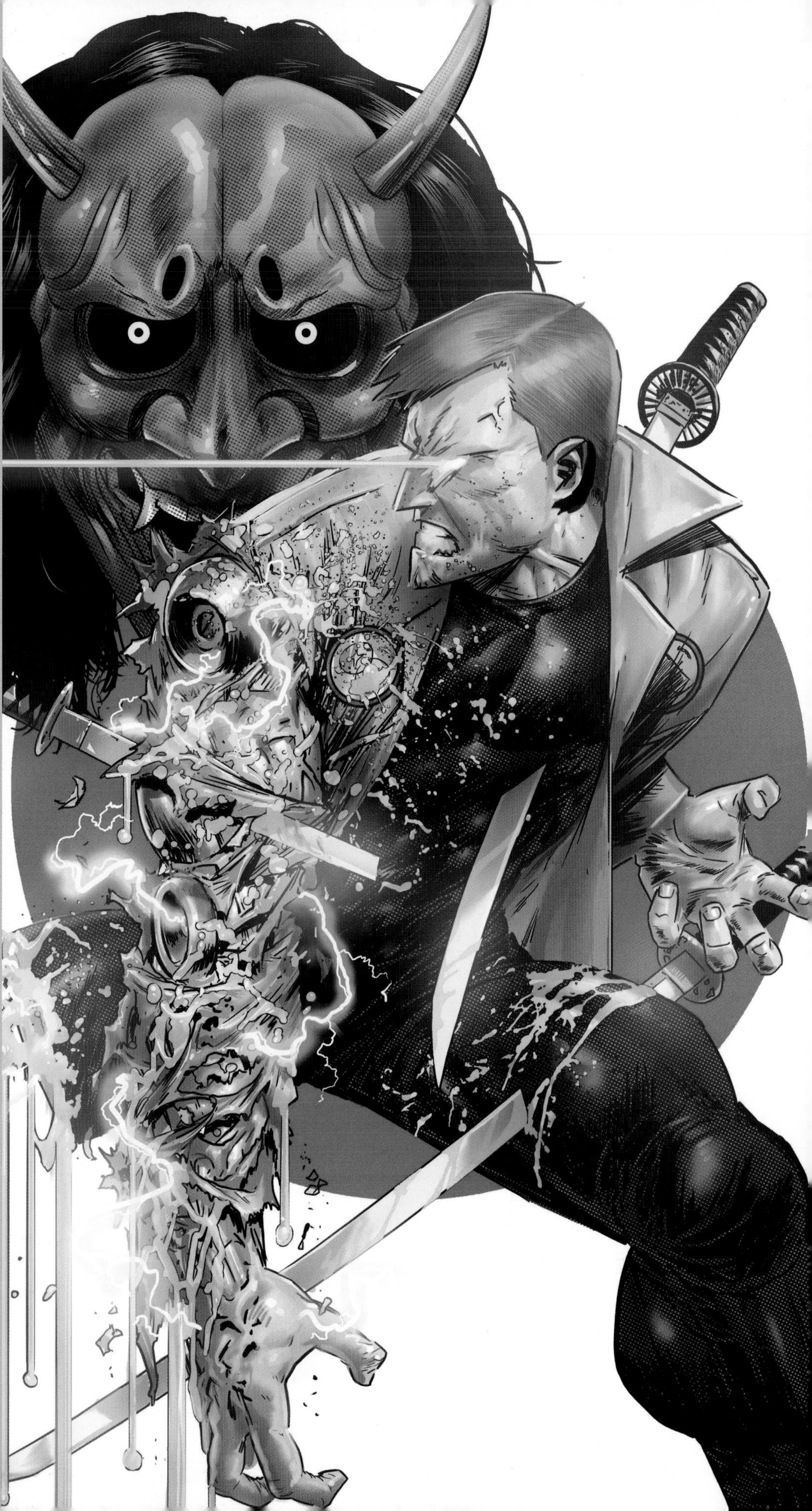

ISSUE 04 VARIANT COVER ART BY JUAN GEDEON

ISSUE 05 VARIANT COVER ART BY DAVID HAHN

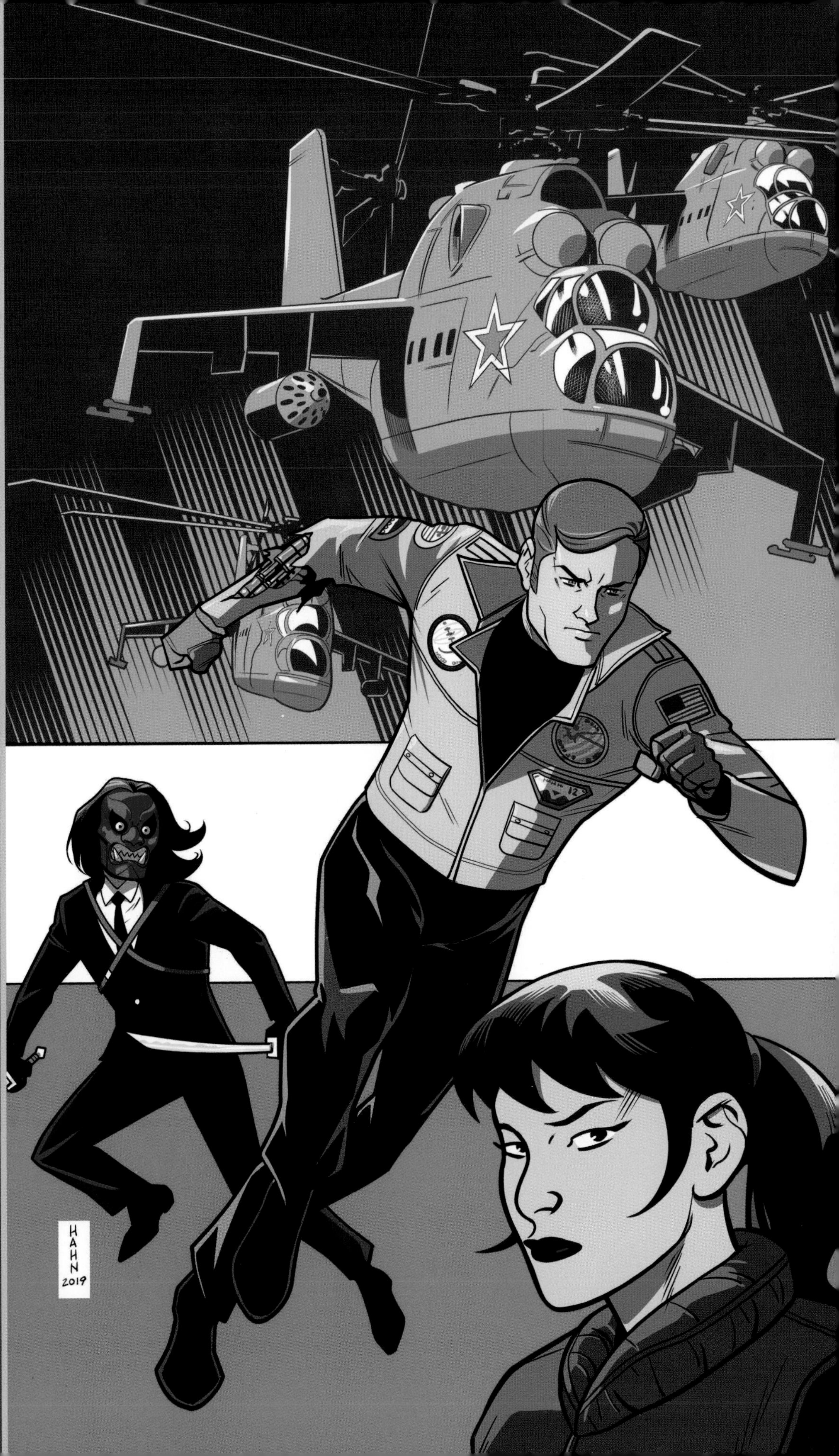
HAHN
2019

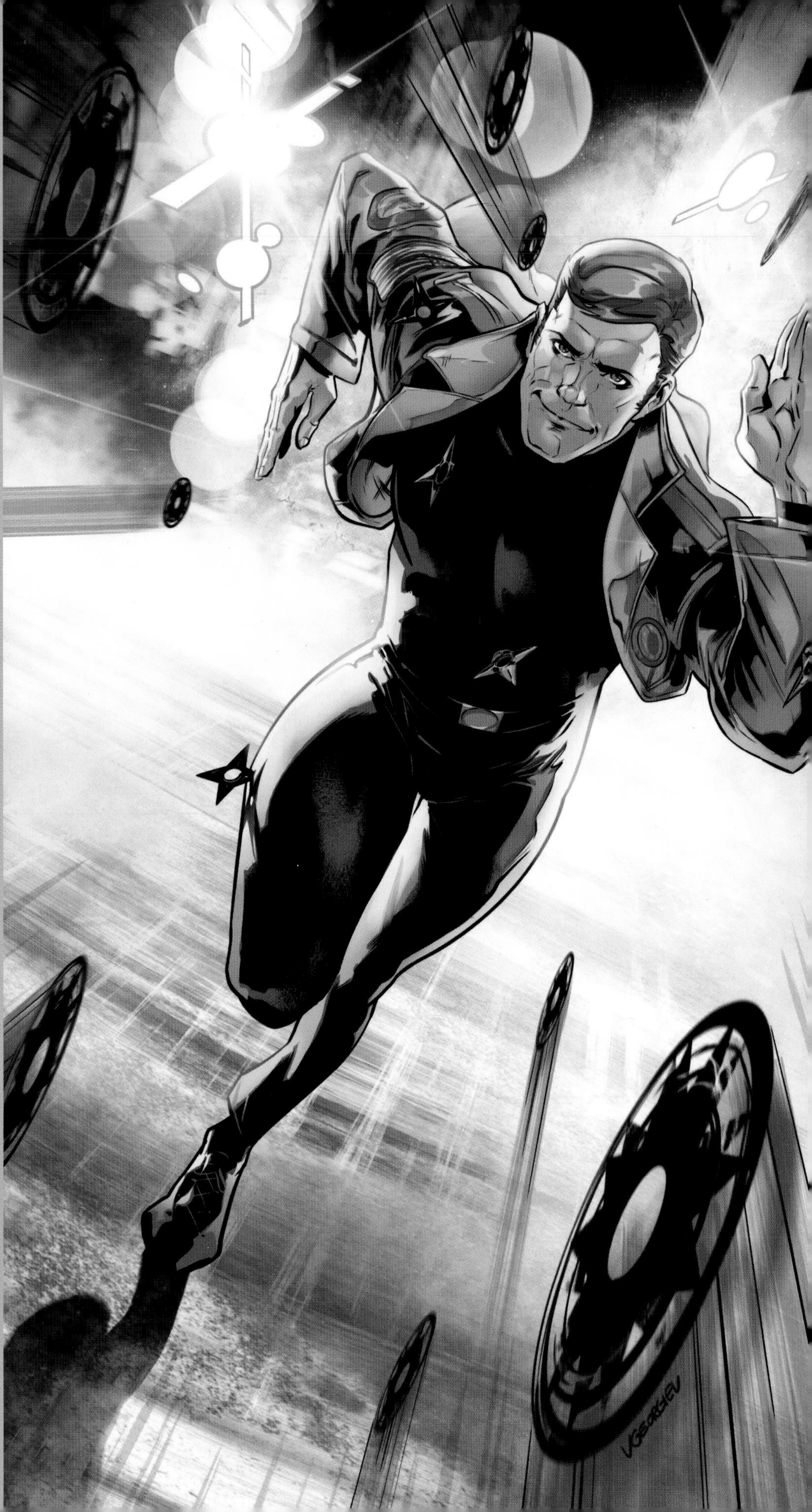
VGEORGIEV

ISSUE 05 VARIANT COVER ART BY VASCO GEORGIEV

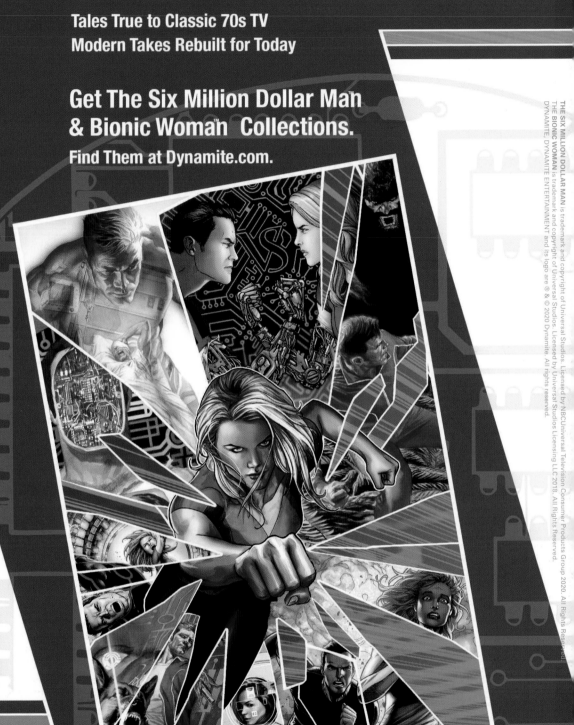   

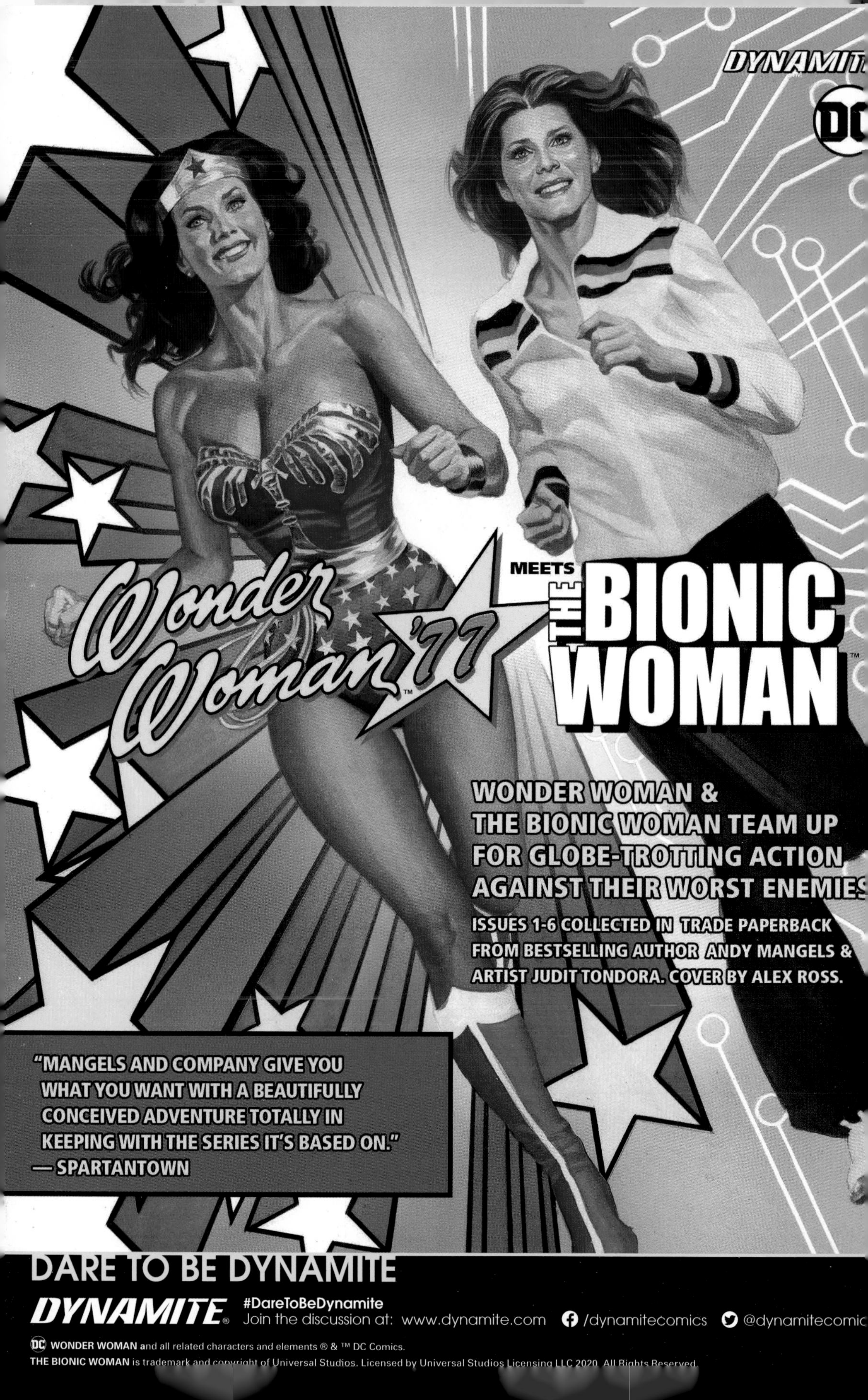
DYNAMITE
DC
Wonder Woman '77
MEETS
THE BIONIC WOMAN
WONDER WOMAN & THE BIONIC WOMAN TEAM UP FOR GLOBE-TROTTING ACTION AGAINST THEIR WORST ENEMIES
ISSUES 1-6 COLLECTED IN TRADE PAPERBACK FROM BESTSELLING AUTHOR ANDY MANGELS & ARTIST JUDIT TONDORA. COVER BY ALEX ROSS.
"MANGELS AND COMPANY GIVE YOU WHAT YOU WANT WITH A BEAUTIFULLY CONCEIVED ADVENTURE TOTALLY IN KEEPING WITH THE SERIES IT'S BASED ON."
— SPARTANTOWN
DARE TO BE DYNAMITE
DYNAMITE
#DareToBeDynamite
Join the discussion at: www.dynamite.com
/dynamitecomics
@dynamitecomic
WONDER WOMAN and all related characters and elements ® & ™ DC Comics.
THE BIONIC WOMAN is trademark and copyright of Universal Studios. Licensed by Universal Studios Licensing LLC 2020. All Rights Reserved.